VOLLEYBALL COACH'S
Survival Guide

• • • • • • • • • • •

Practical Techniques and Materials for Building an Effective Program and a Winning Team

SUE GOZANSKY

PARKER PUBLISHING COMPANY
Paramus, New Jersey 07652

Library of Congress Cataloging-in-Publication Data

Gozansky, Sue
  Vollyball coach's survival guide / Sue Gozansky.
    p. cm.
    ISBN 0-13-020757-8 (spiral-wire) ISBN 0-13-042588-5 (paper)
    1. Volleyball—Coaching. I. Title.
  GV1015.5.C63 G69 2001
  796.325—dc21

Printed in the United States of America

10 9 8 7 6 5 4 3 2 1

ISBN 0-13-020757-8 (spiral-wire)

10 9 8 7 6 5 4 3 2

ISBN 0-13-042588-5 (paper)

PARKER PUBLISHING COMPANY
Paramus, New Jersey 07652

http://www.phdirect.com

ACKNOWLEDGMENTS

This book has been a work in progress throughout my career, taking the form of player manuals and clinic notes. During this time many people gave me their assistance and wisdom. I am indebted to all my past teachers, coaches, and colleagues who directly or indirectly contributed to the shaping of this work.

I am especially grateful to my brother Michael Paul for his patience and constant computer assistance without which I could not have completed this book. I also want to thank him for putting into their final form the majority of the statistical forms and worksheets as well as condensing the information in many of the chapters.

Special thanks go to my colleague and good friend Monica Trainer for her assistance and advice. She spent many hours reading and re-reading my manuscript as well as taking on extra duties in the office to allow me the time to write.

Thanks to Jim Coleman for his helpful comments in the area of statistics and thanks to the many individuals who have contributed to the formation of the statistics that are now commonly used in volleyball. This evolution has helped transform a recreational game into a competitive game on an international scale.

Thanks go to my good friend Rosario Mercado for her unconditional friendship. Her continual support and encouragement helped motivate me to complete this project.

Thanks to all my past and present UC Riverside players. In special memory to Elana Foster, Janet Jones Rodgers, and Margie Himmelberg Stelutti.

Thanks to my past and current illustrators. After much thought I choose to follow the figure illustrations that Karoly Fogassy designed for my first book, *Championship Volleyball Techniques and Drills*. Thanks to David Drew Hatter for his excellent work in this publication.

Thanks to my loving parents who always encouraged and supported my sports efforts.

ABOUT THE AUTHOR

Sue Gozansky, dean of the University of California at Riverside coaching staff, has been at the helm of the Highlander Volleyball program for 31 seasons.

She sports a 607-334-16 record dating back to 1970. During that span, UCR has won the AIAW Small College National Championship in 1977 and two NCAA Division II National Championships (1982, 1986) and had an NCAA-record streak of 20 straight playoff appearances. She has been voted coach of the year in the CCAA five times (1981, 1982, 1988, 1989, 1996). Gozansky also served as head coach for the UCR men's team for five years.

Her national and international coaching history is equally impressive. She has coached at the Olympic Sports Festival as well as the USA women's "B" volleyball team consisting of players being considered for roster spots on the national team and was men's and women's coach for the quadrennial Maccabiah Games (Jewish Olympics) in Israel in 1981, 1985, 1989, and 1993.

Coach Gozansky is a member of the USA Volleyball Coaching Accreditation Program (CAP) and a certified instructor for the Federation International de Volleyball (FIVB). She coached the men's and women's national teams of the Kingdom of Tonga in preparation for the Mini South Pacific Games in the summer of 1997, under the auspices of the FIVB. She has given over 100 clinics in more than 35 countries, including Germany, Malaga, Spain, the island of Dominica, Belize, and Nepal.

Gozansky earned a degree in Physical Education/Social Sciences in 1968 from Cal Poly at Pomona. In 1970 she played on the USA National Volleyball team, and she earned her Master's degree in Kinesiology at UCLA in 1975. In 1981, Gozansky was honored with the Cal Poly Outstanding Alumnus Award, and in 1986 she was again honored with her induction into the inaugural class of the school's athletic Hall of Fame.

She joined the UCR staff in 1970 as head tennis and volleyball coach. During the formative years of women's sports, Gozansky served as the primary representative for women's athletics at UCR and represented the Highlanders at the first Association for Intercollegiate Athletics for Women (AIAW) delegate assembly in 1971. When women's sports became a part of the NCAA in 1981, she served on the first women's volleyball committee. In 1990, she was recognized by the NCAA for 10 years of accomplishments and dedication to Division II volleyball.

Coach Gozansky is the author of topselling *Championship Volleyball Techniques and Drills* (1983, Parker Publishing Company, a Prentice Hall imprint).

ABOUT THIS GUIDE

The sport of volleyball continues to grow in popularity throughout the world. Opportunities abound in U.S. high schools and clubs to play competitive indoor volleyball year-round. For the serious athlete who wants to advance to the collegiate level, scholarships are abundant for the consummate player and often those who display "potential." Elite athletes can play for their national team and/or professionally in a variety of indoor leagues, or on beach tours around the world.

Although the sport of volleyball is over 100 years old, it continues to evolve technically and tactically to significantly higher planes. It no longer resembles the recreation game invented in 1895 by William Morgan. It is a fast-moving and powerful competitive sport for girls and boys and men and women.

Player specialization has become a big part of the game over the years, a move that allows you to utilize more complex offensive and defensive tactics. With the trend toward greater specialization in the passing phase of the game and more variety in serve reception formations, passing skills have become more precise. Consistent passing leads to more attack options and less predictability. This creative style of offense in turn forces the defense to react with more sophisticated and diverse blocking and defensive tactics.

The game is evolving additionally through rule changes that dictate how the game is played. The International Volleyball Federation (FIVB) is the official governing body for all international competition and sets policies on rules. Each country's National Governing Body adopts the majority of FIVB rules that, with few exceptions, become the standard in schools and clubs. The new millennium is a time of great change for volleyball as the leaders of the sport search for ways to popularize the game with fans and make it more television friendly. Recently the FIVB changed from the traditional side-out scoring of 15 points, to rally score of 25 points until the deciding game (which is then rally score to 15).

In addition, the use of the FIVB "libero" player, a defensive specialist, changes the game's substitution policies and gives more opportunities for the smaller player to have an effect on the sport. The FIVB is considering many prospective changes and you must be aware of current rules to effectively do your job. Refer to Chapter 11 for web sites for organizations that provide rules.

I wrote this practical handbook to reflect the technical and tactical changes in volleyball's evolution since my first book, *Championship Volleyball Techniques and Drills*. I hope this book will help players and coaches understand and enjoy the game of volleyball, so they may contribute to its continued growth and success.

All the major aspects of the game are covered in a working format, aimed at the beginning-, intermediate-, and advanced-level volleyball player, coach, and physical educator. Both you and the player will find this book a helpful guide to building a solid foundation of volleyball knowledge, and a useful resource in improving your games.

- Chapter 1 deals with your role as the coach. It gives new coaches their "job description" and gives more experienced coaches the opportunity to evaluate themselves and their philosophy. Coaching requries a mix of responsibilities that go beyond teaching the X's and O's of the game. Excelling at these duties requires periodic self-evaluation and program evaluations—and you'll find a variety of worksheets to assist you in this task. Samples of player policies, contracts, and program goals are included to help generate ideas.

• Chapters 2 through 7 provide information on the six basic technical skills consisting of the pass, set, serve, attack, floor defense, and block. As in *Championship Volleyball Techniques and Drills,* a step-by-step checklist is provided for each skill. In addition, this book supplies tactical checklists that correspond to each individual and team skill.

The order of presentation of skills in this book corresponds to one possible teaching progression. Tough and consistent serving and accurate passing alone win games at the beginning level, and good ball-control skills of passing, setting, and digging contribute most to success at the intermediate level. Attacking and blocking most correlate with winning at the higher levels.

Another method or teaching progression I have found successful is reversing the order; teaching team offense and defense systems first, followed by the individual skills. This style gives the players the whole picture of how the game is played. Then when the individual skills are introduced, the athlete has a better understanding of how the parts fit into the whole.

• Beginning to advanced team defensive and offensive tactics are discussed in chapters 8 and 9.

• Chapter 10 discusses your match responsibilities. Topics include forming the starting lineup, substitutions, timeouts, pre- and postgame meetings, and scouting.

• Chapter 11 deals with statistics that can be used in practice and in the match. Statistics can be an effective way of teaching the game at all levels. Various forms are included for statistical analysis of the six basic skills, individual and team performance, and scouting sheets.

• Chapter 12 discusses the practice and the six main factors in successful practices: preparation, motivation, execution, discipline, learning acquisition, and cooperation. Your role is to plan and manage practices, but it takes cooperation on the part of all coaches and athletes to make practices beneficial. You must constantly give consideration to these concepts when planning and directing practices. Information and checklists are provided dealing with drill concepts and requirements, practice content, how the players can get the most out of practice and out of their teammates, and preseason practice content.

• Chapter 13 discusses training by position. You'll find guidelines for training movement necessary for all players and then specifically how to train the setter, the outside attacker, and the middle blocker. Each position has specific characteristics and responsibilities and it is hoped that this section can be used as a starting point in training players to specialize.

• The book concludes with Chapter 14, the intangibles. Athletes must conquer or at least learn to manage many mental and emotional obstacles in order to play their best game. The chapter discusses the error problem, both personal and tactical, and tips to deal with it. This is followed by an informative and practical discussion of the technique of visualization that is used to enhance physical performance. Individual and guided visualization scenarios are provided. Additional topics dealing with the mental side of the game include communication, dealing with conflict, setting goals, and the ideal player.

A great deal of information is provided in each chapter. Too much information at one time can confuse the athlete and slow down the learning process. It is important that you make decisions about what and how much information is appropriate for your athletes, utilizing the most important information first and saving the other material for another time.

Along the same lines, rather than copying the drills, checklists, or worksheets and reiterating the explanations word for word, it is hoped that you use the information provided as samples to be modified and personalized to meet your specific needs.

I have coached volleyball for the past 30 years, and have come to realize that *teaching should be student driven,* not methodology driven. Human beings are complex. No two are alike. Their differences translate to different methods. All methods are good, but not all are equally applicable to a given person at a given time. Some match some players better than others. It is important to utilize different approaches when players are having difficulty.

The *Volleyball Coach's Survival Guide* presents my approach to teaching and coaching volleyball. It integrates concepts, principles, and philosophies drawn from my coaching experiences. It is a collection of effective volleyball information that I have acquired from coaches throughout the world. I am indebted to all those who have shared with me their knowledge of the game, thus making me a better coach. I am grateful to all my past players who have challenged me to keep learning; by playing for me they have taught me many valuable lessons. I hope to contribute to the creation of better coaches and players everywhere with this book, and to promote the game I love.

Sue Gozansky

CONTENTS

CHAPTER 4   The Server 73

CHAPTER 5   The Attacker .85

CHAPTER 6   The Defender 101

CHAPTER 13   Training by Position 259

CHAPTER 14   The Intangibles 313

CHAPTER 1

YOUR ROLE AS COACH

 "C" is for coaches—they help you learn;
reaching your potential is their concern.

Your primary responsibility as coach is to teach players the game. In the process of developing the technical and tactical skills, however, your role expands to instill values and abilities that can be used on and off the court.

THE MODEL COACH

No two coaches are alike and there is no correct mold. Each coach is a unique combination of personality, beliefs, and life experiences. It is helpful to have had playing experience, but it does not guarantee success, nor does more years coaching guarantee better coaching. Being a successful coach is a continuous process of growth and development through trial and error, reflection, and evaluation. Do you possess the qualities you desire in a coach? Would you want to be coached by you? Do you see the same person in the mirror that others see? Take the time to assess your skills and evaluate those areas you would like to improve.

Reproducible

See the following worksheet reproducible, "Self-Evaluation."

Coach's Worksheet:
SELF-EVALUATION

Know yourself! Assess your strengths and weaknesses, and work to make beneficial changes. Rate yourself in each category:

1 = exceptional, 2 = good, 3 = needs improvement

_____ Knowledge of rules

_____ Technical knowledge of skills

_____ Tactical knowledge of systems and strategies

_____ Knowledge of latest teaching and training methods

_____ Resource utilization: books, videos, professional organizations

_____ Vision and goals for program

_____ Commitment to a quality program

_____ Reliable and dependable

_____ Organization skills and time management

_____ Finance skills and fund-raising abilities

_____ Promotion and public relations skills

_____ Consistency in words and deeds

_____ Leadership skills

_____ Positive role model and mentor

_____ Professional appearance and behavior

_____ Diplomacy and tact

_____ Composure in practice and games

_____ Flexibility to adjust to changes

_____ Communication with athletes, parents, administrators

_____ Listening skills

_____ Inspirational and motivational

_____ Self-confident and decisive

_____ Standard of personal conduct and ethical behavior

_____ Consistent and sustained demand level of athletes

_____ Organization of gym and training athletes

_____ Written preparation of daily practices

_____ Effectiveness teaching volleyball skills

_____ Coaching skills for coach-centered drills (serve, toss, and hit)

_____ Skill analysis and correction abilities

_____ Decision-making and problem-solving skills

_____ Effectiveness of timeouts and tactical match adjustments

_____ Promptness

_____ Sportsmanship

_____ Effective use of personnel: team systems and substitutions

_____ Corrective feedback regarding skills and tactics

_____ Time actively vs. passively coaching in practice

_____ Positive reinforcement of skill, behavior, and effort

_____ Recognition and celebration of players' achievements

_____ Concern for each player's success

_____ Creative and innovative

_____ Enthusiasm, determination, courage, strength

THE B's OF A SUCCESSFUL COACH

Be a Leader

- Every successful team has a strong leader.
- Project confidence in yourself and in the program.
- Sell yourself and your ideas.
- Make athletes feel like winners. Inspire them individually and collectively to commit to the goals and the journey.
- Be a leader all the time. If something needs to be done, take the initiative to make it happen.
- Demonstrate on a daily basis your ability to lead and meet the challenges of the team.

Be a Visionary

- Have a clear picture of what you want for the program and communicate this vision to the athletes, assistant coaches, parents, and administrators.
- Form a partnership with the team and convince them that the vision is doable.
- Get everyone on the same page and heading in the same direction.
- Never lose sight of the objective or what it takes to get there.
- Constantly remind the team of the mission and values of the program.

Be Passionate

- Enjoy the work and strive with passion to reach your goals.
- Put yourself wholeheartedly into the job.
- Love the game, the competition, the athletes, and the coaching.
- Coach from the head *and* the heart.
- Your passion in turn inspires others to work hard and follow the dream.

Be Committed

- Have a high commitment level and a strong work ethic.
- Have a strong belief in your mission and the strength and conviction to work for it.
- Be determined, persistent, and dedicated to the journey.

Be Knowledgeable

- Know the techniques and tactics of the game and stay current with changes.
- Stay up to date with new methods and technology.
- Constantly search for opportunities to expand your knowledge.
- Attend coaching clinics, join professional organizations, and read books or magazines pertinent to the sport.
- Watch as many matches as possible on television and in person, and study the game from an analytical viewpoint.

- Watch other coaches' practices and keep up with what the top junior clubs, collegiate, and national teams are doing.

Be a Role Model

- Athletes want and need good role models.
- You have a very strong influence on players' lives. Make it positive.
- Players are constantly watching and learning from their leaders.
- Maintain high standards of personal and professional integrity in everything you do.
- Dress and act the part. Be fit and healthy.
- Maintain an emotional calmness in difficult situations.
- Be honest and demonstrate high standards of sportsmanship.

Be a Decision-Maker

- Make the majority of the team's decisions. You have the most experience and objectivity.
- Seek and encourage input, but in the end, take the leadership to do what you feel is the best for the individual and for the team regardless of how it is "viewed" by others.

Be a Problem-Solver

- You are the leader and responsible for handling all situations that arise.
- Analyze the problem and find solutions.
- Repair faulty technique, tactics, behavior, and conflicts.
- Understand that there will always be problems regardless of your success or that of the program.
- Accept the responsibility to rectify problems immediately, fairly, and consistently.

Be Confident

- Have confidence in yourself and the courage to stand by your beliefs despite the criticisms or setbacks.
- Your confidence must be so strong that you convince others to follow your lead.

Be Decisive

- Know what you want and communicate it to the team. No one wants to be lead by coaches who are unsure of themselves.
- Clearly state your philosophy, goals, and expectations.
- Let players know what to expect and what you will not tolerate.
- Explain each player's role and how each player fits into the total team picture.

Be a Cheerleader

- Be the team's number-one fan.
- Never give up on a player or the team.

- Encourage players.
- Catch players doing things well.
- Recognize and celebrate players' contributions and achievements.
- Show players their possibilities, *not* their limits.

Be a Teacher

- Provide sound instruction on behaviors, techniques, and tactics.
- You are the expert. Transfer your knowledge to the players.
- Good teaching is not only about what is taught, but also how it is taught.

> *MAXIM: Be interesting or at least be brief.*

Be Flexible

- Be prepared to adjust to many types of personalities and in many situations.
- Teach in any way you can to get the most out of your players.
- Work with every player differently.
- Work within your players' personalities.

Be Creative

- Stay one step ahead of opponents by utilizing your resources and knowledge in a creative way.
- Recognize good ideas and adapt them to meet your own needs.
- Constantly search for innovative approaches to the game. Look inside and outside of volleyball.
- Listen to your athletes. Players can be a good source of ideas.
- Expand your thoughts to see things from different perspectives.
- Take risks. Do not fear change or failure. If it does not work, move on.

Be a Coach–Friend

- Maintain a coach–friend rather than a friend–friend relationship.
- Do not be a peer or a pal.
- Be part of the team and enjoy the player's company.
- Strong leadership functions only when you maintain some distance between the players.

Be Caring

- Display a genuine interest in each player on a personal level.
- Care for the players beyond their skills.
- Acknowledge and support players' accomplishments both on and off the court.
- Take the time to get to know your players and connect with them on an emotional level.

Be "Hip"

- Change with the times.
- Stay in tune with each new generation.
- Stay up to date with what is happening in players' lives and culture.

Be a Disciplinarian

- Know what is necessary for success and set guidelines to demand that these expectations be met.
- Clearly explain your expectations.
- Develop team rules. Define team boundaries and the consequences to going over the line.
- Indicate what is acceptable and what is not—and hold players accountable.
- There should be only one way to do things and that is the way *you* want it.
- If athletes stray off course, they must be disciplined. If they cannot consistently follow the rules, they must be cut from the team.
- Difficult players sap energy and distract the players' and your attention from more productive team issues.
- Do what you feel is best for the individual and the team. Be fair rather than always being equal.

Be Ethical

- Do not compromise the integrity of the program.
- Encourage ethical behavior and good sportsmanship.
- Provide each player with an ethical set of standards (conduct code) that reflect your philosophy and program values.
- Your policies guide your decisions as well as provide players with expectations and standards for every aspect of team life.

Be Credible

- Be honest with players and do not mislead them.
- Be worthy of trust.
- Be reliable and consistent in words, actions, and behaviors.
- Say what you mean and do what you say.
- Be faithful to the program's values and reflect them in all decisions that you make.

Be Communicative

- Communicate clearly, efficiently, and frequently.
- Do what is necessary for athletes to hear and understand the message.
- Speak at the athletes' level and use language they can understand and relate to.
- Be aware of your communication habits and work hard to develop and improve your skills.
- Be aware of the powerful influence of your words.

- Your words and actions affect players in either a positive or negative way; they are generally not neutral.
- Work to control your words in moments of frustration or anger.
- Occasional criticism, yelling, or sarcasm is not harmful; but if it becomes routine, it can hurt the players' feelings and damage their self-esteem.
- Do not avoid interaction in difficult and uncomfortable situations.
- Bad communication is better than no communication at all.

Be a Good Listener

- Keep quiet so you can hear others.
- Listen carefully, attentively, and without interrupting.
- Work to understand how players feel. Seek each player's input.
- Encourage players to express their feelings and let them know you value their opinions.
- Consult players especially the veterans, about individual and team issues.

Be Positive and Energetic

- Capture the mind and spirit of players through your enthusiasm.
- Support and encourage athletes to work hard and give them faith that they can reach their goals.
- Focus on gains, not losses.
- Focus on how to succeed, rather than on why it might not be possible.
- Relate positively with parents, administrators, and the community.

Be Objective

- Evaluate yourself and have others help you do it.
- Ask friends and/or colleagues to observe and evaluate your performance in practice and the game.
- Get an honest picture of how others perceive you.
- Strive to improve your areas of weakness and strengthen your overall ability to coach.

Be Realistic

- Be objective about the prospects of winning and losing.
- Have high, but realistic expectations for the team.
- Understand that although the scoreboard indicates a winner and a loser, both teams can win.
- Define success less by the win–loss record and more on the effort of striving to be one's best and on continual learning.

Be Organized

- Coaching is a multifaceted process that requires extensive organization, planning, and attention to detail.

- Organization insures that the necessary things get done in a timely fashion.
- Stay up to date with paperwork in the office as well as being prepared in the gym.

MAXIM: It is better to aim for excellence and hit good, than aim for good and hit average.

VALUABLE COACHING MOMENTS

Reflecting back on over 30 years of coaching both men's and women's volleyball, I realize that much of my philosophy has developed through my experiences of coaching and the lessons my players have taught me. Each new season offers a new set of circumstances and the opportunity to grow and develop as a coach. Here is a sample of what I have learned over the years.

It's a Great Job, but It's Not Perfect

I began my coaching career at the university level straight from playing on the national team. I had a very short playing career due to a knee injury, but from this experience I felt very confident that I was prepared for the job. The first few years were the honeymoon phase. Everything was perfect. The players were excited to have a knowledgeable coach. They were good athletes, hungry to learn, so much so that they requested additional practice sessions. We were all enjoying ourselves. There were problems, but we were so absorbed in volleyball that we were not aware of them. When I opened my eyes, the honeymoon was over and I could see the whole world of coaching. It is not perfect, but it sure is fun.

You Are the Coach—If It Needs to Be Done, Then You Must Do It

I never enjoyed confrontations—if I could avoid them, I did. It was difficult to communicate with players about serious or uncomfortable subjects. I did not want to be the one to tell them something they did not agree with or did not want to hear. I waited and hoped that the situations would correct themselves, but they did not. In regards to difficult players, I counted the days until they would graduate and these problems would be gone. I waited for the days to be like my first few years, but they did not return. There will always be difficult players and situations and they do not go away by themselves. Someone has to take the leadership in dealing with problems and resolving them. You are that person.

Determine the Skills Before Selecting the Drills

In my first season I ran practices similar to many of my past coaches, but primarily like my club coach for the Los Angeles Renegades, Moo Park of South Korea. This was a fast-paced style to which most of us in the United States were not accustomed. Practices were demanding and fun. I never ran out of drills. Only later did I realize that I could have accomplished a lot more if I had selected my practice goals first and then selected the drills to accomplish them.

Some of My Best Players Have Been the Most Difficult to Coach

Be wary of those players who seem to always say what they think you want them to say; they are not always being honest. Listen carefully to those players who say things you do not always want to hear. Evaluate what they say and see if you can learn from it. The best and most competitive players challenge you to be your best in their struggle to be their best. They keep you on your toes.

Never Underestimate the Power of Desire

Some of my greatest coaching successes have been my biggest surprises. These players did not appear to have the volleyball experience to succeed at the university level, but they taught me that no matter what volleyball skills they lacked, they could make up for it by being coachable and working harder than their teammates to catch up.

Luckily it has never been my policy to cut players. I explain to the players their current role; it is then their decision to remain in the training group or to cut themselves. Those players—who are not members of the traveling squad—do not receive the majority of coaching, but this never deters these special players. They work on their own and fit into drills when the numbers allow it. They listen attentively to corrections and suggestions directed not only to them, but to their teammates. They soak up all the information like sponges. I learned from these players that it is what you cannot see that is often more important than what you can see. They had a tremendous amount of talent, but I was looking past it. If I had realized their tremendous "intangible" talents earlier, I would have been able to help them reach even higher levels.

You Cannot Always Discover Great Athletes—You Must Develop Them

Find a role for your best athletes. If you already have someone in his or her role, find that player another one. One young woman was not effective in the front row as an attacker, but was dynamite in the back row. Her first two years were played as a defensive specialist. She had played on a very successful club team, had good fundamental skills, and was very knowledgeable of the game. She was quick and aggressive and would run through walls to reach a ball. We needed a setter the following year and we trained her to fulfill this role. She did a superb job for her last two years.

One year we had eight outside hitters but only two players for the middle position. I suggested to one player that she train to play middle; she would have a much better opportunity to get some court time in this position. She was tall and strong and had very good footwork. She became one of our best middles and earned All-American honors.

Another year we had a very powerful middle attacker, but we could not set her often enough to make our team successful, so we converted her into a left-side attacker. It took her a fair amount of time to adjust to the new position, attacking a variety of precise and imprecise high sets. We accepted the early errors she made, hoping it was only temporary. The change and our patience paid off. She also earned All-American honors.

In one of our transition years with a very young team, we did not have an experienced setter so the decision was made to train two of our best all-around athletes to set and hit in the 6–2 system. This was a very effective system for us because our best players had the most responsibility. The first year they set and played the left front attack position. The year we won the national championship, they switched to block and hit on the right side, which traditionally is where the setters are positioned.

All Players Should Have the Opportunity to Get into the Game

To this day I regret a decision I made during my first years of coaching. I was coaching both the varsity and junior varsity teams. We had seven players on the varsity and the remaining players made up the junior varsity team. My seventh player on varsity almost never got an opportunity to play. I always wanted to put her into the game, but she was not as consistent as the starters and winning was a big priority for me. She never complained and this made it easy for me to continue to do it. I should have given her the option of playing on the junior varsity team until that time when we needed a replacement—guaranteeing her the opportunity to play.

Years later I had three very capable setters and we were employing a single setter system. I explained the situation to the two substitute setters: One decided to leave the team and I was very comfortable with her decision. A year later the team was in need of a setter and the player returned. Both situations were good, because the player was honestly appraised of the situation and had the choice to decide what was best for her.

Set the Standards and Let Players Know What You Expect of Them and What You Will Not Tolerate

One particularly difficult season taught me the value of written policies and rules. Perhaps I was negligent in distributing the team policy and establishing team rules because for many years my teams had been very responsible and disciplined. This was a huge mistake that I discovered on our first road trip. That Monday the rules were written and penalties were established. Some players must be given guidelines.

No One Player Should Make You Compromise Your Values or Philosophy

It is important as a coach to adjust to the personality of the team, but there is a standard you must uphold. You cannot let one or two problem players distract and sap your energy away from the bigger picture: The program is more important than the individual player. No player is more important than the team and no player is indispensable. Your obligation is to the team. When you find yourself focusing your total attention on one "bad seed" rather than on the team, a change must be made. I have had some tough players to deal with but they taught me to hold fast to my values.

Everyone Is Not Just Like You—And Players Do Not Need to Be to Have a Successful Team

Some players are just "different." Their personalities are not what you are used to. They are not necessarily disruptive or bad, but more flexibility is required to coach them. If you feel these players are valuable to the team, you must learn to "manage" them, *not* change them. These players taught me that it is not always possible to treat everyone equally. Double standards do exist. Here is an example.

The team was in the hotel preparing for our regional championship match that evening. Our captains made the decision to wear the white long-sleeve jerseys and blue shorts. Everyone had the uniforms on when one player emphatically told us that she hated how that uniform fit her and she would not wear it. I immediately went to each room and instructed the players to change into the blue-and-gold uniform. It was easier to ask eleven players to change than to convince one why she had better put on the uniform if she wanted to remain on the team. If she had not been an All-American, I am sure I would not have taken the same course of action.

Not All Teams Are Cohesive—And They Do Not Have to Be

Some of my best teams were not cohesive; in fact, they did not like one another very much. The important factor is that everyone has the same goals and each player can work together on the court to reach these goals. No matter how many team functions you have, some teams will not be so cohesive as others—but it does not mean they cannot be successful.

Find a Way to Sell Your Ideas

One of my players needed to lose weight and she was having a difficult time finding the motivation to do it. One day in practice I had her wear a 20-pound vest throughout the practice to demonstrate to her what it was like to carry around the extra weight. This demonstration definitely caught her attention.

My assistant coach was playing for a semiprofessional team in Italy. Later that week they would be competing against a 6-foot, 2-inch setter who very successfully attacked the second ball with a very quick tip anywhere within the 10-foot line. The setter would alternate the tip with a shoot set to the left-side attacker who attacked with power down the line. The coach was insistent that my assistant playing right back could successfully receive both attacks. My assistant was not convinced that if she were in position to pick up the tip that she could possibly get back to the line to dig a hard-driven spike hit over their short blocker. Practice ended, her teammates departed, and she remained with the two coaches for one last drill. One coach would dump the ball or set it quickly to the other coach who crushed the ball down the line. After 10–15 minutes of constant work, the drill had convinced my assistant that she could do what the coach wanted and needed her to do for the upcoming match.

Never Underestimate the Value of "Heart"

I had two players who demonstrated this more than any others and both were awarded AVCA Division II Player-of-the-Year awards.

Sheri demonstrated her heart to the ultimate in a match against West Texas State at the USAFA Premier Tournament. We were playing for third place but the team was playing without emotion, still disappointed that we were not in the finals. Sheri decided that we were not going to lose—at least if it were up to her. If the team wanted to help, fine; but if not, she would do it by herself. She played her heart out. We won the match and she collapsed. She was rushed to the emergency room where—fortunately after the two intravenous bottles replenished her electrolytes—she completely recovered.

Annie sprained her ankle in the semifinal match of the 1986 national championships and could not finish the match. Fortunately, we won and would play in the finals the next day. That night we went to the emergency room; X-rays did not show a break. The doctor gave her permission to play if she could physically do it without limping. No one thought she would be able to play, especially when she entered the gym the next day on crutches. When Annie got up to stretch and put all her weight on the foot after a whole day of being on crutches, she was in so much pain that she just started to cry. She had worked four years to be able to play in this match. I did not think there was any way she would be able to play, so I adjusted our lineup accordingly. About a half hour before the game began, I saw her running and jumping with no limp, as if nothing had ever happened. She played and we won the championship. She walked out of the gym on crutches and was in a cast for the next two months.

You Must Be Able to Communicate with Your Setter

I was coaching the USA Men's Maccabiah Team in Israel and I had two very good setters. It was difficult to choose between them. One player was tall, left-handed, and could attack the second ball very successfully. The other player was shorter but very smart and good under pressure. The main difference between the two was that I could communicate better with one of them. He was able to run the system and tactics and make adjustments according to our combined decisions. Both setters got an opportunity to play, but the final nod went to the setter with whom I was better able to communicate.

Insist That Players Adopt an Attitude You Feel Is in Their Best Interest and That of the Team

Good teams have competitive players, but when this competitiveness is carried to the extreme, it can become detrimental to the individual as well as the team. On more than one occasion I have had to deal with this situation. In each case I probably waited longer than I should have to confront it, but unpleasant encounters are as hard on the coach as on the player. When I realized that these players' attitudes had to change for the team to function effectively, there was no room for negotiation. Although these players were excellent, it reached a point where I was willing to let them go. Attitude is a decision—if it is important enough to players to be a part of the team, they will change. Fortunately for our program, they all did.

Practice Like You Want to Play

Another player gained our respect and that of her teammates through her extreme training efforts.

No one practiced with more passion, dedication, concentration, and effort. She demanded personal excellence of herself in every drill. She was rarely satisfied with her performance because she knew she could do better. She did not wait for the game to be her best—she demanded it of herself in every drill and scrimmage.

What really impressed me was how serious she took even a simple serving drill. Her goal one day was to serve down the line to zone 1 and to hit the indicated target ten times before two errors. She served ball after ball with the same focused concentration as if it were a championship match. She ran to get the next ball so she would have as many contacts as she could. She was visibly upset when she made an error. She took every drill seriously and got as much out of it as she could.

I recalled this drill after we had just won a match against a rival team where she served six very tough down-the-line serves to zone 1 in a rally score game with our team being down 10–14. A miss would have ended the match and our chances of going to the regional championships. An easy serve would have probably had the same result. She served six tough balls to the target and the receiver was only able to pass with average accuracy. We won the game and match 16–14.

Several weeks later her roommate said to me, "She doesn't do anything halfway. She told me that 'If it's worth doing, it's worth doing right.' I think that is why her side of the room is so messy."

Be Knowledgeable and Prepared—You Will Earn the Team's Respect

It was my first year coaching at the university and I was nervous. The previous coach had given me the rundown on all the returning players so I had a good idea about which ones were going to be easy to work with and which ones might give me problems. When each player introduced herself, I took an especially good look at those the coach had warned me about. It turned out that I did not have problems with any of the players. They were competitive athletes who wanted to be coached. Once I proved to them that I was a knowledgeable coach, they responded to the challenge. If you demonstrate your leadership and ability to coach, your team—whether women or men players—will respond favorably.

Never Underestimate the Value of Competitiveness

It is difficult to teach competitiveness. Many players think they have it and they do, but its levels vary. You can create drills that bring out the competitiveness in athletes, but the amount you can bring out depends on players' personalities and past experiences. One of my best players had average volleyball skills and I thought it was best to start a player with more physical talent. She continued to practice hard and it soon became obvious that she belonged on the court. It was not her physical skills, rather her competitiveness that gave her the edge. She knew how to win. She had played very little volleyball, but she had trained and showed horses for most of her life. She was a winner. She wanted to compete and she knew how. She worked very hard and got the most out of her abilities. She and her teammates won a national championship.

Make Drills and Scrimmages Gamelike

It was our last season in Division II and our last opportunity to compete in the regional championships. The season had been very up and down and we needed to win all nine of our remaining matches. The majority of these wins were comebacks. The players seemed to think a big part of those victories was our scrimmage comeback drills. At the time I did not realize the positive effect the drills had. We made the drills very tough and emotional. Oftentimes the team was not successful and would have to run sprints. The key was they learned to give their best effort even though the possibility existed that they could lose. We finished the season winning nine in a row and qualifying for the regional championships.

Never Underestimate the Value of Commitment

Many of my players have taught me that if your commitment to the program is strong, problems can be resolved. Here is an example. One of my players had a class that ended at 1:00 and practice started at 1:10 on the other side of campus. She always arrived to practice on time. How did she do it? She wore her practice gear to class and ran to practice. One day I was surprised when she entered the gym in a skirt. In moments she had taken off her wraparound skirt to reveal her practice shorts and then she removed her blouse covering a sports bra. She quickly put on her practice jersey and shoes—30 seconds later she was warming up. There's always a solution.

Winning Is Not Based on the Score, but on Giving a Great Effort

I have been very fortunate to have many successful seasons on the scoreboard, but some of our best efforts have not always resulted in wins. In all fairness to your players, success must be measured on attitude, effort, and improvement. Players must understand that the process is as important as the results. I have been very proud of all my teams but especially those I feel have reached their potential and have had the very best season possible regardless of their place finish.

Distinguish Between Good Results and Bad Execution

Players often do not distinguish between talented and weak opponents. If the team or individual is successful, players feel they have done everything correctly. In contrast, when playing against strong teams, players think they are having an off day rather than relating it to the greater obstacles presented by the opponent. One of my players declared to me after a great match against a weak team, "I guess I CAN middle block." It was partially true because against this particular team she had an exceptional performance but she did not have the skills to be successful at a higher level. The results do not always give the whole story. The result can be good, but there are many factors involved to determine if the performance is what is necessary to be consistently successful.

If It's Not Broken, Don't Fix It

One of my best attackers had a very "unique" approach and arm swing. Although it did not fit the championship volleyball "checklist," she was very effective. She hammered the ball and could place it anywhere on the court. She performed consistently not only against weak teams but strong teams as well. Her technique was not the norm but I am glad I was smart enough not to mess with this future All-American's technique.

Consider Carefully to Vote or Select the Captain

One of my biggest errors was allowing the team to vote on captain when I knew the person they would select would not be suitable for the position. She was a very experienced and talented player, but did not buy into the team rules and did not deal well with the coach as an authority figure. When I informed her that she was selected, she told me that I should not have allowed them to vote and she would not be a good captain. My second mistake was not trying to convince her of the importance of her leadership. This was my opportunity to make a difficult situation better by guiding the player to work within the policies of the program and in doing so help the team reach its goals.

Make Instructions Impossible to Misinterpret

I was coaching in the Gold Medal Round of the Sports Festival and we were in the final set two games all. In our previous match against this team, we had followed our game plan and attacked their weaknesses. I had used up my last timeout and I watched helplessly as my setter set five times in a row to an inexperienced outside attacker who was forced to hit against the opponent's strongest blocker with no success. We had discussed the appropriate options but the setter seemed to be focused on only one, the wrong one. I tried to yell instructions to her on the court but to no avail and we lost the match. I take full responsibility because I did not use my last timeout wisely. My instructions should have been more precise. For example: "Set to the middle or right front attacker or set back row. Do not set to the left front attacker."

Every Player Must Have a Role

Many top players begin their careers as practice players and in the games provide water and towels for the "core" players, take statistics, or fulfill other responsibilities. There are many important ways to contribute as a member of the team. Of course all players do not accept their roles even when they agreed to them. On the men's team one year I had a player who I could have cut from the squad but I gave him the option to practice with the team with the understanding he would not be playing in any of the competitions. I asked him if he could live with this and his answer was yes. Several weeks later he complained about not playing and I reminded him of our agreement. He stayed but never did accept the role of practice player. He continued to improve and was not disruptive to the team, so he was allowed to stay.

Never Underestimate the Influence You Have on Your Students

Many team players as well as students in my physical education activity classes return to tell me of the importance volleyball played in their lives. Sometimes it is obvious but I have had many surprises. One of my students returned to campus for his twentieth reunion and came to visit. He was not athletic and had a vision problem that made volleyball difficult for him. His parents said

© 2001 by Parker Publishing Company

he would never be able to play sports and, in fact, had not participated in sports until he entered college and my volleyball class. He was so proud of his volleyball accomplishments and has continued to play in recreational leagues. I never realized how important volleyball was in his life until he returned twenty years later and told me.

Adjust to the Officials

Early in my career I had little patience for poor officiating. It seemed that the player's ability and knowledge of the game was beyond that of the officials. We were playing a match against a rival team that we had beaten earlier in the season and my top setter was being called for a setting violation almost every time she contacted the ball. This was very unusual because she was an excellent setter and no official before or after ever made more than a minimum of calls. My setter was crying in the huddle but I insisted that she continue to use "hand" sets rather than a "forearm" set. My setter was setting correctly and I did not want the official to dictate how the game was played. My setter continued to use her hands and the mishandled ball call was immediate and continuous. I would not relent. I insisted that she use her "hands" even though I knew that if I had permitted her to use a "forearm" set we would have had a good opportunity to win. My stubbornness lost the match.

It is best to adjust to the officials and work to make changes in other ways. Talking to officials between games and/or after the match to give your philosophy, suggestions, and/or interpretations have a much better result.

Define Success for You and Your Players

My competitiveness has not diminished over the years. I still want to win every game and am disappointed when we do not. My definition of success, however, has expanded beyond the win–loss record. Success is about the journey as much as it is about reaching the destination. Success is about uniting a group of individuals to pursue a common goal. Success is about overcoming individual differences in order for the team to achieve its potential. Success is about how much athletes excel on a personal level. Success is about the number of athletes who have enjoyed their overall experience. Success is about teaching through sports the life skills necessary to be a winner.

MAXIM: *We must either find a way or make one.* Hannibal

YOUR COACHING PHILOSOPHY

It is your responsibility to establish a philosophy of coaching and base all subsequent decisions on these beliefs and values. This philosophy is reflected in the program goals, policies, and expectations and must be addressed in the first team meeting. It must be made clear to the athletes that the foundation of the program rests on these principles. The following speech is an example of what might be presented to the team at the first meeting of the season.

The Coach's Commitment.   Your coaching staff loves volleyball and loves coaching. We are motivated day after day to do all we can to make this team successful. We will provide you every opportunity to be as good as you want to be.

Goals. We want you to strive to be your best, to be all-league, all-region, and All-American. Together we want to strive to win a league title, a regional title, and a national championship. We also want you to understand that success is not only measured by awards and wins and losses; just as important as these tangible prizes is the process and what we learn along the way.

We want you to grow as athletes and people. We want you to take the lessons you learn from competing in volleyball and use them to help you achieve in all areas of your life. We want you to be confident in yourselves and know that there is no obstacle that you cannot overcome with hard work. We want you to learn the meaning of commitment, discipline, responsibility, and hard work.

We want you to acquire the skills to get a good-paying job that you enjoy after you graduate. No one is going to give you anything in life. You must work hard and earn it. There are no guarantees you will obtain everything you want, but you will get a lot more if you work hard.

We are proud of the successes of our past teams, but we are most proud of the fact that the majority of our players earned college degrees and are good citizens.

You are student–athletes, and we want you to enjoy both your volleyball and school experience. We want you to take advantage of your opportunity to attend and graduate from this school. We want you to utilize all the resources that the school has to offer.

The Player's Commitment. You must make a decision about your willingness to work with us and commit yourself to the program. We have set high standards. We ask you to buy into this philosophy and follow the ground rules. You must decide if you want to be on the team under these conditions, because these are the rules we are going to play by and there are very few exceptions.

Players' Roles. Each of you has an important role on the team regardless of your playing time. Each player contributes to the success of the team, whether it is on the court, in practice, taking statistics, or cheering on the team. Your role is evaluated every day and can change with individual progress, but you must accept your role for the team to function effectively.

The Substitutes. Playing time will not be equal. The first question you must ask yourself is if you can sit on the bench. Everyone puts in the hours in practice and deserves to play, but only six players are allowed on the court at one time. We have 12 players and we must all be positive and supportive of one another. Unless you can answer this question with a "yes," then you have not made a positive commitment to the team.

Being Coachable. Our job is to coach you. We have a great deal of experience and successes doing this. Although there is more than one way to do things correctly, there are definitely incorrect techniques that will inhibit progress. We expect you to make changes or adjustments according to our decisions. Anyone who is not interested in doing this, we are not interested in having you—regardless of your abilities and experience.

We are not doing our job unless we do everything within our abilities to get the talent out of you so you can use it consistently in practice and the game. If we are on you, correcting you and pushing you, it is because we have confidence in your abilities. We only ask you to do those things that will make you better and only if we think you can do them.

Building Trust. Trust and respect are very powerful elements of a successful team. You must honestly believe that we are doing everything necessary to make you and the team better. Those who have this trust and follow our advice improve greatly; those who do not do not get much out of the program. You must trust us, even if everything is not going your way.

We will give you our respect, but if it is not returned, then you will lose the right to ours. Times will be difficult, you will be frustrated, there will be conflicts between you and your teammates and you and your coaches. We will not always win. You might not always play. You will not always be happy with our decisions. We have rules with which you may not agree. We are open to input, but in an intelligent, courteous, and polite way. We will always listen, but input does not guarantee the decision you desire.

Developing a Work Ethic. The program is built on a strong work ethic. We will give you our best effort and we expect that you will do the same. Everyone wants to win, but very few people are willing to make the commitment and sacrifices to do it. It takes an enormous amount of energy, time, effort, and commitment. You cannot cut corners. If you think you can do it without working, you are wrong. We are going to challenge you to be good every single day, and you must be motivated to give your best. Do not expect us to be happy with you if you are lazy, undisciplined, or selfish. If it is not worth the best you can do, it is not worth your time.

Resisting Temptations. You will encounter many temptations and it is easy to give in to them. You must resist making poor choices, such as going to a party when you should be studying or resting before a game, or stopping conditioning when the going gets tough and you would rather go home and sit on the couch and snooze. You must have the desire and determination to achieve, because there are so many others who are working toward the same goals. If you relax, if you give into temptations, you will be passed by—whether by a teammate or the opponent. We want you to be champions, not merely participants.

No Joking Around. You must take practice and the game seriously. Do not joke or laugh when you make mistakes or lose a point. Show us that it bothers you and make an adjustment the next time.

On Winning. We are happy when the team performs well—whether or not we win—and we are disappointed when we do not play up to our potential. We might not always win on the scoreboard, but we can always be successful. Ten years from now you will not remember the individual wins and losses; rather, you'll remember the experiences you had and what you learned from competing.

Developing Sportsmanship. Be a good sportsperson. Do not hate the opponent—rather, love the game. Play with class. No swearing, trash talking, or finger pointing. Avoid responding to "trash-talking" opponents. Focus on your play and that of your teammates. Celebrate good plays on our side of the net.

Managing Time. To successfully balance athletics, academics, and—for some of you—work, you need to learn to manage your time and set priorities. You must make difficult choices about what activities you are able to participate in and which ones you must forgo. Do not leave studies for last in your desire for a social life. Successful student–athletes take their obligations and responsibilities seriously on the court and in the classroom. You have daily choices and they determine your future success or failure.

Going to Class. You cannot be successful if you do not attend class and do not do the work. We will send out periodic progress reports to your teachers and drop by your classes to see if you are in attendance. We want to see you sitting in the front rows of class, with the top students, not in the back. If we do not see you in class, you do not play and from then on you drop by the volleyball office everyday on your way to class.

No Cheating. You cannot be successful and cheat. Do your own work. Do not ask teammates to do it for you. Attempt to finish your work first before looking at the answers in the back of the book. Read the chapters and answer the questions before the discussions in class.

Setting Priorities. You have one priority while you are here: to be the best student and the best athlete you are capable of being. One is not more important than the other. You cannot be your best in volleyball without practicing and you cannot do your best in the classroom if you do not attend class. If you need more help in either, you work harder and practice more. You must work as regularly and as hard on your academic skills as you do on your sport skills. We want you to compete in the classroom for grades and in the game for points. We want you to be first in sports and first in school.

Choosing Captains. The coaching staff is evaluating team members for the position of overall captain. If anyone has the commitment and desire to fulfill this role, please let us know and/or please inform us of someone you would like to be your captain.

The role of overall captain is a very important one and carries with it a big responsibility. Among other duties, this player is responsible for assisting with team management, maintaining discipline, leading by example, communicating effectively with both teammates and the coaching staff, and addressing any grievances with the coaches.

The captain(s) will be voted on by the team or selected by the coaches and announced within the next several weeks.

Starting Now. The season begins today. Everyone starts at zero with no kills, stuffs, aces, digs, or errors. We have no favorites. We want success for each one of you and will give you our best. It is your responsibility to earn a position on the court in practice. The best 12 players will be selected for the traveling squad. Best is based on skills, attitude, heart, and potential.

Do you understand what it takes to achieve your personal best? Are you willing to discipline yourself enough to do it? We challenge each one of you to answer *yes* to both. Begin today to *become your best.*

COACH'S ADMINISTRATIVE CHECKLIST

Use this checklist as a guideline to help organize your responsibilities for the entire season.

Preseason

❏ **Seek support for the program.** Identify powerful people in the community and sell them on the program values. Enlist them in the effort to reach your goals.

❏ **Select a staff.** Surround yourself with good personnel. Select competent and responsible assistants to help with the program.

❏ **Schedule matches.** Provide the athletes with as many practice matches as possible. Give them game opportunities to learn to compete.

❏ **Schedule beatable teams.** Build team confidence by playing teams you are confident of winning.

❏ **Schedule the best teams.** Schedule top-quality teams even though your team probably cannot win. The team must learn what improvements must be made to be successful at this level and raise its level of play. You must play the best to be the best.

❏ **Schedule teams of equal ability.** Schedule the majority of matches against opponents who are at the same level as your team. These matches will be competitive with either team having the opportunity to win.

❏ **Schedule facilities for practices and matches.**

❏ **Inspect facilities.** Inspect facilities for safety and repairs, such as gym floor, lighting, scoreboard, PA system, and so on. Schedule repairs, if necessary.

❏ **Check player eligibility.**

❏ **Arrange for player physicals, medical clearance, flu shots.**

❏ **Inventory equipment.** Order balls, nets, kneepads, score books, statistical forms, rule books, first-aid kits, and so on.

❏ **Prepare the team budget.**

❏ **Order game and practice uniforms and shoes.**

❏ **Secure sponsors for game programs and pocket schedules.**

❏ **Secure match personnel and officials.**

❏ **Secure ball people for the three-ball rotation system.**

❏ **If necessary, teach personnel how to keep the score book and take statistics.**

❏ **Arrange transportation and lodging for away trips.**

❏ **Prepare trip itineraries.**

❏ **Prepare team play books.** Include policies, guidelines, and expectations for the season.

❏ **Prepare squad phone and address lists.**

❏ **Prepare emergency phone numbers of parents at home and work.**

❏ **Prepare phone list of support people.**

❏ **Prepare squad roster for games.**

❏ **Update booster phone and address lists.**

❏ **Distribute schedules.**

❏ **Take team photo.**

❏ **Pump up balls. Place game balls in separate location.**

❏ **Plan preseason parent–athlete meeting.**

❏ **Plan banquet and awards program.**

Postseason

- ❏ **Prepare final season budget.**
- ❏ **Prepare season summary fact sheet.** Include match results and individual and team awards.
- ❏ **Prepare individual player evaluations.**
- ❏ **Prepare off-season conditioning program.**
- ❏ **Inventory equipment and plan for repairs and purchases for next season.**

SELECTING THE TEAM

The squad size depends on the number of courts and coaches, but generally consists of 12 to 15 players: four setters, four middle blockers, five outside attackers, and two defensive specialists. Six to nine of these athletes form the core of the "playing team."

An important decision for you to make philosophically is whether or not to cut players from the squad. There may be no other option if the numbers are not manageable, but whenever possible it is best to allow players to continue to practice. Those players who are not happy with their roles will cut themselves. Attitude and desire are the most important factors in determining success almost exclusively of one's athletic ability and starting levels. If cuts are made, at times, some potentially very good players can be mistakenly eliminated from the squad. At the same time, if the squad is too large there may not be sufficient time to work with the core team players. A balance must be reached between having too few or too many.

Criteria and Procedures for Selecting the Squad

- Evaluate the six basic skills (serve, pass, set, dig, block, and attack) and movement fundamentals through standard volleyball drills.
- Evaluate players based on their physical and mental characteristics and responsibilities of the position they will fill.
- Evaluate athletes' desire, competitiveness, and toughness. Do drills that mentally and physically tax the athletes.
- Evaluate athletes' ability to be coached. Do drills that test their ability to follow directions and make changes.
- Use physical testing to evaluate athletes' overall athletic abilities, primarily strength, coordination, quickness, and jumping.
- Evaluate inexperienced players more on their athletic ability than their volleyball skills. Their skills can be improved.

Player-Selection Admonitions

- Avoid selecting players to fit a system. Select the best athletes and design a system to fit their needs.
- Do not let players go away feeling they have not been given a fair chance. Give athletes sufficient opportunity to demonstrate their skills.

- Do not make decisions hastily. Know the strengths and weaknesses of each player.
- Do not avoid talking to players who have been cut. Be available to explain specifically why players were not selected and what they need to do to make the team in the future.
- Do not let players leave without thanking them for coming out for the team. Let them know you appreciate their efforts and explain to them that although you would like everyone to be able to play, there are number limitations in each position.

PHYSICAL TESTING

Place tape or a cloth tape measure on the gym floor or on the wall as appropriate. Only one stop-watch is necessary for the timed tests. The timer calls out the seconds for each runner. Two to three trials are allowed for each test.

Vertical Reach

Stand perpendicular to the wall, feet flat with the dominant arm closer to wall. Extend that arm up as high as possible with the palm against the wall on the measurement tape. Record in feet and inches.

Vertical Jump

Position self as for the vertical reach. Allow a comfortable distance from the wall so the jump is not restricted. Crouch down and jump up as high as possible off both feet, swinging the arms back and up to aid in jumping. Touch the measurement tape on the wall with the hand closer to the wall at the peak of the jump. No movement of the feet is allowed before the jump. Record in feet and inches.

Block Reach

Stand facing the wall, with feet flat and toes against the wall. Reach up as high as possible with both hands. Record in feet and inches.

Block Jump

Position self as for the block reach but allow a comfortable distance from the wall so the block jump is not restricted. Crouch down as in a blocking jump, and explode up touching as high as possible with both hands on the measurement tape. No movement of the feet is allowed before the jump. Record in feet and inches.

Approach Jump

Use any type of approach (a three- or four-step approach preferred) and take off on both feet. Reach up with the attacking arm to touch as high as possible on the measurement tape. Using a one-foot take-off disqualifies the jumper. Use a vertex or similar apparatus.

Triple Hop

Stand in a stationary position behind the line. Take three consecutive and continuous two-foot hops (broad jumps) across the floor for maximum distance. The hops must be successive with no pausing or stopping to take extra arm swings between each jump. Hold the final position until the distance has been measured. Falling backwards or using a one-foot take-off disqualifies the jumper.

Medicine Ball Toss

Stand with toes of both feet behind the line. Use a two-handed chest pass motion to throw a 5-pound medicine ball as far as possible. No approach is permitted, but a lunge forward from a crouch is allowed. The ball must be released before landing over the line. A basketball may be substituted if no medicine ball is available.

Nine-Meter Shuttle

Start in a ready position with both feet behind the sideline. On the signal "Ready, go" sprint to the opposite sideline (nine meters), touch it with one foot and hand, and run back to the starting sideline and repeat the procedure. The course is traversed six times as rapidly as possible. Athletes run through the final line. Use groups of three to five.

Prone 18-Meter Sprint

Start by lying on the floor with the nose touching the endline. The hands are palm down and fully extended in front on the floor. On the signal "Ready, go" get up and sprint to the opposite endline. Use groups of three to five.

Agility Run

Set up cones, chairs, or other obstacles on the volleyball court as shown in Diagram 1-1. Athletes stand behind the line in a ready position and on the signal "Ready, go" complete the course as quickly as possible. If an athlete touches or goes over any of the obstacles, he or she must begin again. Always move facing the indicated direction without turning around. More than one station can be set up depending on the number of athletes.

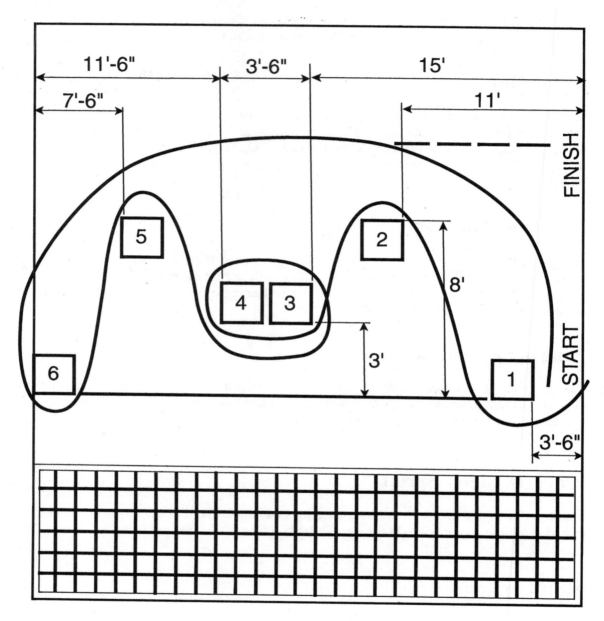

Diagram 1-1.

ASSISTANT COACH CHECKLIST

Selecting assistant coaches is as important as the selection of players for the team. They must be qualified and benefit the program. Their selection should be based on personal qualities as well as their knowledge of the game—and once selected they must be given specific responsibilities within the team. Use this checklist as a guideline to determine those factors you feel are important.

General

❑ Be a mature leader.
❑ Display knowledge of volleyball.
❑ Have good communication and repertoire with players.
❑ Show empathy for players in a competitive situation.

Season

❑ Help plan and run practices.
❑ Monitor equipment and uniforms.
❑ Secure transportation for away trips.
❑ Supervise home-game setup.
❑ Assist with administrative tasks.
❑ Call game scores to media.
❑ Assist with scouting opponents.
❑ Assist with recruiting duties.
❑ Assist with camps, clinics, promotions, and fund-raisers.
❑ Supervise weight-training program.

GAME-PROMOTION CHECKLIST

It is the responsibility of the volleyball staff to assist in the promotion and marketing of their product. It is important to educate young coaches, players, and spectators about the game and in doing so influence them to become fans and follow your team.

Promotion and Marketing Ideas

❑ Sponsor one big match with a top team.
❑ Sponsor one international match whenever possible.
❑ Give clinics and speeches.
❑ Establish a boosters support group. Do not start by asking for money or making it a big effort; just get people involved.
❑ Invite parents to pre- and postgame chalk talks.

❏ Invite parents to see a practice and explain what each drill is attempting to accomplish. Explain the team's offensive and defensive systems. Have a team BBQ afterwards.
❏ Have an aggressive season-ticket campaign.
❏ Give away brochures, pocket schedules, and tickets.
❏ Give tickets to local sports stores, radio stations, newspapers, the YWCA, health clubs, and so on.
❏ Have a media match and luncheon to teach reporters about the game and about the team's statistics.
❏ Mail out personal invitations to special guests for individual games.
❏ Sponsor single-sex and coed alumni games.
❏ Wear something special on game days to promote the games, such as arm bands, hats, team T-shirts. Carry helium balloons.
❏ Wear buttons that say "Watch volleyball—you'll dig it!"
❏ Have a volleyball exhibition at half time of a basketball game.
❏ Sell volleyball team T-shirts.
❏ Train and use a great announcer.
❏ Select different people to sing the national anthem or play it on a musical instrument.
❏ Get families to come and adopt a player.
❏ Get the pep band to play at the games.
❏ Have serving contests between the second and third games.
❏ Have a local fast-food chain sponsor "If we win, you'll receive a free ice cream with this ticket stub" or "If the opponent scores less than 25 total points, we'll buy you a soda" promotions.

Sponsor Special Promotional Nights

❏ Plant night ("Grow with our team.") The first 50 fans receive a plant
❏ Door prizes
❏ Costume night
❏ Tattoo (washable) night
❏ School colors night
❏ Patriotic dress night
❏ Parents admitted free with child night
❏ "Watch now, pay later if you liked what you saw" night

Reproducibles

Successful coaching requires the development of a personal philosophy. The following worksheets are designed to help you do this through (1) an evaluation of the actions and behaviors of coaches or teachers you have known, (2) evaluating yourself as a person, and (3) making decisions about your goals and how you will manage your team.

Coach's Worksheet:
POSITIVES & NEGATIVES

List the positive and negative actions/behaviors of coaches who have influenced your philosophy.

Positive Actions/Behaviors
Example: Coach Moo sat calmly on the bench during the game, encouraging us even when we made unforced errors.
•
•
•
•
•
•
•
•
•
•

Negative Actions/Behaviors
Example: Coach Zero only encouraged those players who were experienced and played club volleyball.
•
•
•
•
•
•
•
•
•
•

Coach's Worksheet:
YOU AS COACH

List five adjectives that describe the ideal coach.
-
-
-
-
-

List five adjectives that describe you.
-
-
-
-
-

List three reasons why you are coaching.
-
-
-

List three things necessary to satisfy your ego.
-
-
-

List three of your best coaching qualities.
-
-
-

List two coaching qualities you would like to improve upon.
-
-

How would someone else describe you as a coach?

-

List three of your practice-management strengths.

-
-
-

List two practice-management weaknesses you want to improve.

-
-

List three of your game-management strengths.

-
-
-

List two game-management weaknesses you want to improve.

-
-

List five duties for your assistant coach.

-
-
-
-
-

List four of your coaching goals.

-
-
-
-

List four obstacles you might encounter in reaching your goals.
•
•
•
•

List three ways to build team spirit.
•
•
•

Coach's Worksheet:
YOUR PHILOSOPHY

List five program goals.
•
•
•
•
•

Define the difference between winning and being a winner.
•

List four things that must happen for the season to be a success.
•
•
•
•

List five team rules and penalties for infractions.
•
•
•
•
•

List four player behaviors that you will not tolerate.

-
-
-
-

List four methods you would use to cut the squad (when necessary).

-
-
-
-

Give an example of how to deal with athletes who use profanity.

-

List four ways to keep up team morale when the team is losing.

-
-
-
-

List three penalties for athletes who are late or miss practices.

-
-
-

List four ways you will work on conditioning inside or outside the gym.

-
-
-
-

Give an example of when you might have two sets of rules (a double standard).

-

Will the overall captain be selected by a vote of the team or by the coaches?
Circle one and justify.

-

Will the court captain be selected by a vote of the team or by the coaches?
Circle one and justify.

-

Give an example of some comments you would make to the players at the first team meeting to establish your role as the coach.

-

Give an example of some comments you would make to the parents at the first promotional BBQ explaining your philosophy of the program.

-

List four things you need from the administration to make the program successful.

-
-
-
-

Justify why each is important.

-
-
-
-

© 2001 by Parker Publishing Company

Coach's Worksheet:
CHARACTERISTICS OF EFFECTIVE TEAMS

Successful coaching involves two dimensions—content and process. Content deals with the technical and tactical aspects of the game, and process deals with the player's personal needs. The more effective you are as a coach who meets the athlete's needs, the more effective the group will function. The team's success is contingent upon the group's volleyball skills as well as a positive social structure. Through the process of completing this worksheet, you will understand more clearly the process of effective coaching.

You are the leader of the team. List four LEADERSHIP qualities you possess.
•
•
•
•

List four ways to build LEADERSHIP WITHIN THE TEAM.
•
•
•
•

Players need to feel a strong AFFILIATION with the team. List four ways to make players feel a part of the team.
•
•
•
•

List two emotional events you can provide to help the team BOND.
•
•

List three ways you can help avoid CLIQUES and widen friendships within the group.
•
•
•

Players need to INFLUENCE some aspect of their team life. List three situations in which players will be involved in the decision-making process.

-
-
-

All teams want to be COMPETENT. Players must buy into the training system. List three ways to sell your program.

-
-
-

There must be a strong TASK COMMITMENT in the pursuit of a common goal. This unified effort helps build cohesion. List four team goals.

-
-
-
-

Each player must have a ROLE to feel a part of the team. List the current role for each nonstarter.

-
-
-
-
-
-

To be their best, players must feel good about themselves. List three ways you can build players' SELF-ESTEEM.

-
-
-

FAILURE and errors are part of the game. List three ways to help players deal with these setbacks.

-
-
-

To be most successful players must feel comfortable in their training ENVIRONMENT. List four ways to achieve this.

-
-
-
-

Players learn best when they are APPRECIATED and know you care. List four ways to show your appreciation.

-
-
-
-

List three TRADITIONS the program has or you will establish to foster a strong bond to the team.

-
-
-
-

Coach's Worksheet: TEAM TACTICS

To determine tactics, you must first determine your team's strengths and weaknesses.

List four team strengths.

-
-
-
-

List four team weaknesses.

-
-
-
-

List five ways to best utilize your personnel offensively.

-
-
-
-
-

List five ways to best utilize your personnel defensively.

-
-
-
-
-

Every player must have a role. These roles are obvious for the starters. Define the roles for the six nonstarters.

-
-
-
-
-
-

Circle your offensive system (4–2, 6–2, 5–1) and justify.

-

What type of defensive system do you use?

-

Justify.

-

Describe your side-out offense.

-

How will the plays be called?

-

Describe your free ball offense.

-

How will the plays be called?

-

Describe your transition offense.

-

How will the plays be called?

-

Name your overall captain.
•
Justify.
•
Name your court captain.
•
Justify.
•
Name your exercise leader.
•
Justify.
•

Name a statistic you will use.
•
How will it help the team?
•

Name a statistic you will use.
•
How will it help the team?
•

Name a statistic you will use.
•
How will it help the team?
•

Diagram the starting line.

Justify the placement of the players.

-

Diagram the placement of each player in the serve receive formation (use numbers) for each of the six rotations.

Rotation 1	Rotation 2	Rotation 3

Rotation 4	Rotation 5	Rotation 6

PROGRAM GOALS

Provide participants with written goals, policies, and expectations prior to the first practice.

- Have FUN and ENJOY the game.
- Make it a quality experience.
- Be a WINNER. Be a CLASS ACT.
- Be your best athletically and academically.
- Strive for continuous improvement.
- Improve with each match and within the match.
- Represent yourself and the team in a positive fashion.
- Respect and accept coaches' and teammates' individuality.
- Support teammates and coaches.
- Contribute to the total team effort at all times.
- Deal with conflicts head-on through open communication.
- Be responsible.
- Be disciplined. Give 100% effort in practice, during the game, and in the classroom.
- Stay in shape mentally and physically.
- Be honest with yourself, teammates, and coaches.
- Learn from your mistakes and handle them positively.
- Never surrender or turn against yourself.
- Play with pride and poise and PLAY TO WIN.
- Love the battle, the competition, and the challenge.
- Win league, regional, and national titles.
- Work as a team to achieve these goals through dedication to the program.

PLAYER POLICIES AND EXPECTATIONS

COACH'S POLICY: Whatever is best for the team, we do!

Personal Conduct

- Attend all practices, physical conditioning workouts, games, fund-raisers, and promotional events.
- In the event you are unable to attend any function due to work or personal emergency, contact the coaches immediately.
- All players on the squad are required to attend all home matches and assist with home team responsibilities.
- If you miss a practice or function, you will be expected to make it up by contributing in other areas at another time.
- Be on time to every team function. It is inconsiderate to teammates and coaches to be late and it will not be tolerated.

- Make volleyball a priority in your life. Manage your time accordingly so that there is no conflicts.
- Conduct yourself in such a manner that you bring credit and honor to yourself, your teammates, the team, and your school.
- Do all assignments requested by the coach whether or not you feel they are important. Failure to do this will result in additional conditioning, and inability to practice and/or play.
- Report all injuries to the trainer. Minor injuries not properly treated can become serious.
- Do all therapy prescribed by trainers or physicians.
- Treatment may not be done during practice unless you have received prior approval. It must be taken care of before or after practice.
- All twelve players on the roster are required to fill out a match evaluation form after each match and turn it in before practice the following day.
- No swearing in practice or in the games.
- Treat teammates, coaches, officials, and opponents with courtesy and respect even when you are down or in a bad mood.
- Never criticize teammates to their faces or behind their backs, on or off the court!
- Work out personal conflicts with teammates immediately. Avoid passing on rumors or gossip. If the problem cannot be resolved, all parties must meet with the coaches until it is resolved.
- Do not sulk. If you have a problem or complaint, speak to the team captain(s) or coach.
- Drinking, smoking, or the use of drugs of any amount will be dealt with severely.
- Maintain good nutrition. Continue to cut down on junk food while working on improving your diet.

Academics

- Make academics a priority in your life. Attend all classes, and do all assignments on time and to the best of your ability.
- Remember the difference between HOMEWORK and STUDYING. You may finish your homework, but there is always some studying to do.
- Do your homework twice. The second time you will get a lot more out of it.
- Meet every academic obligation.
- Stay academically eligible.
- Discuss class conflicts with teachers as soon as you are aware of them.

Practice Expectations

- Come to the first practice of the season in shape. It hurts you and the team when you are not able to practice at full strength.
- Come to every practice. This is "your" and "our" opportunity to improve.
- If you know you will miss practice, communicate this in writing to the coaches.
- All missed practice sessions, except for an excused illness, must be made up and a substitute practice form must be turned in the following day.
- Be on time to practice. This means long hair tied, shoes and kneepads on, and ankles and fingers taped, if necessary.

- Be mentally ready to practice. Leave your problems outside of the gym.
- All players share in the net set-up and take-down responsibilities. Court set-up is ready by the hour of practice.
- Dress in official practice gear with shirts tucked in.
- Do not use practice as a time to socialize with teammates.
- Practice conversation should be directly related to the practice session.
- Inform visitors that they are welcome to attend practices, but they are not allowed to talk to or approach the athletes or coaches.
- Check in with the coach immediately if you arrive late.
- Notify the coach if you must leave practice.

Uniforms

- Uniforms are to be worn for approved events only. You are financially responsible for any items lost or stolen.
- You are responsible to turn in uniforms upon request. Failure to do so in a prompt fashion will result in fines.
- Fold and place sweats on the bench or in your bags.
- Place bags in an orderly fashion behind the bench.
- All jerseys are to be tucked in.
- Only official team gear is worn at practices, scrimmages, and matches.
- Do not wear jewelry in practices or the games.
- Turn in practice gear to be washed daily.
- Turn in game uniforms immediately after home games. Do not wear uniforms home.
- After away games, uniforms must be returned before 10:00 A.M. the following morning. Never wash your own uniform.

Travel

- Arrive before the departure time. We will leave without you if you are late.
- Everyone travels with the team. The only exception is that you may travel home with your parents after the game.
- Everyone is responsible for keeping the van's or bus's interior clean. Pick up your own trash.
- Your personal appearance and dress are important. The emphasis is on neatness and cleanliness.
- Locker rooms are to be left clean. Dirty towels, tape, paper cups, and so on, are to be placed in the proper areas.
- When help is required to carry additional items, assignments will be made for each specific trip. When an assignment is made, you are responsible for the item for the entire trip.
- Players are responsible for loading their own gear into the vans or buses.

Lodging

- The coaches will make up the lodging assignments. There will be no unapproved room changes.
- Those individuals in the room will pay any additional room charges.
- Be courteous to other guests by being quiet in the halls and in the rooms at all times.
- Comply with the stated curfew.

MATCH EVALUATION FORM

Match evaluation form for _____

Match date _____ Opponent _____ Site _____

Winner _____ Scores _____

Give a brief evaluation of why we won or lost.

_____

_____

_____

_____

List opponent's technical or tactical strengths. Be specific. Indicate individual players by name or number.

_____

_____

_____

_____

List opponent's technical or tactical weaknesses.

_____

_____

_____

What worked for you that will repeat when we meet this team again?

_____

_____

_____

What did not work and you will change?

_____

_____

_____

_____

What was your physical ( ) and mental ( ) effort level in this match on a scale of 1–10?

VOLLEYBALL PLAYER CONTRACT

Here is a sample player contract you should consider using with your athletes.

I understand that, as a member of the _____ Volleyball Team, I will
be expected to make ACADEMICS *and* ATHLETICS a priority in my life.
team name

I will not be satisfied with less than my best effort on the court or in the classroom.

I will strive to earn A's & B's in all my classes.

I understand that if I do not maintain an overall GPA of 2.5, I will be expected to attend team study-hall sessions.

I will attend every class. *I will* arrive on time for each class and I will turn in every assignment on the assigned date.

I will take advantage of the Learning Center and Tutorial Services.

I will attend all practices, games, fund-raisers, and promotional events. In the event I am unable to attend any function due to work or personal emergency, I will contact the coaches immediately.

I understand that if I do miss any volleyball function, I will be expected to make it up by contributing in other areas at another time.

I will be on time to every volleyball function. *I understand* that it is inconsiderate to my teammates and coaches to be late.

I will treat my teachers, coaches, and teammates with courtesy and respect, even when I am down or in a bad mood.

I will give 100% effort in every practice and game, as it is my intention to become the best volleyball player that I can be.

I understand that for my personal success, and the success of the program, I must follow these guidelines and, furthermore, encourage my teammates to do the same.

I have read and agree to the above guidelines. I understand that failure to meet the requirements of the contract may result in loss of opportunities to continue as a member of the _____ Volleyball Team.
team name

Signed/dated _____

TEAM CAPTAIN CHECKLIST

The role of the captain is very important to the overall success of the team. Responsibilities can include that of court captain if he/she is a starter. If not, another player can be chosen. Use this checklist as a guideline to help in your selection of the captain.

- ❏ Exemplifies the highest standards of a student–athlete.
- ❏ Has great work ethics.
- ❏ Is mature, positive, intelligent, and articulate.
- ❏ Sets the standards for all players.
- ❏ Confronts teammates who are not meeting team standards.
- ❏ Is positive and supportive of teammates.
- ❏ Is a likable person whom teammates and coaches can turn to for help.
- ❏ Serves as liaison between coaches and players.
- ❏ Meets with coaches on a regular basis to relate team problems and concerns.
- ❏ Assists coaches when necessary.
- ❏ Helps in scheduling activities and selecting roommates.
- ❏ Serves as team representative at official functions.
- ❏ Takes the initiative to "lead" in all team activities.
- ❏ Provides leadership on and off the court.
- ❏ Calls team meetings, without coach, if necessary.
- ❏ Is responsible to see that the gym is set up for practice.
- ❏ Leads warm-ups if an exercise leader is not designated.
- ❏ In matches has the responsibility to address the official.
- ❏ Knows the volleyball rules completely.
- ❏ Communicates with the official with courtesy and respect.
- ❏ After match thanks the officials and tells them they called a good match.
- ❏ Knows his or her role is vital to the team's success.
- ❏ Takes his or her responsibility as team leader seriously.
- ❏ Knows that it is an honor to be captain.

CHAPTER 2

THE PASSER

 "P" is for passer, who sends the ball to the setter; when the passes are good, the offense can be better.

The goal of the passer is to receive the serve and free ball, and direct it accurately and consistently to the setter. The perfect pass is one that allows the setter to run the offense and utilize all set and attack options. A team that cannot pass accurately will not be able to effectively execute its offense.

ATTRIBUTES OF SUCCESSFUL PASSERS

Good Vision and Hand–Eye Coordination

Tracking the ball from the server's hand to the passer's arms requires good hand–eye coordination and good depth perception. The passer must quickly calculate the speed, trajectory, and placement of the ball in order to assume the proper position. These calculations are done with the eyes. Players with poor depth perception have a very difficult time passing accurately.

Good Movement and Technique

Successful passers have good movement and pass mechanics. Accurate passing relies on good movement that puts the passer behind and under the ball. Although it is not always possible for the passer to assume the perfect body position in relation to the ball, the better the positioning, the more accurate and consistent the passing.

Aggressiveness

Successful passers do not wait for the ball to come to them; instead, they pursue it. They want to pass. They move aggressively to play all balls that are within their reach.

Mental Toughness

Successful passers do not shy away from playing the ball when the game is on the line. They are mentally tough and confident to accept the responsibility to pass the ball in all situations.

FOREARM AND OVERHAND PASSES

The forearm and overhand passes are used to receive the serve and free ball. The advantage of the "hand" pass is that its trajectory allows the ball to arrive to the setter more quickly and speeds up the offense. Mechanically, it provides a longer contact period potentially allowing for better accuracy and control. It also allows better court coverage because passers may position themselves midcourt to protect against the short ball and still have good range to receive deeper balls.

The main difference between the overhand pass and the set is its function. The technique of the overhand pass (described in Chapter 3) and the set is almost identical except that the posture for the overhand pass is more forward leaning rather than erect. The setter must maintain an up-and-down balanced posture prior to the set to disguise the set type and direction.

CHECKLISTS

Use these tactical checklists for yourself and/or provide them to your players as a guideline of tactical responsibilities. Some players like to read the checklists as a review prior to practice or a game.

FOREARM PASS CHECKLIST

See Figure 2-1.

Ready Position

✓ Stand with medium high posture, facing server.
✓ Use wide base, with feet spread not less than shoulder-width apart.
✓ Put weight on the balls of the feet and distribute equally.
✓ Relax arms and extend them out from the body.

Read Sequence

✓ See the toss and see the server contact.
✓ Track the ball from the server's hand.
✓ Evaluate the ball's direction, speed, and trajectory before it reaches the net.
✓ Hurry with the feet to put the body behind the ball.

Figure 2.1.

Figure 2.2.

Pre-Contact Position

> *MAXIM: Preparation is key. The pre-contact position determines success or failure.*

✓ Put the body behind the ball with the feet and hips facing the server.
✓ Stand with feet shoulder-width apart with the right foot slightly forward of the left.
✓ Flex knees about 90 degrees with the weight on the inside balls of the feet.

Platform

✓ Form and extend the platform behind and under the oncoming ball simultaneously as the lower body assumes the pre-contact position.
✓ Join hands when the arms are straight. (See Figure 2-2.) The heels of the hands are together and parallel. The thumbs are even and pressed together. The tips of the thumbs point toward the floor on the contact and follow-through.
✓ Extend the arms straight and lock at the elbows.
✓ Position the forearms even to form a solid platform.
✓ Turn the hands and wrists downward to facilitate a locked and straight arm position.
✓ Angle the arms toward the target by raising or lowering the shoulders and hips.
✓ For the most part, keep the arms straight before and after pass execution.

Contact

✓ Contact the ball on the arms between the wrists and the middle of the forearm.
✓ Contact the ball out from the body in front of the hips, and in a low position just off the thighs.
✓ Contact the ball at the body midline when passing to a target directly in front of the body. (See Figure 2-3.)
✓ Contact the ball to the left of midline when passing left to right (right foot forward). (See Figure 2-4.)
✓ Contact the bottom of the ball. Direct the swing upward for balls played close to the net with arms parallel to the floor. (See Figure 2-5.)
✓ Contact the back and the bottom of the ball for balls deep in the court. Direct the swing forward and upward. (See Figure 2-6.)
✓ Swing the arms out from the shoulders, according to the speed of the oncoming ball. The slower the serve, the more swing necessary to propel the ball.
✓ Cushion balls coming at very fast speeds by bringing the arms back toward the body at contact.

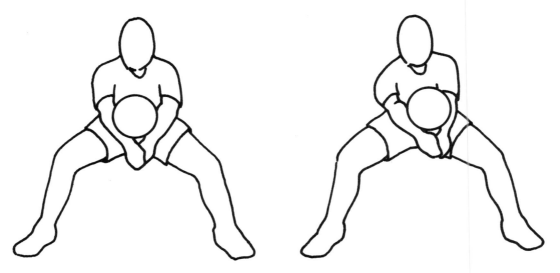

Figure 2.3.   **Figure 2.4.**

✓ On contact, strive to be stopped and balanced with the right foot forward.
✓ Keep the head still. Follow the ball into the platform with the eyes, but without any movement of the head.
✓ Have the target, platform, and ball in vision simultaneously.

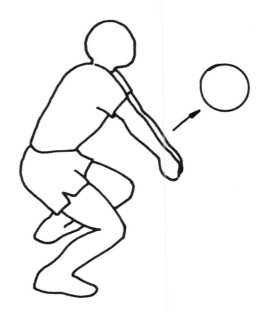

Figure 2.5.   **Figure 2.6.**

Figure 2.7.　　　　　　　　　　**Figure 2.8.**

Follow-Through

✓ Maintain a low and balanced position.
✓ Maintain a position with the platform and body leaning toward the target.
✓ Momentarily freeze to target.

High Balls/Misjudged Balls

✓ **Kick back pass.** Quickly kick back pushing off the left foot while kicking the right knee up and almost simultaneously passing the ball. The movement facilitates the passer in positioning the body behind the ball and playing it at a higher position. (See Figure 2-7.)
✓ **Lateral pass.** Step back to get the body out of the path of the ball and replace the arms with the chest. The shoulders and hips are raised or lowered to position the platform to face the target. (See Figure 2-8.)

> **KEY:** Use a breadboard to aid in teaching the pass. The passer extends the arms holding onto the sides of a breadboard. The breadboard represents the platform. The passer gets behind the ball, faces the server, and angles the breadboard for the ball to rebound to the target. The key is the position of the breadboard (arms) in relation to the target at the moment of contact.

MAXIM: If at first you don't succeed, you are running about average. M. H. Alderson

SERVE RECEIVE TACTICS CHECKLIST

✓ Know where you are on the court relative to the sideline and endline.

✓ Judge whether the ball is in or out according to your base position.

✓ Scout servers to determine their tendencies.

✓ Adjust your court position immediately after a difficult reception or "ace" by the opponent.

✓ Never stand so deep in the court that you give up an "ace" in front of you.

✓ Understand and be aware of position overlaps.

✓ Call "mine" early and move aggressively to the ball.

✓ Avoid calling "yours." This call often triggers a teammate to relax, assuming that you are playing the ball.

✓ Nonpasser(s) nearest the ball calls "in or out" on all balls close to the line.

✓ Nonpassers "open up" to the receiver ready to play an errant pass.

✓ As pass accuracy improves, lower the trajectory of the pass.

✓ A low trajectory quickens the offense and allows the setter to simultaneously see the ball, the attackers, and the block.

✓ Do not pinpoint difficult passes. Pass high to the middle of the court.

✓ Passing responsibilities come first! Then think attack!

CHAPTER 3

THE SETTER

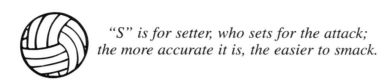

"S" is for setter, who sets for the attack;
the more accurate it is, the easier to smack.

The team setter(s) has primary setting responsibility, but the greater number of players who can set effectively, the stronger the team's attack potential. All players should perfect the skills of the front and back sets, but the team's setter(s) must be proficient in setting a variety of sets as well as be able to attack with a tip and/or spike on the second contact. The role of the setter encompasses many additional skills. It is a demanding job—both physically and mentally—and selection of the primary setter(s) is vital to the success of the team.

ATTRIBUTES OF SUCCESSFUL SETTERS

Good Condition

Setters must be in great physical condition because they are involved in virtually every play, touching every second ball.

Athletic

Setters must have strong athletic skills. They must have quick feet to get to all balls. They must be agile and have good spatial orientation to maneuver around the net and around teammates. It is valuable to have good height and/or jumping ability to block, set, and attack the ball on the second contact.

Left-Handed

Left-handed setters have an advantage in that the traditional setting target is toward the right sideline. Biomechanically it is easier for them to spike the second ball from this position.

Good Technique

Successful setters have good set mechanics. Solid technical skills translate into consistent setting and good ball control. Setters must be able to deliver accurate sets beyond the ability of other players, on good as well as difficult passes, and they must make very few errors.

Tactically Smart

Setters run the offense and must understand the game both from a player's and a coach's perspective. They must be aware of what is going on—on both sides of the net. They must be able to assimilate tactical information quickly, draw the necessary conclusions, and apply this information in the appropriate way. They must have good and rapid decision-making ability. They must execute on the court the desired offensive tactics of the coach, and they must be aware of their own attacker's psychological state to make good decisions of where to direct the set.

Poised

Setters must be in control emotionally in order to manage and lead the team. They must be able to think clearly and maintain a positive and fighting spirit no matter how difficult the situation. Setters have no time for emotional breakdowns or to let personal disappointment interfere with how they play the game. They are in charge. They must instill confidence and challenge the team to respond positively.

Leadership

Setters quarterback the offense and provide overall leadership for the team. They must have a strong affiliation with their teammates and the coaches. They must work hard to gain the team's confidence and respect and must always be supportive. They must have complete confidence in themselves and know that they can do the job. They must feel that no matter how tough the situation, they can lead the team to victory.

Good Communication Skills

Running the offense is a cooperative effort and setters must communicate well with both coaches and teammates to execute the game plan. They must seek input from attackers to give them exactly the type of sets they feel will be successful for them. Setters must also make it clear verbally and nonverbally that they will set the ball.

> **MAXIM:** *The setter is the heart of the team. If you cannot find a ready-made setter with the necessary attributes, search for an athlete who does have the attributes and train that player to set.*

FRONT SET (OVERHAND PASS) CHECKLIST

See Figure 3-1. Also see Chapter 2 for a description of the technique.

Ready Position

✓ Stand with medium high posture.
✓ Stand with feet shoulder-width apart with knees slightly flexed.

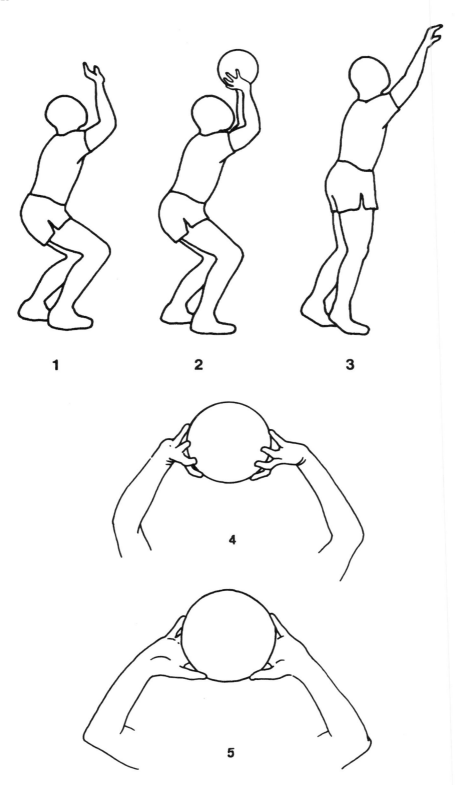

Figure 3-1.

✓ Keep weight on the balls of the feet and distribute equally.
✓ Hold hands comfortably at chest level.

Pre-Contact Position—Lower Body

✓ Get feet and forehead to a position behind and under ball.
✓ Maintain a balanced, neutral body position that looks the same for all sets.
✓ Square the shoulders and hips to the target prior to the set. (Advanced systems' target is zone 4.)
✓ Keep feet shoulder-width apart, with right foot forward and knees bent to push into set.
✓ Set the body, then set the ball.

Pre-Contact Position—Upper Body

✓ Simultaneously with movement to the ball, move hands up into a ready position above the forehead.
✓ Move hands up close together, no wider than the ball.
✓ Keep hands up and in position early, several moments prior to contact.
✓ Open hands wide, with fingers spread and rigid.
✓ Form a triangle with thumb and index finger above and in front of the forehead. Fingers are not more than a few inches apart.
✓ Tilt back wrists; point thumbs back toward the eyes and opposite shoulders.
✓ Tilt back head to see ball through this triangle or viewfinder.

Contact

✓ Keep wrists flexible and relaxed, and fingers firm to cushion oncoming ball.
✓ Although weight and impact of ball brings wrists back slightly, do not attempt to drop the wrists back once the ball is in the hands.
✓ Extend wrists and elbows in a forward and upward direction immediately on impact with the ball.
✓ Create the soft touch in the wrists.
✓ Simultaneously push and extend legs and arms forward and upward into ball.
✓ Contact the ball above and in front, but close to the forehead.
✓ Contact the ball on the pads of the fingers and the outside portion of the thumbs.
✓ Strive to have all ten fingers contact the ball, but the main contact points are the thumb and first three fingers.
✓ Ball comes close to but does not contact the palms.
✓ Speed of acceleration into ball controls ball distance and height of set.
✓ The greater the distance from the target, the more acceleration and greater use of the legs.
✓ Body angle also controls distance. The more the body is inclined, the greater the distance.

Follow-Through

✓ Extend with arms and legs through the ball to the target.
✓ Transfer the weight into the ball and onto the front foot.

✓ Finish with hands close, even, and within the shoulders.
✓ Point index fingers in the direction of target.
✓ Point thumbs up and away from body.
✓ Freeze to target momentarily.

BACK SET CHECKLIST

See Figure 3-2.

✓ Position the ball as in the front set. Do not give away intention to back set.
✓ Maintain a neutral position and delay movement to back set as long as possible.
✓ Just prior to contact, throw hips forward and under ball.
✓ Arch back and transfer weight to forward foot.
✓ Use flexibility of wrists and forearm to flick the ball back.
✓ Follow-through with the body in the direction of the set.
✓ Follow flight of the ball with head.

Figure 3-2.

THE SIDE SET

The side set (see Figure 3-3A) can be used to set balls passed tight to the net in order to avoid netting with the elbow or the side of the body. The set can be made from a position facing the net or with the back to the net, depending on the setter's preference and/or dictated by the originating position of the setter. Some tight passes can be set with a traditional front or back set; but immediately after the set, the setter must turn to a parallel position facing the net to avoid netting on the follow-through and/or recovery.

The side set can also be utilized advantageously to set the right front attacker when the pass draws the setter off the net. The setter moves to the ball, squares off to face the left side and middle attacker, and quickly pivots to the right just prior to the set to side set the ball over the right shoulder to zone 2. This movement allows the setter to see the target as the set is being executed and, thus, aids the setter in achieving greater accuracy as well as making the set more deceptive and difficult to read. (See Figure 3-3B.)

Left and middle back defenders can also effectively use the side set to set deep balls to the left front attacker when the setter digs the first ball. Sets originating from the back row are coming from a difficult angle for right-handed players attacking from zone 2. Unless a left-handed player is positioned in that zone, the easier set to attack off deep balls is from zone 4.

Figure 3-3A.

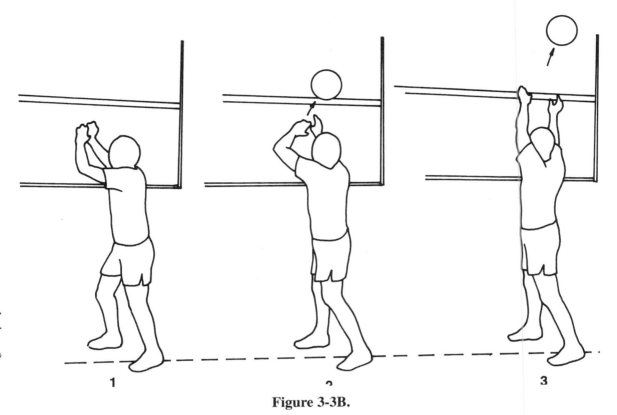

1   2   3

Figure 3-3B.

SIDE SET CHECKLIST

✓ Position body directly to the side of the ball.
✓ Dip shoulders in the intended direction of the set.
✓ Contact the ball evenly with both hands.
✓ Shift weight and lean body from the waist in the direction of the set.
✓ Follow-through with hands high and together toward the target.

JUMP SET CHECKLIST—TWO-FOOT TAKE-OFF

See Figure 3-4.

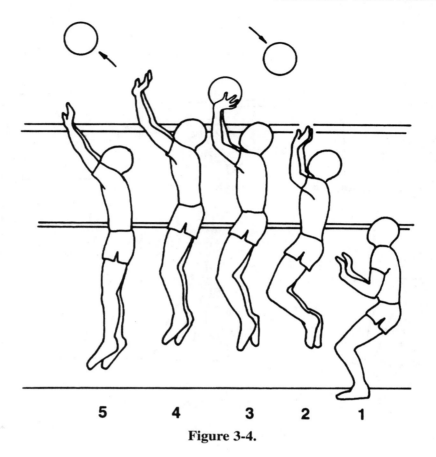

Figure 3-4.

Function

✓ Used to set balls passed tight to the net and to intercept balls going over the net.
✓ Used to get the ball to the attacker quickly to speed up the offense.
✓ Used to present a constant threat of attack by the front-row setter. Once in the air, the setter has the option to set or attack the ball.

Technique

✓ Move to a position behind and under the ball.
✓ Jump up and square off in the air to face the intended direction of the set.
✓ Meet the ball in the air at the peak of the jump, above the plane of the net.
✓ Contact the ball high above the forehead.
✓ Execute the set with the wrists and a quick extension of the arms.

JUMP SET CHECKLIST—ONE-FOOT TAKE-OFF

See Figure 3-5.

Function

✓ Used when the setter is moving off the net, beyond the 10-foot line to chase down a pass, and there is not sufficient time to square off to face zone 4 prior to the set with a traditional two-foot plant.

Technique

✓ Run full speed to a position behind the ball.
✓ The last step to the ball is with the right foot.
✓ Push up and off the floor with the right foot, and kick the left knee upward toward the chest to gain height in the air.
✓ Pivot the body in the air to face the left front attacker.
✓ Contact the ball at the height of the jump and set forward to zone 4; or, with a slightly greater rotation in the air, side set the ball to zone 2.

1   2   3   4   5   6

Figure 3-5.

SETTING LOW BALLS CHECKLIST

See Figure 3-6, which shows two different methods to recover.

✓ Strive to hand set all balls.
✓ Drop under the ball or lunge with the last step to reach and get under the ball, holding the hands high.
✓ Transfer the body weight to the forward leg as the body continues to move under the ball.
✓ Pivot the feet and square the shoulders to the target.
✓ Execute the set with a quick extension of the arms.
✓ The legs hold their upright position momentarily on the set.
✓ Strive to set ball before falling to the ground.
✓ Recover and return to play as quickly as possible.

1.   2.   3.   4.

Figure 3-6.

ONE-HAND SET CHECKLIST

See Figure 3-7.

Function

✓ Used for tight passes that cannot be reached with a two-handed set.

Technique

✓ Set with the hand closer to the net.
✓ Hand, fingers, and wrist are firm and opened with the palm facing the hitter.
✓ Block the ball from going over the net and push the ball back to the hitter.
✓ Contact the ball on the fingertips and, if possible, the thumb.
✓ The attacker is in the air at the same moment as setter contacts the ball.

Figure 3-7.

FOREARM SET CHECKLIST

See Figure 3-8.

Function

✓ Used when the ball is too low to hand set.

Technique

✓ Bend the knees and position the arms behind, under, and to the side of the ball.
✓ Step forward with the leg that is closer to the net and transfer the weight to that side and toward the target.
✓ Raise the shoulder farther from the target to allow the platform to face the target.
✓ Swing the arms in a controlled fashion upward and forward while extending the legs.
✓ Lift and extend the legs and arms upward and forward to the target.
✓ Platform faces the target at the moment of contact. Do not pivot or swing to the side to direct the ball.
✓ Follow-through with arms above the shoulders and the legs fully extended.

Figure 3-8.

FIRST-TEMPO SET CHECKLIST—SETTER RESPONSIBILITIES

Definition

✓ A first-tempo set is where the attacker is in the air just prior to the set.

Movement to the Target

✓ Arrive to the setting target area as quickly as possible and call for the pass.
✓ Give passers a visual and verbal target.

Pre-Contact Position

✓ Establish a body position insuring the quick set is possible. Poor positioning allows the middle blocker to release to another attacker.
✓ Establish a body position that allows vision of both the attacker and the opposing middle blocker.
✓ See the middle blocker in your peripheral vision, as the attacker approaches and just prior to setting the ball.
✓ See the quick hitter in front of you and the other attackers in your peripheral vision.

Technical

✓ Set from a balanced position. Avoid forcing the quick set when moving or off balance.
✓ Jump set all passes within four feet of the net.
✓ On standing sets, set from a tall body position.
✓ Keep the hands high.
✓ Set primarily with the wrists and release the ball quickly.
✓ Adjust the set to the position, height, and speed of the attacker.
✓ Set to the height of the attacker's jump. Set "up" to the hitter.
✓ Get the ball to the attacker as quickly as possible.
✓ Set off the net.
✓ Allow the attacker an unrestricted arm swing and the ability to hit around the block.
✓ The farther the pass is off the net, the higher the set.
✓ When the attacker is late, delay the set by bending the knees, dropping the hands, or setting the ball higher.
✓ When the attacker is early, jump set and/or stretch up to the ball with the arms extended.
✓ Use a soft, arching set for smaller players, allowing the ball to hang in the attack zone longer.

Tactical

✓ Use the middle as a decoy on tight passes.
✓ Set quick on average passes and in transition.
✓ Set in front of the attacker's shoulder or body midline to allow the hitter to determine the direction of the hit.
✓ Help direct the attacker to hit around the block by setting to either side of the middle blocker.

SETTER AS ATTACKER CHECKLIST

Second contact attacks by the setter are commonly referred to as the dump or tip. The tip can be performed with the right or left hand or with both hands. (See Figure 3-9.) Good tip placement is generally more effective than a weak attack.

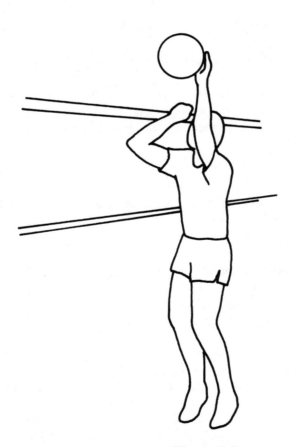

Figure 3-9.

Technical

- ✓ Learn to tip with the right hand, left hand, and both hands.
- ✓ When positioned in the back row and on balls passed off the net, use the two-hand dump. At the last moment rather than set an attacker, send the ball to the opponent's court.
- ✓ When positioned in the front row, jump to play all balls passed within four feet of the net and be prepared to set, tip, or hit.
- ✓ Jump to set the ball and—just prior to contact—reach with one hand and tip the ball softly over the net.
- ✓ Tall setters can reach with one hand and contact the top of the ball and put it to the floor more rapidly.
- ✓ Contact with one hand is made with an open and firm hand, with or without wrist action.
- ✓ Contact with the ball is made high and in front of the body, with little or no elbow bend.
- ✓ On tight passes that are impossible to set or tip, be aggressive. Turn, and with a block motion, push it back to the opponent's side joust-style.

Tactical

- ✓ Always pose a threat to attack whether in the front or the back row.
- ✓ Keep the attention of the block and defense. Force them to position themselves defensively to play the second contact.
- ✓ Be deceptive and unpredictable in sending the ball to the opponent's side.
- ✓ Attack the second ball as an offensive weapon on a good pass and use it as an emergency tactic on tight passes.
- ✓ Establish the first tempo attack and move the quick hitter to various positions along the net to open up the tip.
- ✓ Focus on placement and surprise.

Placement

- ✓ Learn to tip to a variety of spots on the court.
- ✓ Evaluate the blockers' initial positions and tendencies to assist in placements, that is, does the outside blocker help block the first tempo attack or the dump, or wait toward the antenna for the outside set?
- ✓ Use peripheral vision to see blockers. Learn to tip the ball around, between, and over the block.
- ✓ Evaluate the opponent's back row defense to assist in placements.
- ✓ Tip to the middle of the court against a perimeter defense.
- ✓ Tip to the sidelines when the defense pinches toward the center of the court.
- ✓ Tips with the left hand are more deceptive due to the range of positions the ball can be directed.
- ✓ Tips behind the setter to the left front corner can be done most easily with the right hand.

SETTER TACTICS CHECKLIST

General

✓ Visualize and analyze set strategy prior to each game.

✓ Visualize "what if" situations.

✓ Have plans to get out of stressful situations.

✓ Over-talk stressful situations. Be poised, competitive, and aggressive.

✓ Know attackers' set preferences, speed, height, and distance from net.

✓ Know who to set in tough situations.

✓ Read attackers' reactions to repeated errors and pressure and know which attackers you can go back to.

✓ Assume all attacks will be blocked and cover. Give the attacker a second opportunity to hit.

✓ Play defense first in transition, then prepare to set.

Choices

✓ Base set choices on individual past performance evaluated through statistics as well as current game statistics and block weaknesses.

✓ Set equally early in the game to keep the attackers alert and the offense unpredictable.

✓ Experiment early in the game to learn which attackers are most successful. Utilize these players at the most critical times late in the game.

✓ Think in terms of how to best utilize each attacker in the front and back rows.

✓ Take advantage of what we do best, *now.*

✓ Identify the "hot" attacker in each game or match.

✓ The hot attacker is not always the team's best attacker, but the best attacker *at the moment.*

✓ Feed the hot attacker, not every time, but a large majority of the time and when the team needs a kill.

✓ Know that when attackers are hot, it might be more effective to set them, even though everyone knows that they will receive the ball.

✓ Make the easy set in difficult situations.

✓ Never force a difficult set to the hot attacker. It might result in a mishandled ball or a poor set.

✓ Distinguish between risk-taking situations and percentage plays and know when to do each.

Patterns

✓ Set in random patterns. Be unpredictable in position and type of set. Do not make it easy for blockers to know what you plan to do.

✓ Set in predictable, sequential patterns. Lure the blockers to commit to a specific pattern.

✓ Alter the pattern once the block adjusts.

✓ Set quick until the opponents can stop it.

✓ Set outside once the middle blocker commits to the quick attacker.

✓ Establish an effective first-tempo attack first, before running second-tempo play sets.

✓ Force blocker movement inside, then set wide, forcing the blocker to reach away from the court or float out to block the ball.

✓ Think in terms of setting middle and right and then middle and left.

✓ Think in terms of a ratio of sets to the middle and to the outside in each rotation.

✓ Think in terms of game phases, that is, beginning, middle, and end.

Opposites

✓ Movement forward, set back. Movement back, set forward.

✓ After an attack is "covered" from one outside attacker, set to the outside hitter on the opposite side of the court.

✓ Direct the counterattack in transition to the opposite side from the opponent's attack.

✓ See and perceive blocker movement and set the opposite direction.

Adjustments

✓ Think in terms of game adjustments—serve receive formations, plays, and position of attackers.

✓ Set the ball higher, deeper, and faster, inside or outside as the situation dictates.

✓ Set the ball off the net to reduce the effectiveness of a big block.

✓ Change the game rhythm with first-, second-, and third-tempo sets and/or by attacking the second ball.

Block Considerations

✓ Keep blockers honest by constantly varying the direction, height, and placement of sets.

✓ Strive to outguess the block. Where does the block think the ball will be directed?

✓ Direct the attack to a weakness in the opponent's block.

✓ Consider the initial start positions of blockers, that is, spread toward sidelines or pinched inside.

✓ Make blockers move. If blockers are pinched inside, spread the block by setting the ball wide to the sidelines.

✓ Do blockers overload (double or triple block) specific attackers?

✓ Do blockers make adjustments during the match?

✓ What are the middle blockers' abilities and tendencies?

✓ Does the middle blocker commit on the first-tempo attack?

✓ Does the middle blocker remain in a neutral position in the middle of the court or follow the setter during the pass?

✓ If the pass goes to the far right side and the middle blocker follows, set quick to the left front attacker.

✓ Is the middle blocker slow to the outside?

✓ Force slow middle blockers to move to the outside with lower and quicker sets to the antennae.

QUICK TACTICAL GAME CHECKLIST

✓ What are my options in this rotation?

✓ What are the positives and negatives of each option?

✓ Evaluate the pass. What are my options now?

✓ Am I predictable?

✓ Am I accurate?

✓ Where are my opponent's weakest blockers?

✓ Which blockers should I avoid?

✓ What are the best set and play combinations for us?

✓ Who are my most effective attackers?

✓ Is everyone getting a reasonable share of sets?

✓ What were my last five sets?

✓ Do I "own" the middle blocker?

✓ What is the score?

✓ Is our best attacker getting the most sets?

✓ Should I alter the serve receive formation?

✓ Am I doing my best to make a bad pass *better?*

✓ Can I justify each set selection?

Chapter 4

THE SERVER

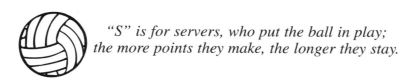

"S" is for servers, who put the ball in play;
the more points they make, the longer they stay.

A good serving team can neutralize an opponent's attack and—although it might be "overmatched" in size or experience—with tough serving, the team has the opportunity to be competitive.

ATTRIBUTES OF SUCCESSFUL SERVERS

Good Technique

Successful serves have good serve mechanics. The simpler and cleaner the serve action, the better. Good technique is the best assurance for consistent performance, especially in pressure situations.

Accurate Placement

Successful servers can place the ball accurately to the six zones on the court. They can tactically pinpoint the serve to specific targets to disrupt the opponent's offense.

Tactically Smart

Successful servers are tactically smart. They recognize critical game situations in which a tough, but controlled serve is more appropriate than risking an error. They know that missing a serve on a "big point" can either reduce the team's chances of a comeback or give the opponent an opportunity to get back into the match.

Consistent

Successful servers have a consistent serve. They reach a balance between serving "too easy and too tough." They understand that "playing it safe" gives the opponent an easy opportunity to side-out, or score a point in rally score, and that attempting too "risky" a serve causes excessive errors.

Successful servers know their ability and serve within it. They serve at a controlled speed and leave some room for placement errors by aiming higher above the net and to a larger area of the court away from the lines. They serve too deep rather than too short, too high rather than too low, and too far inside the court rather than outside the court.

Aggressive

Successful servers use the serve as an offensive weapon. Their goal is to reduce the opponent's best attack options. Many athletes define a tough serve as fast and hard. Successful servers define it as a combination of speed, accuracy, and a low trajectory. They understand that without topspin, the ball can only be served so hard before gravity can no longer pull it back into the court. Attempting to serve too aggressively causes needless errors.

Mentally Tough

Successful servers are confident in their ability to perform in both relaxed and pressure situations. They want to be the one to serve at important moments in the game. They might be nervous, but it does not affect their ability to do the job.

> *MAXIM: It's what you learn after you know it all that counts.* John Wooden

© 2001 by Parker Publishing Company

THE UNDERHAND SERVE

The underhand serve (see Figure 4-1) is recommended for young players in the very early stages of the game. The slower trajectory of the serve facilitates better serve reception, and allows for more continuous and exciting rallies without the serve dominating the game. The underhand serve is relatively easy to perform; it not only reduces the number of serve errors, but also creates more opportunities to place the ball and introduce serve tactics. The adoption of a more advanced serve is recommended as soon as the strength and ability of the players increase.

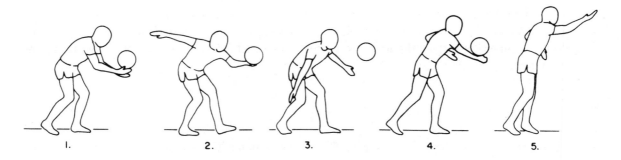

Figure 4-1.

UNDERHAND SERVE CHECKLIST

Ready Position

✓ Face net and intended target.
✓ Assume a medium high and balanced posture.
✓ Flex knees slightly.
✓ Stagger the feet with the foot opposite the hitting arm slightly forward.
✓ Put weight on back foot.
✓ Hold ball in the palm of the nonhitting hand at waist level.
✓ Place hitting arm down by the side ready for the back swing.

Mental Preparation

✓ Compose yourself.
✓ Take a deep breath and relax.
✓ Use positive self-talk.

Aim

✓ Select a serve target.
✓ Eye check to target.
✓ Focus on the ball and the contact.

Arm Position and Toss

✓ Just prior to toss, take a small step forward with the lead foot in the direction of the target.
✓ Toss ball out from body and up to chest level.
✓ Bring hitting arm back behind body with elbow slightly bent.
✓ Transfer body weight forward as arm moves forward to contact ball.

Contact

✓ Contact ball at waist level in front of body.
✓ Contact behind and under the ball.
✓ Contact through the ball to the target.

Follow-Through

✓ Momentarily freeze and hold serve position.
✓ Face feet and hand toward intended flight direction.
✓ Put weight on the forward foot and be balanced.
✓ Move quickly into a defensive position.

THE FLOAT SERVE

The float serve is the most common of the advanced serves in today's game. This serve is similar to the knuckleball in baseball because it travels (floats) through the air without spin, moving side to side or up or down in unpredictable patterns. These unpredictable flight patterns make it difficult for the receiver to establish good pass position.

There are two styles of float serves. The American floater is executed with the body facing the net, while the Asian floater is executed with the side to the net. The advantage of the Asian floater is that its technique generates greater arm velocity on contact, enabling a small or weaker player to serve aggressively. The Asian floater is used by beginners as well as Olympic-level players, and is an effective tool for coaches in coach-centered drills.

The effectiveness of the float serve lies in its execution, rather than in the style. The toughest serves have a flat, low-line trajectory and are placed tactically to an advantageous position. Velocity is important, but must be controlled, because only gravity will pull the ball into the court.

AMERICAN FLOAT CHECKLIST

See Figure 4-2.

Ready Position

✓ Face net and intended target.
✓ Assume a high, balanced posture.

© 2001 by Parker Publishing Company

Figure 4-2.

✓ Stagger feet with the foot opposite the serving arm slightly forward.
✓ Put weight on back foot.
✓ Keep hips and shoulders slightly open to the target.
✓ Hold ball in the palm of the nonhitting hand, comfortably out from body at chest level with elbow slightly bent, similar to a food server holding a tray.
✓ Hold ball in front of the hitting shoulder.
✓ Hold the hitting arm up, extended almost straight and above the hitting shoulder.
✓ Lay the hand back, with fingers and thumb together, in a firm and closed position.
✓ Flex wrist back and lock.

Mental Preparation

✓ Compose yourself.
✓ Take a deep breath and relax.
✓ Use positive self-talk.

Aim

✓ Select a serve target.
✓ Eye check to target.
✓ Focus on the ball and the contact.

Arm Position and Toss

✓ Just prior to the toss, take a small step forward with the lead foot in the direction of the target.
✓ Transfer the weight forward.
✓ The step is optional. If no step is taken, transfer the weight forward with the toss and contact.
✓ Almost simultaneously with the step, toss (lift) the ball out from the body, above the head, and over the hitting shoulders.
✓ Lift the ball into the air from shoulder level.
✓ Release the ball when the tossing arm is above the head.
✓ Place (lift/toss) the ball in the air with no spin.
✓ Toss high enough to allow contact at full extension of arm.
✓ After the toss, the tossing arm remains extended at waist level or higher.
✓ Rotate shoulders back to allow for body rotation into contact.
✓ Rapidly rotate shoulder and arm into hit with the body weight transferred forward.
✓ Elbow leads and remains high.

Contact

✓ Contact ball high, above the head, with the arm extended and in front of the serving shoulder.
✓ Accelerate arm and rotate shoulders into contact, hitting through the center (or just below the center) of the ball.
✓ Contact ball on the palm of the hand.
✓ Keep hand rigid and flat.
✓ Hand and forearm act as one unit.

© 2001 by Parker Publishing Company

✓ Keep wrist firm and locked.
✓ Contact through ball to the target.
✓ Contact is short and controlled.
✓ Do not fully extend the arm.

Follow-Through

✓ Momentarily freeze and hold the serve position.
✓ Face feet and palm of hand toward intended flight direction.
✓ Keep weight on forward foot and maintain balance.
✓ Quickly move into defensive position.

ASIAN FLOAT CHECKLIST

See Figure 4-3.

Ready Position

✓ Maintain high posture with side to net.
✓ Keep feet shoulder-distance apart and bend knees slightly.
✓ Hold the ball at chest level out from body and parallel with the net.
✓ Hold hitting arm in a relaxed position, slightly bent, at body's side, with hand near hip.

Mental Preparation

✓ Compose yourself.
✓ Take a deep breath and relax.
✓ Use positive self-talk.

© 2001 by Parker Publishing Company

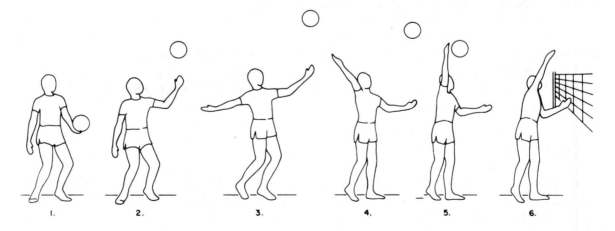

Figure 4-3.

Aim

✓ Select a serve target.
✓ Eye check to target.
✓ Focus on the ball and the contact.

Arm Position and Toss

✓ Toss ball above head, in front of body, parallel to net.
✓ Simultaneously with toss, lean body backwards as both legs bend and the hips rotate back.
✓ Rapidly rotate the hips forward, followed by extending the hitting shoulder forward and upward.
✓ Have shoulder of hitting hand lead arm. Forearm and hand remain slightly behind arm.
✓ Swing hitting arm upward in a windmill motion.
✓ Simultaneously with hip and arm movement, extend legs up and transfer the weight forward to the leg nearer the net.
✓ Move tossing arm down and shift weight to forward foot.

Contact

✓ On contact, open body to net—face hips and shoulders forward.
✓ Contact on palm of the hand with the wrist remaining firm.
✓ Contact high, above head and forward shoulder.
✓ Slightly bend elbow.
✓ Contact below center on back of ball.
✓ Contact through the ball to target.

Follow-Through

✓ Use short follow-through with palm facing target.
✓ Balance body with weight on foot closer to net.
✓ Move quickly into a defensive position.

> **MAXIM:** *Eliminate unnecessary movements in the service motion. The fewer the variables, the more consistent the serve.*

THE SHORT FLOAT SERVE

Regardless of the style of float serve used, the technique changes necessary to serve short are very similar. The toss is made farther back so that contact can be made near the bottom of the ball rather than the center, and the arm swing slows just prior to contact.

The short serve has a small arc that allows it to clear the top of the net and drop near the 10-foot line. Although the lower the arch, the more deceptive the serve, a slightly higher arch prevents errors and makes it easier to serve close to the net. The most effective elements of a short serve are accurate placement and deception, catching the receiver(s) off guard, and giving the setter less time for decision-making. The serving team's block and defense must be prepared to respond quickly to the opponent's attack.

THE JUMP SERVE

The jump serve imitates the approach and arm swing of the spike. Basically, it is an attack with a self-toss from 30 feet off the net. It is an aggressive and risky serve tactic, but when executed well, it is a very effective weapon. Although the trajectory of the ball is easily determined, its rapid movement can make it difficult to pass. Consideration must be given to the server's ace:error ratio to determine in what situations this serve should be utilized. It is important to hit the ball hard; otherwise, it is relatively easy to pass. Whether or not the jump serve is utilized in the game, it is recommended for practice as an effective method of training the attack.

JUMP SERVE CHECKLIST

Ready Position

✓ Assume a comfortable standing position.

Mental Preparation

✓ Compose yourself.
✓ Take a deep breath and relax.
✓ Use positive self-talk.

Aim

✓ Select a serve target.
✓ Eye check to target.
✓ Focus on the ball and the contact.

Toss

✓ Toss with the left, right, or both hands—with or without spin.
✓ Release the ball at head height.
✓ Toss the ball high in front of the body and in line with the hitting arm.
✓ Let a poor toss drop or hit a controlled serve to keep the ball in play. (Check current rule regarding toss.)

Chase

✓ After ball is released, chase it down with the approach.
✓ Use a straight or diagonal spike approach.

Jump

✓ Take off from behind the endline and broad jump into the hit.
✓ The more movement forward, the more power generated.
✓ Get the arm up into a hitting position immediately on takeoff.

Contact

✓ Contact the ball as close to the net as possible, at minimum above the endline.
✓ Contact the ball above or slightly behind the head.
✓ Contact as high as possible with arm fully extended.
✓ Contact the ball with entire hand; wrap fingers over the top of the ball.
✓ Snap the wrist up and over the top of the ball to impart spin.
✓ Snap up and out sufficiently to give the ball height to clear the net, understanding that the top spin pulls the ball down into the court.
✓ Follow-through forward and on the same side of the body as the hitting arm in the spike.
✓ Move quickly into a defensive position.

MAXIM: Success is built on solid fundamentals. Stress the basics.

SERVE TACTICS CHECKLIST

Start Position

✓ Base initial serve position on quickness to the defensive position and the ability to serve tough and consistently.
✓ Position toward the right, center, or left sideline and any distance from the endline.
✓ As the server moves farther back from the endline, power becomes more important than placement.

Preparation

✓ Assume a ready position.
✓ Compose yourself. Take a deep breath and relax.
✓ Use positive self-talk.

Select Serve Target

✓ Prior to the serve, look to the coach for the hand signal (numbers 1–6) indicating the zone placement, or . . .

✓ Select a serve target based on previously discussed game tactics, or . . .

✓ Select a serve target based on your best serve.

> **KEY:** Use common sense in instructing athletes to serve particular zones. Although tactically specific placements are warranted, consideration must also be given to the server's ability. Make an appropriate call that allows the server a good opportunity for success.

Aim

✓ Eye check to target.

✓ Focus on the ball and the contact.

Toss

✓ If permissible (check current rule) do not attempt to "go after" a bad toss. There is too big a risk of a serve error. Repeat the toss.

Placements

Serve Weak Passers

✓ Serve in the direction of the weakest receivers. Make them move to their right, left, short, or deep.

> **MAXIM:** *Once weak passers are identified, continue to "go after them."*
> *Do not let them off the hook.*

Serve Areas to Weaken the Offense

✓ See open spots on the court rather than receivers.

✓ Never serve directly to a player. Make the receiver move.

✓ Serve seams and open spots, forcing receivers to decide who should pass.

✓ Serve toward the sidelines. Make receivers move away from the court.

✓ Serve as close as possible to the opponent's endline.

✓ Serve away from the strongest attacker if the setter is weak. Make it difficult for a weak setter to get the ball to his or her strength.

✓ Serve in the path of the penetrating setter.

✓ Serve short or deep to front row attackers to take them out of their normal approach routes.

✓ Serve zone 2, making it difficult for the setter to see the quick attacker.

> **MAXIM:** *Once weak areas are identified, continue serving them until the opponent makes an adjustment.*

Serve to Psychologically Strain a Receiver

✓ Serve toward the player who has just erred.
✓ Serve toward the new substitute.
✓ Serve toward a player who is upset or tired.
✓ Serve repetitively to one player, striving to "wear them down" and to "break them."
✓ Use a combination of short and deep serves.

> **MAXIM:** *Keep the pressure on opponents. After scoring a succession of points, strive to keep the ball in play rather than serving harder. The opponents are in a psychologically disadvantaged position.*

Serve Tough but Conservative

Serve . . .
✓ After a teammate before you in the rotation errors.
✓ After opponents take a time out. They are in trouble. Keep the pressure on them to earn their points.
✓ On match point or in rally score.
✓ After opponents miss their serve.
✓ After a substitution or time out.
✓ After opponents have scored a series of points.
✓ After your team wins an inspiring rally.
✓ When opponents are in their weakest rotation.
✓ When you are in your strongest rotation.
✓ When either team is within three points of winning the game.

Train to Be Successful

✓ Employ all tactics and serve expectations in all drills.
✓ Give serving drills your full attention.
✓ Limit conversation in serving drills to acknowledgment of teammates' good serves.
✓ Discipline self to never make two serving errors in succession.
✓ In pregame serve–receive warm-up, get a feel of the gym and how much the ball floats. Progressively serve tougher.

Train to Make Teammates Successful

✓ Serve tough in drills. Help teammates become good passers by giving them the opportunity to receive tough serves.
✓ Serve tough but consistently in serve–pass combination drills. Frequent errors disrupt drill flow.
✓ In pregame serve–receive warm-up, serve controlled balls to allow passers to develop a passing rhythm and confidence. Progressively serve tougher.

CHAPTER 5

THE ATTACKER

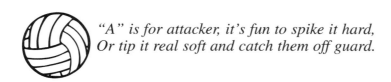

"A" is for attacker, it's fun to spike it hard,
Or tip it real soft and catch them off guard.

Winning at the advanced levels correlates best with hitting. The name of the game is to strive for good attack percentages and—at the same time—keep the opponent's percentages low.

ATTRIBUTES OF SUCCESSFUL ATTACKERS

Height and Jumping Ability

The majority of successful attackers are tall and strong and rely on power and speed. The game is played at a high level above the net; thus, it is very important that if the attacker is not tall, he or she must have good jumping ability.

Good Technique

Proper technique gives the attacker the best opportunity to be consistently successful. Good technique in the approach increases the jump, and a good arm swing permits the attacker to hit with power and finesse.

Good "Ball-Control Skills" Attacking

It is common to hear of a player with good ball control on the ground in the skills of setting and passing; less common, but just as important, is ball control in the air—attacking. Successful attackers control the ball with the arm, wrist, and hand. Proper positioning and solid contact on the palm of the hand allow for use of a variety of shots and accurate placements.

A Variety of Weapons

The attack encompasses a variety of options and the most effective attackers, small and tall, utilize these options to beat the blockers and defenders. Attackers with good height and jumping ability can be successful at certain levels hitting just with power; but at the more advanced levels, power alone cannot make an attacker successful. Smaller attackers rely less on power and more on a variety of shots for their success.

Block and Defense Awareness

Successful attackers see the block and know their tendencies. To properly utilize the options, attackers must see around the ball to the obstacles that the opponent presents. Successful attackers consider the position and strength of the block as well as the defense behind it. They know what defense the opponent is using, and the location of the open spots.

Smart and Consistent

Attackers can have "moments of brilliance," but they will not be successful unless they can be effective on a consistent basis. Consistency is a product of good technique and good choices, that is, hitting smart. Successful attackers hit the ball with their *brain*. They have the ability to hit the right shot at the right time.

Attack opportunities can be categorized as good, bad, or neutral. Good opportunities favor the offense, whereas bad opportunities are risky and favor the defense. In neutral situations, neither the offense nor the defense has the advantage and success is a product of execution. Smart attackers distinguish between "good" and "risky" situations and select the options that are most appropriate. They "go for the kill" when the percentages favor it, and are more conservative when the chances of making errors are the greatest. All attackers make errors, but successful hitters make fewer mental errors or poor choices.

Experience

Successful attackers understand the game and the factors that contribute to the success or failure of each option and placement. They have had the training and experience to recognize each situation and respond to it quickly and correctly by executing the proper option.

> **MAXIM:** *Errors win games. Attempt to have them on the other side of the net.*

ATTACK OPTIONS

> **MAXIM:** *The more humble a player's physical data, the better technique and tactics are needed to play effectively at the net.*

Power Attack

This is a ball attacked with maximum power around, through, or off the block. The best hitters combine this power with various "shots" and placements.

Tip

This is a ball that is tapped softly over or to the side of the block. The tip is most effective when used by those attackers who have established the threat of hitting with power first and then catching the defense off guard by mixing in a soft shot. Tight or low sets can force the attacker to use the tip option, but it still can be very effective if placed to a weakness in the defense.

The action leading up to the tip imitates that of the power attack, but as the arm uncoils, the motion is slowed just prior to contact. Contact is made at full arm extension, on the pads of the fingers of a firmly opened hand. Although the contact is short, the ball is guided "up and over" the block to the target. There is very little or no wrist movement.

The tip is one of the easiest, yet most effective attack variations. It is advantageous to have the ability to tip with either the right or left hand. Many wide sets outside the antennae can be saved and effectively attacked with the ability to play the ball with either hand.

Deep Tip

© 2001 by Parker Publishing Company

This is a ball tipped forcefully and rapidly over the block and directed deep into the court in a horizontal trajectory with as little arch as possible. After the threat of the short tip has been established and the receiver moves up anticipating it, a deep tip to the corner is very effective.

Roll Shot

This is a change of pace ball hit off-speed and generally directed over the blocker's hands toward the middle of the court. Placement is emphasized over speed and deception over power. The action leading up to the roll shot, as in the tip, imitates that of the power attack. Just prior to contact, the arm swing slows and the hand rolls from under to over the top of the ball imparting top spin. The elbow is slightly bent and follows through to a more extended position.

> **MAXIM:** *Tip or roll shot too high and too deep rather than into the net or into the block.*

Wipe-Off/Tool (Lateral)

This is a ball hit or tipped off the blocker's hand(s) and out of bounds. It is a useful option against big blocks when the ball is set tight to the net and near the sideline. The attacker contacts the side of the ball, hitting it partially into the block, aiming for the blocker's hand and arm closer to the sideline and following through out-of-bounds. For example, for left-side tools, right handers would contact the ball a little right of center. For right-side tools, contact would be made a little to the left of the center of the ball with a wrist-away style shot. The follow-through is with the arm and the wrist turning toward the outside of the court.

> **DANGER:** Do not force the tool by aiming for the hands on balls that are set deep. It is easy to miss the block and hit out-of-bounds. Aim for the line, just inside the antennae. The ball will usually contact the blocker and go out-of-bounds; if not, the ball still has a good chance of being in.

Wipe-Off/Tool (Vertical)

This is a ball hit high, hard, and flat off the top of the blocker's hands. It is an effective option against a strong and well-formed block, especially when the ball is set a little off the net. The attacker aims for the hands and/or for the endline so that if the ball does not touch the block, it will still land inside the court.

> **MAXIM:** *When faced with a strong block, be aggressive and attack it. Successful attackers "hit the court for kills" and "hit the hands for kills."*

Rebound Shot

This is a ball tapped into the top of the block with the intention of receiving it after it "rebounds" back to the attacker's side. It is a last-resort option when it appears that the ball will be blocked and no other options are available.

> **MAXIM:** *Only those attackers who can see the block can become effective at the higher levels of the game. Learn to see the ball and the blocker's hands.*

Back Row Attack

This is a ball attacked by a back row player taking off from a position behind the 10-foot line. Effective back row hitters use a full and powerful approach and arm swing. Emphasis is on jumping high and forward, broad jumping to contact the ball as close to the net as possible. The closer the ball can be attacked in relation to the net, the more aggressive and effective the hit can be.

Although not so aggressive an attack, back row hitting is still effective when the attacker is not able to contact the ball in front of the 10-foot line or near the net. Emphasis is on contacting the ball above or slightly in front of the head and at full arm extension. Contact with the ball is on the palm of the hand, hitting over and through the ball with good wrist-snap creating top spin.

ATTACK PLACEMENTS

Successful attackers use a variety of placements. (See Diagram 5-1.) The ability to do this is based on good "ball control" hitting, that is, the ability to control the ball with the hand, wrist, and arm, and placing the ball to the desired spot on the court.

Deep Corners

This is an attack directed to the deep back corners of the court, hitting in the direction of the line or cross-court. Emphasis is on contacting the ball high and hitting deep, avoiding the block completely or getting a piece of the block resulting in a deflection. Contact is made behind the ball rather than on top and with good wrist snap creating top spin. This variation allows all players the

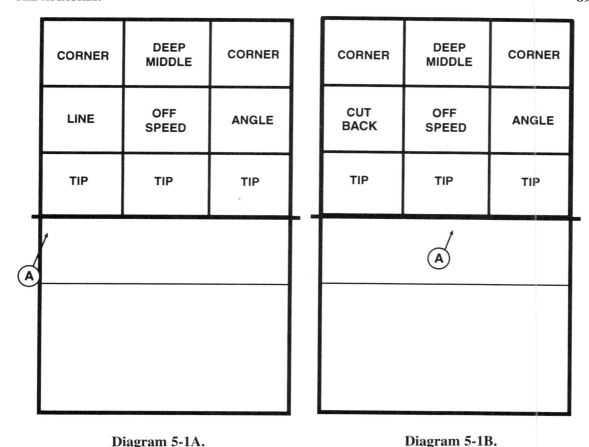

Diagram 5-1A.   **Diagram 5-1B.**

ability to attack effectively against a strong block. These placements can be difficult to defend, especially when the receiver is playing an intermediate position. From this position inside the court, deep hits can be deceptive and difficult to determine if they are going in or out.

Angle (Cross-Court)

This is a ball attacked at the sharp or deep cross-court angle. The sharp angle hit is directed near or in front of the l0-foot line. The attacker approaches either at the angle or straight in and increases the severity of the angle by dropping the opposite shoulder to allow the upper body to face the angle prior to contact. The sharper the angle, the less time the defender has to react; at the same time, however, there is less court and more margin for error.

Cut Shot

This is a ball hit with power or off-speed that travels just over and almost parallel to the net. A right-hander hitting from zone 4 dips the shoulder nearer the net (left) and uses a wrist and forearm action from the elbow to cut the ball inside the block. Instead of striking the back of the ball, contact is made on its left side. The action of the arm is away from the body. The arm follows through to the extreme right side of the body with the thumb facing down. It is most effective to reach outside the bodyline and contact the ball before it reaches the right shoulder, and before it travels in front of the block.

Cut-Back

This is a ball hit from the middle of the court to the opposite angle that the body is facing. Emphasis is on a quick and deceptive turn with the forearm and wrist swinging across the body. Emphasis is on deception rather than on power.

Line

This is a ball directed straight ahead toward the sideline. The line attack is generally utilized when the ball is set near the antennae and the block is positioned to take away the angle shot. It is important for right-handers hitting line on the right side to let the ball drift past the midline of the body until it is in line with the hitting shoulder. This allows the attacker to hit straight ahead down the line. (The reverse is true for the left-handers attacking the line on the left side.)

Seam (High/Low)

This is a ball directed toward the space between the blockers. Attackers look "for daylight" and hit toward the openings or seams of the block. This is potentially the weakest part of the double block.

> **MAXIM:** *Everyone needs options to be effective, but everyone doesn't need "every" option.*

THE APPROACH

Consistent and effective attacking requires a solid and aggressive approach that gets the attacker to the ball at the proper time and generates sufficient speed to aid in the jump. Successful hitters adapt their approach by varying the speed and/or the size of the steps to allow them to get to all sets, consistent or inconsistent in height and location.

Number of Steps

The most common approaches use three or four running steps prior to the take-off. Most first-tempo middle attackers use the three-step approach. Both the three- and four-step approaches are used by outside hitters.

Final Plant

Approaches are further designated by the style of the final plant. In the step–hop approach, the attacker terminates the run with a "hop" on both feet into the take-off. In the step–close method, the attacker plants with a step–close sequence.

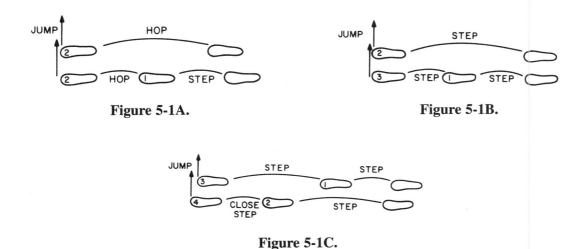

Figure 5-1A.   Figure 5-1B.

Figure 5-1C.

Four-step sequence for right-handers: R-L-RL. Four-step sequence for left-handers: L-R-LR.
Three-step sequence for right-handers: L-RL. Three-step sequence for left-handers: R-LR.

In the step–close approach, emphasis is on a right–left foot sequence into the plant for right-handers with the left foot being slightly forward of the right (opposite for left handers) and the body facing the "range point." (See the range point section in this chapter.) Emphasis is on a heel-to-toe plant (a rocking motion), converting the horizontal speed into the vertical jump. The first steps of the run are short reading and timing steps. The last two steps are breaking and closing steps and occur almost simultaneously. (See Figure 5-1.)

Goofy-Foot

Attackers who use a reverse footwork sequence are commonly referred to as goofy-foot. Biomechanically it is more difficult to hit all options and placements with power with this reverse foot position.

Recommendations

The decision to use three or four steps or the step–hop or step–close plant depends on one's personal preference. The step–hop is, however, recommended for beginners because it is simple to learn. It is also effective for attackers with difficulty learning the proper step–close sequence. The benefit of the step–hop approach is that the foot sequence is not important because the run is terminated on both feet and biomechanically the body is properly opened up to the attack.

BASE POSITIONS

Once serve receive and/or defensive responsibilities have been met, attackers tag up to a base position to prepare for the attack. Traditional base positions for all attackers (right-handers) begin near the 10-foot line. The left-side attacker begins one or two feet outside the court, while the right-side attacker tags up one or two feet inside the court. The middle attacker starts near the center of the court. The attacker "reads" the set trajectory and placement prior to beginning the approach. The earliest a player should start the approach for second- or third-tempo sets is after the ball has left the setter's hands. (See Diagram 5-2.)

RANGE POINT

Range point is a term that indicates a point of reference. On the plant and take-off, it is easiest biomechanically to hit all options and placements with power when the attacker's body initially faces the range point. For right-handers, it is the left back corner of the opponent's court; for left-handers, it is the right back corner. It is equally important that the proper footwork sequence is used in the step–close approach in order to enable the attacker to open the hips and shoulders to the ball, which in turn allows them to use all the body's power in the attack. (Refer to Diagram 5-2.)

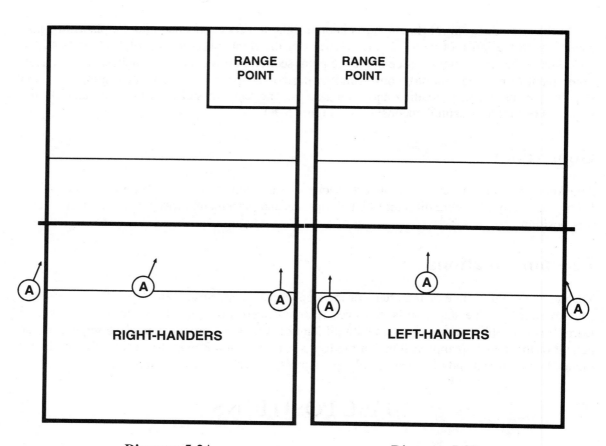

Diagram 5-2A.   **Diagram 5-2B.**

APPROACH ROUTES

Traditional approach routes are from the outside of the court to the inside (outside–in) for right-handers attacking from left and middle front, and inside–out or straight in for right-handers attacking from the right side. (The reverse is true for left-handers.) This approach places the attacker in a position facing his or her range point. (Refer to Diagram 5-2.)

Another option is for right- and left-handers to use the inside–out approach for all positions at the net. These approach routes are most commonly used in the side-out portion of the game when attackers receive serve from various locations and transition to attack from inside the court. It is a popular tactic to have the best passer receive from the middle of the court and swing to hit left, middle, or right. (See the swing option in Chapter 9.)

The disadvantage of the inside–out approach pattern is that it limits the range of some attackers. The approach route often does not allow the attacker to plant in a position with the feet, shoulders, and hips facing the range point. Biomechanically, attacking to all angles with power from this position can be very difficult or impossible for players without strong jumping abilities and upper body strength.

ATTACK CHECKLIST

See Figure 5-2.

Tag Up

✓ Prepare for the attack after pass and defensive responsibilities are complete.
✓ Tag up to the base position.

Ready Position

✓ Wait in a high track start position.
✓ Lean the body forwards slightly, arms relaxed, feet staggered, and weight on the opposite foot of the first step to aid in proper foot sequence.
✓ Read the trajectory, speed, and placement of the set to determine when to begin the approach.

Approach

✓ Strive to approach the ball in the same way each time.
✓ The first steps are reading and timing. Start slow and finish fast, attacking the approach.
✓ Emphasis is on a continuous movement, accelerating into the plant and take-off.

Plant and Take-off

✓ Plant and take off quickly. The less time spent on the ground during lift-off, the higher the jump.

Figure 5-2.

✓ Plant at an arm's distance behind the ball, lining the ball up at the hitting shoulder.
✓ Take off from a balanced position from both feet.
✓ Lift off by simultaneously extending up with the arms and the legs.

Arm Swing

✓ Lift up arms early into an attack-ready position.
✓ Place the hitting arm in a throwing position with the elbow high and hitting shoulder rotated back. A high elbow generally means a high contact point.
✓ Keep the nonhitting arm up, bent, and held at chest level.
✓ Keep hitting hand open, with wrist loose and flexible.
✓ Throw hitting hand up at the ball with the elbow leading the shoulder rotation into the hit.
✓ Generate speed by rotating the hips, shoulders, and arm into the hit.

Contact

- ✓ Strive to see simultaneously on contact the ball, the block, and opponent's court.
- ✓ Contact the ball at maximum reach, in front of the body and over the hitting shoulder.
- ✓ Contact the ball on the palm of the open hand, fingers wrapped around the ball.
- ✓ Contact the ball with a whip-like motion. Snap vigorously with a loose wrist to create top spin.
- ✓ Imagine that the ball is the face of the clock. Direct the ball by contacting it on different sides.
- ✓ Contact the ball at 12 o'clock to attack the ball straight ahead.
- ✓ Contact the ball at 10 o'clock to hit a sharp angle to the right and at 2 o'clock to cut back to the left.

Follow-Through

- ✓ Abbreviate the swing on tight sets, but always follow-through. Snap the wrist in a direction along the net or abbreviate the swing by bending the elbow on contact.
- ✓ Body follows arm and rotates to face the direction of attack.
- ✓ Thumb faces down on angle shots and up on line shots.
- ✓ Arm follows-through on the same side of the body.
- ✓ Land softly on both feet, cushioning with toes and knees.

SLIDE CHECKLIST

See Figure 5-3.

| 1 | 2 | 3 | 4 | 5 |

Figure 5-3.

✓ Tag up near the middle of the court within the 10-foot line.

✓ Run parallel to the path of the ball.

✓ Approach more parallel to the net when the setter is close to the net, and more diagonal as the setter moves toward the 10-foot line.

✓ Run! Accelerate through and into the take-off.

✓ Take off at a point behind the ball and float into the hit.

✓ Take off on one leg similar to a basketball layup.

✓ Do not pivot with the foot or hip on take-off. Point toe to antennae or sets wide to the antenna (slide C) or toward the net on tight sets (slide A). See Chapter 9, Team Offense.

✓ Pivoting to the angle on take-off is stressful on the knee and limits the jump, the float in the air, as well as the ability to hit the line.

✓ Elevate the nonsupport leg for a higher take-off. The higher, the better.

✓ At lift-off, thrust upward with the leg farther away from the net. The higher the leg, the higher the jump.

✓ Simultaneously while elevating the leg, thrust the arms upward and cock arm ready to hit.

✓ Turn toward the hitting target after the jump.

QUICK ATTACKER CHECKLIST

See Figure 5-4.

Figure 5-4.

© 2001 by Parker Publishing Company

Pre-Approach Preparation

✓ Open up to the setter and the pass.
✓ Keep the ball and the setter in sight.
✓ Allow the setter to go to the ball.
✓ Whenever possible, transition off the net to base-hitting position.

Approach

✓ Evaluate and adjust approach to the trajectory and speed of the pass.
✓ Take a full approach on a high pass.
✓ Accelerate into the approach. Let the pass beat you and then chase it down.
✓ As the pass moves off the net, open up to the setter by moving a corresponding distance away from him or her.
✓ Do not cross the imaginary line established by the setter's feet and shoulders.
✓ Be unpredictable in positions attacked at the net.
✓ Approach away from or in the seam of the blockers to attack the gaps.
✓ Be vocal. Convince the blockers that you will be set.
✓ Readjust and call for another set when a quick set is not possible.
✓ Do not fake the quick attack when no set is possible.

Plant and Take-Off

✓ Take off in a position where the setter can deliver the ball to you.
✓ Take off one to two feet off the net and allow for some float. Float toward the net rather than horizontally toward the setter.
✓ Stay off the net to allow for a set out of the blocker's range.
✓ Take off an arm's distance from the setter. Allow the setter space to deliver the ball to all attackers.
✓ Take off facing the range point to allow power hits in all directions.
✓ Jump hard and drive up with the arms.
✓ Be in the air and available when the setter has the ball.
✓ Force the middle blocker to commit in order to block the ball.
✓ Jump on tight passes with the setter ready to attack.

Arm Swing and Contact

✓ Create a target for the setter by getting the arm up and cocked early.
✓ Be ready to attack when the setter has the ball.
✓ Use a short backswing and small shoulder rotation.
✓ Hit with a quick and compact motion, utilizing a strong wrist and forearm action.
✓ Reduce the amount of body snap.
✓ Hit at the peak of the jump and the set.
✓ Contact the ball high and in front of the body.

ATTACKER TACTICS CHECKLIST

Be Aggressive

✓ Be ready to attack on every set, in the front and back rows.
✓ Be aggressive and "hungry for the ball."
✓ One must attack, attack, and attack to win. Never pass up an opportunity.
✓ Attack balls close to the net on the first and/or second contact.
✓ Strive to jump on every hit to prevent the opponents from moving into a free ball formation.

Evaluate the Options

✓ Evaluate the blocker's initial start positions as well as positions of weak blockers and defenders.
✓ Take another look at the opponents during the approach as the set ascends.
✓ Evaluate the set. What options are possible based on the quality and location of the set?

Use the Options

✓ Don't be one-dimensional. Think tactically. Think choices.
✓ Keep the defense guessing. Choose the option in the air.
✓ See around the ball to the block and defense.
✓ Direct attacks toward weak blockers and back row defenders.
✓ Look for openings in the block. Attack the gaps.
✓ Perceive blocker movement and hit toward the moving blocker.
✓ Hit hard into the seam or the inside hand of a late middle blocker.
✓ Hit "high and flat" off the hands of a strong and tall block.
✓ Hit or tip off the blocker's hands on tight sets near the sideline.
✓ Tip to the corner of the second blocker on a center attack.

Make Smart Choices

✓ Contact the ball intelligently.
✓ Distinguish between sets that you can go for the "kill" and those you must "keep in play."
✓ Go hard on a good set with the intention of scoring.
✓ Keep the ball in the court on difficult sets. Go for percentages.
✓ Tip or off-speed the ball too high or too deep rather than into the block or into the net.
✓ Reevaluate the options when ineffective.
✓ Analyze each attack to determine future strategy: "This was effective" . . . or "Next time I will. . . ."
✓ Watch the defense as teammates prepare to hit and call out attack suggestions as well as use information for your future strategy.

Setter Considerations

✓ Call for the set vocally while the pass is between the passer and the setter. Reconfirm or audibly call to adjust to a bad pass.

✓ Be especially vocal when positioned behind the setter (for backsets); the setter cannot see you.

✓ Make a loud and aggressive call. Make the setter feel that you want the ball and will be successful.

✓ Do your best with any set you receive. Hit the ball—don't judge it.

✓ Encourage the setter with positive comments.

✓ Never blame the setter for a bad set.

✓ Never "count" sets. Volleyball is a team sport.

CHAPTER 6

THE DEFENDER

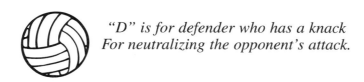

"D" is for defender who has a knack
For neutralizing the opponent's attack.

Defense is the key to winning games at all levels. If the ball does not touch the floor, a point cannot be scored. The more digs a team has, the more opportunities it will have to mount a counterattack.

ATTRIBUTES OF SUCCESSFUL DEFENDERS

Great Attitude

Successful defenders are determined, aggressive, fearless, relentless, and passionate about pursuing the ball. They not only keep the ball "alive," but the team's spirit as well.

Good Ready Position

The fastest and most efficient way to initiate movement is from a ready position. When a ball drops near a player who is unable to react, the error may not be due to lack of desire but rather lack of the proper ready position. Successful defenders live in an active ready position with the eyes and the feet always alert. These defenders are disciplined to maintain a good body position and never lose sight of the ball. They are always ready. They are never caught standing. They prepare to receive every ball even though often times they will not be the ones who make the play.

> **MAXIM:** *You can't play good defense if you are not READY.*

Good Reading Skills

Successful defenders read the cues to help determine the ball's direction and improve their defensive judgments with each play. The greater their knowledge and experience level, the greater their ability to select a position that allows the best chance of receiving the ball.

> **MAXIM:** *Good reading skills maximize a player's defensive skills.*

Functional Technique

Defense is a reaction skill. Although some techniques are definitely better than others, there are many varieties of successful methods. Successful defenders find a way to keep the ball in the air, getting it sufficiently high for a teammate to make a second contact, and recovering in such a way so as not to be injured.

READ SEQUENCE CHECKLIST

One of the keys to successful defense is the ability to read and respond to the visual cues given by the ball, the pass, the setter, the set, the attacker, and the positions of teammates' blocks. Players move to the next cue after each "read" in order to adjust the ready position and establish the appropriate final court position.

Identify the Attackers

✓ Identify the front and back row attackers. Is the setter front row?
✓ Vocalize and physically communicate this information to teammates.
✓ Share information about setter and attacker tendencies.

Read the Pass

The position and quality of the pass dictate the attack. The attack options are revealed once the pass is evaluated.
✓ Watch the pass to the apex.
✓ Evaluate the trajectory and speed of the pass. How quickly will it arrive to the net?
✓ Evaluate the quality of the pass. Which options are available to the setter and attackers?
✓ Will the pass be an overpass, tight, off the net, or directly to the setter?
✓ Is the quick set, dump, or combination play possible?

Read the Setter

✓ Know the setter's options tendencies and strengths.
✓ Read the setter's body position for clues to set placement.
✓ If the ball is far in front of the setter's head, expect the set to go outside.
✓ If the ball is over or behind the setter's head, expect a backset.

Track the Attackers

✓ Track movement of the attackers. Are they changing zones?
✓ Communicate this information verbally to teammates.

Read the Setter's Release

✓ See the ball released from the setter's hands.
✓ On first-tempo sets, focus on the setter's release, the quick attacker, and the ball at the same time.

Read the Set

✓ On second- and third-tempo sets, follow the ball as long as necessary to determine its speed, placement, height, and depth.
✓ To whom and from where will the ball be attacked?
✓ Is the set high or low, good or bad, tight or deep, inside or outside the antennae?
✓ What does the set allow the attacker to do?
✓ Balls set off the net are generally hit deep in the court. Move back.
✓ Inside sets are generally attacked cross-court. Move over.
✓ Good hitters generally hit close sets down. Move in.

Read the Attacker

✓ Switch focus as quickly as possible from the ball to the attacker.
✓ Focus on the attacker's body position and line of approach.
✓ Read the position of the ball in relation to the attacker.
✓ Expect the cross-court hit if the ball is inside the attacker's shoulder.
✓ Expect the line or seam shot if the ball passes the midline of the attacker's body.
✓ Expect the sharp angle shot or tip if the ball is tight to the net.
✓ Epect the attacker to attempt to hit off the block if the ball is tight and near the sideline.
✓ Expect a high-flat or off-speed shot if the attacker runs under the ball.
✓ Return the focus back to the ball.

Read Teammates' Blocks

✓ Evaluate the position and quality of the block.
✓ Eliminate where the ball cannot go and defend the other areas.
✓ Stop and assume a final court position and focus on the ball just prior to attacker contact.

DIG CHECKLIST

MAXIM: *Focus on proper technique. It's important for safety and consistent ball control.*

See Figure 6-1.

Figure 6-1A.   **Figure 6-1B.**   **Figure 6-1C.**

Ready Position (see Figure 6-1A)

✓ Stand with feet wider than shoulder distance apart, parallel or with the right foot slightly ahead of the left.

✓ Keep toes and knees straight ahead or turned in slightly.

✓ Put weight forward on the balls and the insides of the feet, with very little space between the heels and the floor.

✓ Bend trunk forward with back straight. Keep shoulders over knees, and knees over toes.

✓ Relax shoulders and hold arms out from body.

✓ Bend elbows, and keep hands apart at knee-to-waist level.

✓ Raise hand position as defender nears attack. Movement of the hands is quickest from the shoulders to the knees, rather than the reverse.

✓ Balance your weight. The center of gravity is low and slightly forward, and the legs are fired, ready to spring in any direction.

✓ Be stopped, but maintain an "active" rather than "static" position.

✓ Keep the muscles fired.

> **MAXIM:** *Pre-contact movement and pre-contact position is critical to success.*
> *Contact with the ball is limited.*

Platform

✓ Extend out with the arms and legs simultaneously to form the platform behind and under the ball.

✓ Avoid reaching just with the upper body.

✓ Move one arm to meet the other and then put the heels of the hands together. Do not move them as one.

✓ Angle the platform to the target by dropping or raising the shoulders and hips. (Bellybutton faces target.)

Contact

✓ At contact, the platform of the arms faces the target.

✓ At contact, see the ball and the target.

✓ Contact the ball first, the floor second, or both simultaneously.

✓ Play the ball first, then find a way to land safely. Focus on making a good contact.

✓ Contact the ball in front of the hips. Put the body behind the ball and block it.

✓ Do not swing or pivot the body. Do not allow the platform to face away from the target.

✓ Strive to play the ball with two hands. Play the ball with one *only as a last resort.*

✓ Channel easy balls to the target and tougher balls to the middle of the court.

✓ Cushion hard hits and swing on the slow ones. The greater the velocity, the smaller the arm movement. On impact, give in with the arms and body on hard hits. Relax the arms to absorb the power.

✓ Dig the ball high. Allow the setter time to reach the ball and run the offense.

✓ The longer the ball is in the air, the better the chance of someone playing it.

✓ Follow the ball with the eyes with little head movement.

MAXIM: Keep the ball off the floor.

DIG VARIATIONS

Floor defense encompasses a variety of skills that are used to receive the attack and redirect the ball to the setter in preparation for the counterattack. The general term referring to the reception of an attacked ball is the dig. Terminology describing dig variations include the run-through, the "J" pass, the extension or sprawl, the barrel roll, and the dive.

"J" Pass

The "J" pass (see Figure 6-2) is used to receive attacks that are low and in front of the body. At best, there is time for one step to the ball, but often times the movement must be made directly to the floor. The arms and the legs almost simultaneously drop to and under the ball, but the arms contact the ball first, followed by the knees touching the ground. The legs are completely flexed and the weight is forward on the toes. The elbows and wrists are flexed to allow the forearms to go to the floor, under the ball, and scoop or curl the ball upward. This "J" formation with the arms creates the correct rebound angle. The thumb, knuckles, and wrists—rather than the forearms—are often the main point of contact.

Overhand Pass

High and slow balls above the waist are passed with the hands as described in the overhand pass and set checklists in Chapter 3.

Overhand Dig or Reverse "J"

On balls that are near or above the shoulders, direct the ball with the reverse "J" or overhand dig. (See Figure 6-3.) Form a large flat surface with the hands and place this surface behind and under the ball. The hands and wrists are open and firm. The elbows are bent to enable the hands to get under the ball and redirect the ball forward and upward. Reach out to receive the ball in front of the body with the body weight forward, rather than waiting for the ball and possibly playing it behind the body.

High Lateral Dig

On balls that are moving fast and above the level of the waist, dig it by pivoting the body to the side of the ball and replacing the arms with the body. (Refer to Figure 2-8 in Chapter 2.) The outside shoulder is higher than the inside shoulder, the weight is forward, and contact with the ball is in front of the hips.

Over-the-Head Dig

The over-the-head dig (see Figure 6-4) is used in situations where the defender is moving away from the court and must dig the ball over the head to a teammate or send it directly over the net. The ball is contacted at chest level with the arms straight and elbows locked. On contact, the back is arched slightly with the hips forward and the knees bent slightly. The follow-through is short with the hands pointing upward above the head. The legs remain flexed.

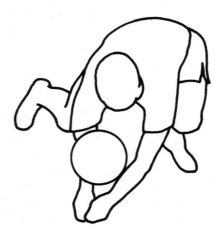

Figure 6-2.

Figure 6-3.

Run-Through

The run-through is used to reach distant balls. (See Figure 6-5.) Defenders run as fast as necessary to the ball and—simultaneously with the run—redirect the ball to the target by angling the platform or with a controlled swing bending the arms at the elbows and curling the ball back to the target. After contact, defenders run-through the ball along the pursuit line, gradually slowing down and returning as quickly as possible to their defensive position. It is important that defenders do not pivot or attempt to face the target prior to contact. This reduces their speed and jeopardizes their ability to reach and/or control the ball.

Extension Checklist

See Figure 6-6.

✓ Used to extend the body's range to receive fast-hard attacks hit directly in front or to the side of the body.
✓ Drive out to the ball with a long and powerful step.
✓ Move in a diagonal path toward the ball. Cut it off before it gets too wide.
✓ Push with the legs to get full extension and spring out to reach the ball.
✓ Simultaneously extend the arms to and under the ball with the platform angled up toward the middle of the court.

Figure 6-4.

Figure 6-5.

✓ Contact the ball on the forearms of both hands whenever possible.
✓ If the ball is not reachable with both arms, continue reaching with one and contact the ball on the forearm or with a cupped or fist-like hand position.
✓ Flick the wrist or bend the elbow to redirect the ball up.
✓ After playing the ball and prior to the knee touching the floor, the hand opposite the lead foot touches down with the palm flat, to help lower the body to the floor.
✓ Almost simultaneously, the lead foot pivots inward to allow the body to extend out on its side.
✓ Both arms extend out sliding along the floor, followed by the body.
✓ Recover as quickly as possible, hopping onto the feet and back into a ready position.

Barrel Roll Checklist

See Figures 6-6 and 6-7.

✓ Used to recover from the extension movement after a run. The momentum created from the run dictates a roll as the easiest and quickest method of recovery.
✓ The barrel roll is recommended over the shoulder roll because of the reduced risk of injury and simplicity to master.
✓ Run directly to the ball.
✓ Just before the ball is going to fall to the floor, time exists for one last step.
✓ On the last step, drive the legs and arms out to and under the ball. Do not pivot or turn prior to contacting the ball.
✓ After contact and just before the knee touches the floor, pivot the lead foot to allow the body to extend out on its side as in the extension.
✓ Follow-through by rolling onto and over the flat of the back.
✓ After the roll, place one foot flat on the floor and push up with the hands back to a ready position.

Dive

In this defensive maneuver, the defender runs and dives to reach the ball, contacting it while the body is "flying" through the air. (See Figure 6-8.) After the ball is dug, the body falls to the ground, contacting the floor first with the hands followed by the chest, stomach, and legs. The body is arched with the knees bent and the head up. There are two common methods of landing. The most common is called the "dive and slide." The diver pushes with the arms in a backward motion upon landing, creating a sliding motion that dissipates the shock of landing throughout the chest and abdomen area. The second method is the "dive and catch" where the diver catches him- or herself and supports the weight of the body upon landing with the arms and lowers the body to the floor. This requires a great deal more upper body strength than the first method.

It is important to start low and dive "out" rather than up to reach the ball. Emphasis is on kicking the heels up and arching the back while keeping the chin up. Emphasis is on catching the body with the weight equally distributed on both hands to avoid shoulder injuries.

> **MAXIM:** *I'm a great believer in luck, and I find the harder I work, the more I have of it.*
> Thomas Jefferson

Figure 6-6.

Figure 6-7.

© 2001 by Parker Publishing Company

Figure 6-8.

NET RETRIEVAL CHECKLIST

✓ Intercept the ball prior to its contact with the net whenever possible.

✓ Once the ball is in the net, drop quickly to a position as low to the floor as possible.

✓ Assume a position off the net that allows room to adjust to various rebounds.

✓ Play the ball from a balanced and stationary position. Movement is with the hands and the arms.

✓ Let the ball drop below the net to allow time to make a controlled contact and avoid a net foul.

✓ Learn how the ball "rebounds" from each net, depending on the tension of the net and speed of contact with net.

✓ Generally a ball that contacts the bottom of the net rebounds out and away, while the ball contacting the top of the net generally drops straight down.

✓ Contact the ball with two hands when the ball rebounds out of the net slowly and/or away from the net.

✓ Use a one-handed contact with the hand closer to the net when the ball remains close to the net.

MAXIM: *The only time the athlete is not physically involved in the play is when he or she is on the bench.*

DEFENDER CHECKLIST

✓ Expect the ball, even when it appears it will not be hit in your direction.

✓ Maintain an "active" ready position.

✓ A body at rest will take a little longer to get going.

✓ Stay low. The lower you are, the more time you have to react.

✓ Focus on good movement to your position and in your position.

✓ Hold the defensive ready position until the ball direction is "seen."

✓ React to where the ball is going—*not* where you think it "might" go.

✓ Never "guess" the ball's direction.

✓ Discipline yourself to go after the ball with two hands.

✓ If you make an errant pass, follow and encourage your teammate who is chasing it down.

✓ Always think of digging the ball up, even if you think it is going to hit you. Be tough and redirect it.

✓ Go after every ball. Don't let it hit the floor alone.

✓ Have the "nothing hits the floor but us" attitude.

✓ Be aggressive but under control.

✓ Stay on the feet whenever possible, but not at the expense of controlling the ball.

✓ Do not give up. Every opportunity is a possibility.

✓ Give an all-out effort to reach every ball.

✓ Wear down the other team through tenacious defense.

✓ Challenge the attacker to hit something you cannot dig.

✓ Play an area, not a spot.

✓ Know defensive responsibilities for yourself and teammates.

✓ Be aware of your position on the court in relation to lines and to teammates.

✓ When the ball is "alive," you have a movement responsibility whether contacting the ball or preparing for the next action.

✓ There is no single skill in volleyball. Each one is linked together in a chain of movements. Constantly think of the next action.

✓ Prepare to attack once defensive responsibilities have been met.

SERIOUS DEFENSIVE CRIMES CHECKLIST

✓ Not being ready.

✓ Not being disciplined enough to be in a ready position that allows you to go for every ball.

✓ Being caught with your weight on your heels.

✓ Being caught with your weight on the wrong foot. Be balanced.

✓ Not being low.

✓ Reaching for the ball with one hand when you could have reached for it with two.

✓ Not going down for a playable ball.

✓ Judging the possibilities of success or failure in receiving the ball. Do not judge it—just go for it!

✓ Contacting the floor first rather than the ball.

✓ Falling or diving for anything slightly out of reach rather than taking a step or running the ball down.

✓ Losing sight of the ball.

✓ Hesitating or looking to someone else to play the ball.

✓ Making token moves. Honestly pursue the ball.

✓ Standing up when a teammate plays the ball. Be low and ready for a second contact responsibility.

✓ Not making any movement in the direction of a ball that you were responsible for receiving.

✓ Reacting to the ball with only the eyes and the head.

CHAPTER 7

THE BLOCKER

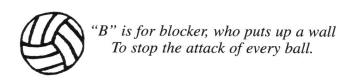

"B" is for blocker, who puts up a wall
To stop the attack of every ball.

The block is the first line of defense to stop the attack. Successful blockers are not only those players who intercept the ball and return it to the opponent's side for an immediate side-out or point, but also those who give the defense the ability to counterattack. These blockers channel the attack into an area of the court that is well defended or deflect the ball upward, slowing it down, allowing the defense an opportunity for successful transition.

ATTRIBUTES OF SUCCESSFUL BLOCKERS

Height and Jumping Ability

The taller the athlete and the better his or her jumping ability, the more opportunities the player has to force an opponent error or block the ball. Height alone, however, does not guarantee blocking success. Height above the net must also be combined with good penetration over the net and proper positioning in relation to the attacker. Although taller blockers may gain more points directly off the block, smaller blockers can be very effective focusing on the goals of channeling and deflecting the ball.

Good Technique

Good blocking does not only depend on height, but on good technique as well. Poor mechanical execution of the block is not only ineffective, but can also place receivers at a disadvantage by making it difficult to select a defensive position around a moving block and/or by making them chase down poorly deflected balls caused by reaching blockers. It is generally more effective to dig the ball directly, without a block, than to play defense behind a mechanically poor one.

Tactically Smart

Blockers may have great technique but if they are not in the correct block position, they will have little opportunity to block the ball. Good positioning not only increases the chances of a successful block, but also elevates the level of back row defense by better defining where the ball will be directed. Good positioning is a product of good reading skills (see the Read Sequence Checklist in Chapter 6) as well as learning about the opponent's offensive tendencies.

Positive Attitude

Good blockers actively go after the ball and the attacker. They are aggressive and confident in their pursuit. They do not go through the motions passively. They block with the intention of being successful.

FOOTWORK PATTERNS

The best method of movement to the block position varies depending on the distance the blocker must cover and the time to do it. Research indicates that when time or distance is a factor, crossover footwork is superior to slide steps. Although lateral movement is fastest utilizing slide steps, the gathering and takeoff portion of the jump takes additional time and is slower overall in getting the blocker off the ground and into a blocking position in the air.

Slide Step

The slide step is the preferred method for covering short distances as well as longer distances when time is not a factor. The advantage of the slide step is that the blocker maintains a parallel body position to the net. The feet slide along the ground, maintaining the same center of gravity throughout the movement. Initial movement is made with the foot nearer the movement direction, and the trail leg immediately slides along the floor to follow. During the movement, the feet remain apart.

Two-Step Crossover

The two-step crossover is a useful option for outside blockers when their initial start position is pinched inside to block the quick attack and the ball is set wide to the outside attacker.

Step One.   The blocker, from the ready position, pivots and runs by stepping with the inside foot, crossing in front of the lead leg toward the new outside block position.

Step Two.   The blocker reorients the body (shoulders and hips) to a position parallel to the net. The outside foot plants, stopping the horizontal movement, and converts it to a vertical one. The plant and liftoff is almost simultaneous. The blocker stops, plants, gathers, and explodes up into the block.

Three-Step Crossover

The three-step crossover is a common option for middle blockers when they need to move quickly from the middle of the court to the outside. The movement is a three-step sprint to the outside block position. (See Figure 7-1.)

Figure 7-1.

Step One.   From the ready position, the blocker quickly transfers the weight to the leg opposite the movement direction, pivots, and pushes off the trailing foot while taking a big running step with the lead leg into the new direction. Emphasis is on a long and powerful first step from the ready position.

Step Two.   The trailing foot crosses in front of the lead foot and takes a second big running step parallel to the net. The toes are turned somewhat toward the net on the plant.

Step Three.   The lead foot swings behind the other foot to re-orient the body to a position parallel to the net. The outside foot plants, stopping the horizontal movement, and converts it to a vertical one. The plant and lift-off is almost simultaneous. Emphasis is on being balanced and square to the net prior to the jump. When it is not possible to complete the squaring-off process on the ground, the process is completed in the air. In place of the step-close as stated above, the blocker can terminate the run with a two-foot hop into the final plant, landing on both feet.

To go left, the blocker pushes off with the right foot and takes a running step with the left, crosses over and runs with the right, and squares off by planting the left foot.

BLOCKER CHECKLIST

See Figure 7-2.

Ready Position

✓ Stand with feet shoulder distance apart, toes pointing straight ahead or slightly out.
✓ Maintain a neutral weight position.
✓ Keep the weight on the balls of the feet, knees slightly flexed.
✓ Maintain a high body and hand position, parallel and near the net.
✓ Extend the arms almost straight, above the head and in front of the shoulders.
✓ Keep hands about a ball's-width apart.
✓ The closer the ball is to the net and the quicker the offense, the higher the ready position because there is less time to prepare.

Figure 7-2.

Movement Concepts

✓ Get to the block position as quickly as possible, allowing time to make small positional adjustments and take a maximum jump.
✓ Move parallel to the net.
✓ Keep the hands high throughout the movement to the block position as well as in the jumping phase.
✓ On arrival to the take-off position, establish a pre-jump base with the feet shoulder-width apart and balanced for take-off.

Timing Concepts

✓ Generally, jump just after the attacker jumps.
✓ Vary the timing of the jump according to the speed of the attacker's take-off, arm swing, and height of jump.
✓ Vary the timing of the jump according to the height, speed, and distance the set is from the net.
✓ The closer the ball is set to the net, the earlier the jump and vice versa.
✓ Position the arms over the net to block before the attacker's arm is up and beginning to go forward to attack the ball. The attacker accelerates into contact very quickly.

Jump Concepts

✓ On first-tempo sets or dumps, jump directly upward from the starting position with very little knee bend. Do not drop into a squat position.
✓ On second- and third-tempo sets, bend the knees to a half-squat position and explode up.
✓ Use a rapid and dynamic counter movement, i.e., squatting down just prior to take-off.
✓ Squat and get off the ground quickly. Do not hold the counter movement in the lowered position.
✓ The faster the counter movement, the higher the jump.
✓ Experiment with the depth and speed of the counter movement—it differs for each athlete. Too much or too little can affect the jump height.
✓ Use more legs than arms in the jump. A vigorous arm swing may improve the jump slightly, but does not outweigh the potential errors it causes.
✓ Be on-balance on take-off with the body weight between the feet.
✓ Jump up off both feet.
✓ Jump square to net.
✓ Keep the hands in front of the body and above the shoulders. The jump increases with high hands at take-off.

Go Up and Down

✓ Be balanced in the air.
✓ Do not float forward or to the sides.
✓ Block where you are. Once positioning is established, block in that position.
✓ Do not drift sideways. It gives the attacker the opportunity to hit into a moving target and "use" the block.
✓ It also makes it difficult for defenders to establish correct court positions.

Block Within the Shoulders

✓ Block within the shoulders. This is the strongest block position.
✓ Do not reach away from the court. It weakens the block and gives the attacker a target to "tool."
✓ Do not reach for the ball. This forces defenders to play difficult deflections.
✓ Only reach outside the bodyline if you can seal the net.

Keep Hands and Arms Quiet

✓ Get the hands and arms over the net quickly.
✓ Extend the arms over the net in one motion.
✓ Do not swing. Swinging causes incorrect timing, nets, and unseals the net.
✓ Spread and tense the fingers. Point thumbs to 11 o'clock and index fingers to 1 o'clock.
✓ Hold hands a ball's-width apart, palms facing toward the middle of the court.
✓ Lock the elbows and make the forearms rigid.
✓ Extend the arms by shrugging the shoulders and elevating the shoulder blades.
✓ Keep the hands, arms, and shoulders strong, firm, forward, and parallel to the net.
✓ See the back of the hands in front of you.

Wrist Position

✓ The position of the wrists depends on the block goal, position of the ball, and height of the blocker.
✓ Generally, on good sets, flex the wrists back slightly. The wrists are firm and locked in this position for best height.
✓ Flex the wrists forward on tight sets and redirects, with the rebound angle facing downward into the opponent's court.
✓ Bend the wrists backward on soft blocks to deflect the ball into the air. Place the hands as high as possible and near the top of the net, and tilt the wrists back as far as possible with the palms facing the ceiling.

Penetrate

✓ Reach over the net as far as possible.
✓ Strive to contact the ball on the opponent's side of the net.
✓ Create a tight seal with the net. Leave as little space as possible between the hands, arms, and top of the net.
✓ Strive to keep the ball between the hands and the floor.
✓ Be aggressive on balls set on top of the net and get the hands on the ball as quickly as possible, denying the attacker or setter an opportunity to make a play.

> **MAXIM:** *The farther the blocker extends over the net, the more area taken away from the attacker.*

Block Outside–In

✓ Press the body to the middle of the court with the hips, shoulders, arms, and hands.
✓ Keep the head forward and look up with the eyes. When the head tilts back, the arms are pulled off the net.
✓ Keep the eyes open. Focus on the attacker and ball simultaneously.

One-Hand Blocks

✓ Learn to block with each hand independently. A well-positioned one-hand block is better than reaching incorrectly with two.
✓ On late blocks, reach as far as possible with one hand toward the attacker and over the net. The extension is greater with one arm. (See Figure 7-3.)
✓ Use one hand to close the block when proper position has not been established.

Abdominal Muscles

✓ Tighten the abdominal muscles.

Follow-Through

✓ Sustain the block as long as possible.
✓ Stretch the body in the air.

Figure 7-3.

✓ Hold the follow-through. The longer the hands remain over the net, the better the opportunity to contact the ball.

✓ Finish the block before turning off the net.

✓ As the ball passes the block, follow it with the eyes, the head, and the body.

Landing

✓ Draw the arms back to a parallel position.

✓ Land on both feet, square to the net and in the take-off position.

✓ Cushion the landing by bending slightly with the knees on impact.

✓ Listen to the landing—it should be soft and silent.

✓ Land ready to play the next ball.

> **KEY:** Feedback is critical for blocking success. The coach must focus on footwork, technique, court positioning, and position of contact with ball in relation to the net. If the coach does not give feedback, blockers will only feel successful when they block the ball back to the opponent's court—and at any level this is not frequent. Good observation points for the coach are 1) the referee stand, to see block penetration or lack of it, and 2) on the opposite side of the blockers to evaluate the blockers' eyes. Are they open? If so, are they focused on the attacker or the ball?

GENERAL BLOCKER TACTICS CHECKLIST

Knowledge

✓ Learn the abilities and tendencies of opposing setter(s) and attackers.

✓ Learn offensive patterns of opponents in each rotation.

✓ Keep track of the last five sets the setter made.

✓ Keep track of the last five attacks made by attackers for which you are responsible.

✓ Consider the score and who will most likely be set.

> **MAXIM:** *Perfect block technique is useless if the block is positioned improperly.*

Positioning

✓ Position the block to take away one attack option.

✓ Most attacks are directed at the angle of the approach. Block this angle.

✓ The faster the set, the less opportunity the attacker has to change the direction of the ball. Block the attacker's angle of approach.

✓ Take away the attacker's favorite shot and force him or her to hit a weaker one.

✓ Keep the attacker guessing. Do not exclusively block the line or angle.

✓ Fake your intentions. Assume a base court position and—just prior to the attacker's approach—reposition the block. Start in and move out or vice versa.

✓ Work in combination with the diggers. Establish a solid block position that enables them to select a position to defend behind the block.

✓ Work in combination with other blockers. It is the responsibility of each blocker to close the seam between the block.

✓ Surround the ball with the hands on sets tight to the net. Reach over the net as far as possible to intercept (stuff) the ball back immediately on the attacker's contact.

✓ Do not allow the setter the opportunity to set balls that are on top of the net. Get your hands on the ball first.

✓ Move the block inside on deep sets and challenge the attacker to hit the line.

✓ Do not block on bad sets or weak attackers when the ball can be easily controlled with the dig.

✓ Soft block the ball for small blockers or taller players on late blocks or mismatches.

✓ Take the short tip when the ball is within one step of the block, but do not fall to the floor for it. The digger may be attempting to receive the ball.

> **MAXIM:** *Less focus on the ball and more on the attacker will result in more successful blocking.*

OUTSIDE BLOCKER CHECKLIST

✓ Block your corresponding attacker and/or those attackers who enter your zone.

✓ If attackers leave your zone, move to block in another zone or back off the net to dig.

✓ Be prepared to block first-, second-, and third-tempo sets within your zone.

✓ Press hands to the middle blocker to protect the seam and close the block.

✓ Generally block cross-court: (1) when the attacker is chasing the ball on an inside set, (2) on quick sets, and (3) on deep sets.

✓ Block the attacker's angle of approach when the ball is set tight.

✓ Block the line on good attackers, tight sets, and on balls to the antennae or beyond.

✓ Avoid reaching out toward the sideline and giving the attacker an easy target to "tool."

✓ Do not reach out of the court or outside the bodyline to attempt to block a ball that is directed to the line. Block the line or channel the ball to the line for the diggers.

✓ Do not follow wide sets outside the antennae. Do not land outside the sideline.

✓ Block parallel to the net. Do not face the angled outside attacker, and thus be facing outside the court.

✓ Move the arms outside in toward the inside of the court.

MIDDLE BLOCKER CHECKLIST

✓ Assume a base position in the middle of the court until the set direction is determined when the opponent's middle attacker primarily hits from the middle of the court and/or when the opponent most successfully attacks from the outside; or . . .

✓ If the middle attacker is effective the middle blocker must follow them anywhere along the net. The middle blocker can either read or commit block if the middle attacker is set. The disadvantage of this tactic is when the middle attacker moves to an attack position to the far right or left of center and the set is directed outside. It will be difficult to cover the additional distance.

✓ Readjust the start position based on the possibilities allowed by the pass.

✓ Be prepared to block all front and back row attackers.

✓ Prepare to block first-tempo sets first. Focus on quick adjustment steps to front the attacker's hitting shoulder in the direction of his or her approach or hitting tendency.

✓ Never give up. Maintain the attitude that a block or deflection is always possible.

✓ Move to the outside blocker on outside sets and press back into the middle of the court with the arms and body.

✓ Be disciplined to cover your area and not try to reach over the outside blocker's space.

✓ Use a one-hand drop move when late, that is, drop the arm farther from the ball and reach to the ball/fill the gap with the other. You gain more reach and height with one arm than two.

✓ Allow the setter to get to the ball and set after the block.

✓ Prepare to transition for the attack after the path of the setter is determined.

✓ Call the best audible for the attack according to the position of the pass.

✓ Strive to move to an attack position away from the opponent's middle blocker and/or move to a position of block weakness.

✓ Be unpredictable in the attack position along the net and type of set.

TEAM TACTICAL BLOCK OPTIONS

Team block tactics encompass a variety of options from simple to complex and conservative to risky. They can simply react to the offense or take a more proactive stance, working actively to stop or disrupt it. In order to employ a system that is effective, the opponent's offensive tendencies, strengths, and weaknesses in each rotation are first identified. *For example:* Which attackers are most effective? What are their most common types of attacks? Is it necessary to block all their attackers? Second, decisions must be made on where it is best to employ the block and with which players. Scouting reports give a tactical beginning and observations during the match are utilized to make immediate adjustments.

Decision 1: Number of Blockers

Tactically the first decision that must be made is how many blockers to employ against specific teams and/or individual attackers. The single block is used against attackers who do not pose a strong hitting threat, and the double and triple block is used to defend strong attackers. (See Chapter 8 on team defense.)

> *MAXIM: Do not require players to block who cannot get their hands above the net.*

Decision 2: Setting the Block

A decision must be made as to who sets the block. It is a common tactic for the blocker closest to the attack to set the block and provide the focus for the remaining blocker. Generally, the outside blocker sets the block on all outside sets and the middle blocker sets the block for center hits. The primary blocker (the player who sets the block) lines up with the attacker's hitting shoulder in the direction of the approach, blocking the approach angle or tendency.

Decision 3: Tactical Options

Player-to-Player Block.   Each blocker is responsible for his or her corresponding attacker. Generally this system is employed when the opponent's offensive system is not using crossing-combinations patterns.

Zone Block.   Blockers are responsible for blocking all attackers who enter their zone, whether they are attacking first-, second-, or third-tempo sets. This system is employed when attackers use the whole net from antennae to antennae and cross paths, rather than attacking consistently in straight-ahead patterns. Traditionally the middle blocker is responsible for participating in all blocks. In this system outside blockers assume many of the characteristics of middle blockers and are responsible for blocking middle as well as their outside attacker.

Area Block.   Blockers are responsible for taking away an area of the court from the attacker with the intention of reducing a player's effectiveness by forcing the attacker to hit a nonfavorite shot or forcing the attacker to attack where the defense is waiting to receive the ball.

- *Block angle.* It is advantageous to block angle against attackers who have a difficult time hitting down the line. The blockers take away the cross-court shot and invite the attacker to hit the line. If the attacker continues to hit angle, more blocks are probable. If the attacker attempts to hit the line, the block is forcing a weaker shot and possibly the attacker will make more errors.
- *Block line.* It is advantageous on good sets to block line and force the cross-court shot against attackers who can successfully hit the line. There is more time to read and react to the cross-court attack than a line shot, and can be more easily defended with at least two receivers.
- *Setting the block.* To block line, the end blocker is not always positioned at the sideline. In general terms, the blocker's position is determined in relation to the position of the ball, that is, the outside blocker sets the block by placing the inside hand in front of the ball. The outside blocker places the outside hand on the ball to block angle.

Block Signals.   Blockers prior to the serve can use hand signals to indicate to the diggers which area of the court they plan to "take away" on a specific hitter. The signal, given behind the back, indicates the blocker's intention to block "line" (1 finger) or "angle" (2 fingers) if the set is good. Hand signals are effective at all levels because they encourage blockers to think about tactics and communicate this strategy to the defense.

Read Block.   The read block tactic is an option used primarily by the middle blocker when defending first-tempo sets. The blocker "reads" the quick set and reacts to the quick hit just after the set is made. Emphasis is on a quick rather than high block and getting "deflections" rather than "stuffs." The blocker's arms are extended over the head with the hands leading quickly over the net. The jump is off the balls of the feet (tiptoes), with very little leg flexion. A good quick attacker is difficult to stop in the read system. Emphasis is placed more on assisting with the higher second- or third-tempo sets.

Commit Block.   The commit block is the most effective way to stop first-tempo attacks. The blocker "commits" or jumps with or slightly before the attacker—before it is determined that the specific attacker will receive the ball. If the attacker is set, the blocker has a good opportunity to stop it; but if the ball is directed to another attacker, it is very difficult—if not impossible—for the blocker to participate. The commit block is effective in the following situations:

- On tight passes where the setter has few options and it is difficult to set another attacker.
- After the outside hitters have been ineffective and it is probable that the setter will go to the middle.
- When the blocker is physically inferior to the attacker in size or jumping ability. This is the only possibility of blocking successfully.

Match-Ups.   In traditional blocking tactics, players specialize by blocking right (zone 2), left (zone 4), or middle (zone 3) based on their blocking and attacking strengths. Match-up tactics place blockers in positions based on their strengths and those of the opponent. The concept is to "match-up" the best blockers against the opponent's best and most probable attackers and avoid a successful attacker hitting against a weak blocker.

Match-up tactics require more flexibility in roles because players must block and attack in more than one position. *For example:* Outside blockers might be performing roles much like that of the middle blocker, that is, blocking first- and second-tempo sets and covering more than one attacker within their zone. Middle blockers might be blocking on the right and the setter blocking on the left.

Match-up tactics can be utilized at any time during the game, but are most easily employed when the team is in the serving phase defending against the side-out attack. While the offense is striving to get mismatches in height or ability, the defense is working to get the best blocker to defend the best and most probable attacker.

Positional Overload and Release Block.   Players wait to see where the ball is directed in traditional blocking schemes and move after the set direction is determined. Blockers in this tactic move prior to the set (release) to double or triple block (overload) the most effective and most probable attacker(s), and "invite" the opponent to set a weaker player who is not so well defended. The concept is to play the percentages. Attackers are prioritized according to their effectiveness. All attackers are not equal and successful attackers should be better defended than weaker ones.

For example: If the opponents are scoring the majority of their points with the left-side attacker, the middle blocker "releases" to the outside block position before the setter has the ball. This places two blockers in position early to block the strongest attacker. The tactic is considered successful if the best attacker is stopped or made less effective as well as when the weaker hitter is set. Generally a weak attacker can be adequately defended with a single block.

MAXIM: *Even if you are on the right track, you'll get run over if you just sit there.* Will Rogers

---

CHAPTER 8

TEAM DEFENSE

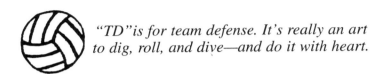

*"TD" is for team defense. It's really an art
to dig, roll, and dive—and do it with heart.*

The goal of the defense is to block the ball back to the opponent's court or to receive the ball in such a way that successful transition to the attack can be made.

> **MAXIM:** *Great defense alone is futile. It must be combined with the
> counterattack to score points.*

The best defensive system is one that places players in a position where they can utilize their strengths. These individual efforts must be coordinated within the constraints of the team defense. No one system is perfect. The success of the team defense is dependent on the individual abilities of the defensive players rather than on a specific system. If players' individual skills are poor, no system can be successful.

> **MAXIM:** *Personalize tactics to meet your needs.*

DECISION 1: BASE POSITIONS

All defensive systems begin from a base position on the court. Every time the ball crosses the net to the opponent's side on the serve or in a rally, players return to these initial positions. Starting positions are based on what can happen first before time allows for further adjustments and reflect the system and tactics employed in the team defense. Base positions are adjusted according to the opponent's tendencies and style of play and, thus, are not necessarily the same in every rotation or against every opponent.

Block Base Positions

Standard. Standard block base positions have the left front blocker (zone 4) pinched inside. This tactic is used when the opponents primarily attack with first- and second-tempo sets to the middle or right side. The right front blocker (zone 2) remains wide near the antennae to block third-tempo sets on the outside and have no responsibility to block quick or combination attacks. (See Diagram 8-1.)

© 2001 by Parker Publishing Company

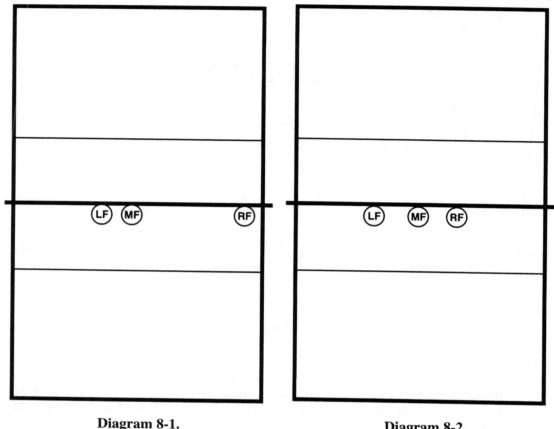

Diagram 8-1.   **Diagram 8-2.**

Pinched.   Pinched block base positions have both left and right front blockers (zones 2 and 4) pinched inside. This blocking tactic is utilized when the opponent's strength is in the middle attacking with first- and second-tempo sets and combinations all across the net. If the set is directed outside, end blockers have the responsibility to reposition themselves to defend this attack. (See Diagram 8-2.)

Wide.   Wide block base positions have both left and right front blockers (zones 2 and 4) positioned wide toward the antennae. This tactic is used when a high percentage of sets go to the outside and the middle can be effectively defended with a single block. Outside blockers concentrate on blocking the outside attacker and have no responsibility in the middle. (See Diagram 8-3.)

This tactic is also employed when the opponents have been effective "tooling" the outside blocker. This adjustment helps the blocker to better position the block to redirect the ball back into the court.

Adjustments from Pinched to Wide.   Positional adjustments are made once it is determined that the pass will not allow first- or second-tempo set options. End blockers assume a wide base position near the antennae to prepare for the outside attack. (See Diagram 8-4.)

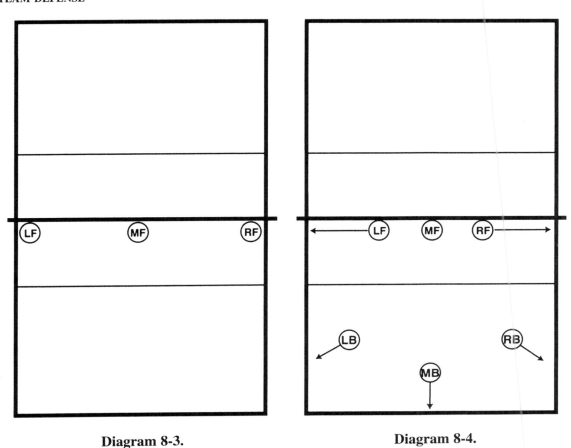

Diagram 8-3.   Diagram 8-4.

Back Row Base Positions

Pinched. Back row base positions that are used to defend first- and second-tempo attacks have the right and left back wings (zones 1 and 5) pinched in near the 12-foot line and middle back (zone 6) inside the endline and toward the tendency of the attacker. (See Diagram 8-5.)

Wide. Back row base positions that are used primarily to defend third-tempo high sets have right and left back (zones 1 and 5) deeper in the court and wide near the sidelines. Middle back stays deep near the endline in the middle of the court or at the attacker tendency. (See Diagram 8-6.)

Adjustments from Pinched to Wide. Positional adjustments are made once it is determined that the pass will not allow first- or second-tempo set options. Back row wings assume a wide base position near the sideline to prepare for the outside attack. (Refer to Diagram 8-4.)

   KEY: It is a common strategy to show one tactic and switch to another, that is, start with blockers or defenders pinched inside and—during the pass—move to a wide base position.

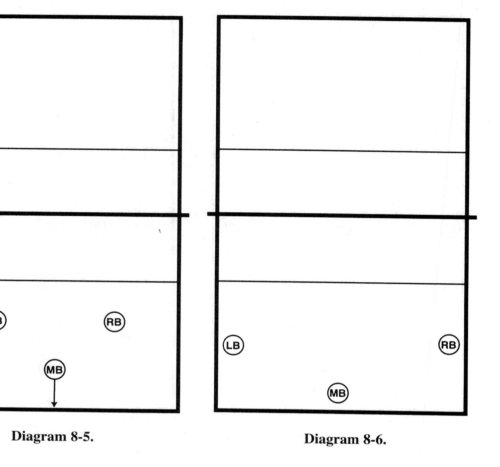

Diagram 8-5.   Diagram 8-6.

DECISION 2: NUMBER OF BLOCKERS

The first system decision is whether to defend with one, two, or three blockers. This next decision is based on the strengths of your blockers as well as on the opponent's offensive strengths and tendencies. How effective is the opponent's attack? Does it warrant a double or triple block? What are your blocking abilities? Assign functions to players that they are capable of performing, rather than asking them to do something physically they cannot do. If players are not tall enough to present a solid block, utilize them to play defense.

Single Block

The single block is frequently used against attackers who do not pose a strong hitting threat.

Double Block

The double block is used to defend strong attackers. In the traditional system, all three front row players assume a ready position at the net to block. (See Diagram 8-7A.)

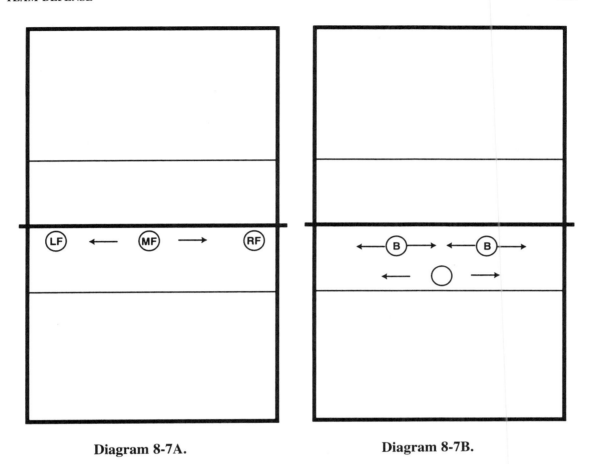

Diagram 8-7A.　　　　　　　　**Diagram 8-7B.**

In a situation when one front row player is not an effective blocker, the two remaining blockers can split the court and double block against all three of the opposition's attackers. The non-blocking front row player assumes a position under the block to cover the tip or moves to the back row for defense. (See Diagram 8-7B.)

Triple Block

The triple block is used to intimidate and defend strong attackers. It can be used on both middle and outside attackers. It is especially effective on the left side attacker when it is obvious that the ball will be directed to that side. The outside blocker takes away the line on the left side attack, leaving the attacker very few options other than the tip. (See Diagram 8-8.)

DECISION 3: SYSTEMS BEHIND THE BLOCK

The primary decision is to use either a "player-back" or a "player-up" tip coverage defense. Consideration must be given to the type of attacks most often being defended. How often do op-

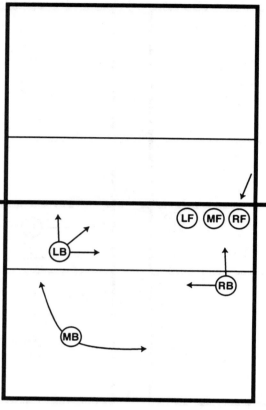

Diagram 8-8.

ponents tip and what is the player's ability to receive tips with only "deep" court coverage? Also, which areas of the court are most frequently attacked? It is best to position receivers in those areas most often attacked rather than necessarily balancing the court.

It is not necessary to play within only one system. A combination of systems may be employed according to the strengths and weaknesses of your personnel as well as the opponent's in each specific rotation. Other options include matching up your best defensive blockers and diggers to defend against their strongest and most probable attacker.

Player Back Defense

The player back defense is also referred to as a zone 6 deep, perimeter, or read defense. The court is squeezed from the outside–in with receivers remaining deep and near the sidelines. Defenders must move in to play the tip or off-speed shots. The team might be forced to move into an "up" system if the opponent begins to tip effectively.

Single Block.   The player back defense used with a single block has the advantage of both strong back row and tip coverage. (See Diagram 8-9.) It is employed when the opponent's attack is weak and/or when a team does not have strong blocking skills or sufficient numbers of solid blockers to utilize a double block.

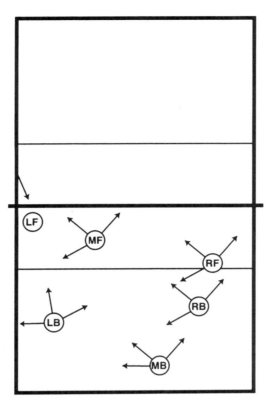

Diagram 8-9A.

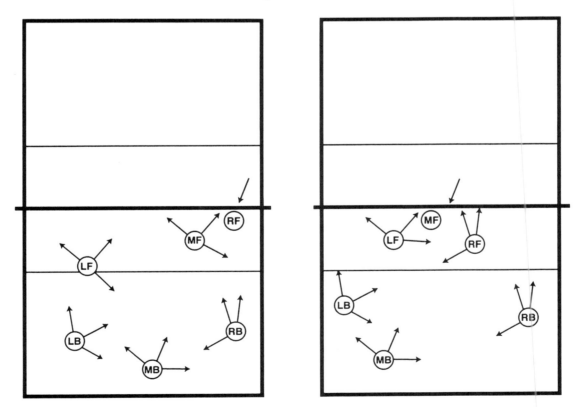

Diagram 8-9B.   **Diagram 8-9C.**

To defend against the outside attack, right or left front blockers position themselves for a one-on-one block, lining up at the angle in which the attacker approaches. Middle front is positioned behind the block and near the 10-foot line to receive tips. For the center attack, middle front blocks and both right and left fronts position themselves for the tip. All other positions are identical to the player back system for the double block with the exception that back row players have more area to defend around the block and they have no tip responsibility.

MAXIM: *Every attack has its own life and possibilities. Evaluate the options according to the attacker, the set, and the position of block.*

Double Block.   Diagram 8-10 indicates the defensive formations against a right, left, and middle attacker. The following is a detailed explanation of the position and responsibilities of the defenders against the left side or zone 4 attacker. The positioning is just the reverse for the right side or zone 2 attacker.

Blockers are responsible to block line or angle according to the team's tactics as well as in relation to the position of the ball and the ability and approach of the attacker.

Right back (zone 1).   Right back is responsible for defending the line hit and tip, balls hit off the block toward the sideline and/or out-of-bounds, and the dump or off-speed shot toward the center of the court.

Right back starts in a base position ready for the dump or quick attack. When it is determined that the pass will not allow the quick set or dump, or when the setter release indicates a high set, right back moves back and out toward the sideline with the right foot on the line and slightly forward of the left. The body and platform are turned to channel the ball into the court. Movement is outside–in, assisting in digging the ball into the court, rather than reaching toward the outside to play a ball. Right back must evaluate the attack options and the placement of the set in relation to the net and position of the block. If right back sees the ball and the attacker clearly around the block, he or she remains back to defend the line attack. Right back releases for the tip and/or off-the-block attack on good sets when the block appears "solid," and the ball or attacker cannot be seen. Right back can automatically release for the tip when the ball is set beyond the antennae because no line shot is possible; or, if the opponent rarely tips, right back can move toward middle back to defend a deep angle hit over the block. Right back also releases for the angle tip on inside and center sets when the blocker in front is involved in the block. Right back should communicate his or her "up" position to the blockers to discourage them from reaching back to play a tip.

Left front (zone 4).   Left front is responsible for the sharp cross-court power attack, the off-speed shot, deflections, and tips within the 10-foot line. The attacker must prove he or she can hit the power angle, or left front should assume more responsibility for the soft attack.

Left front begins at the net in a blocking position. As the direction of the set is determined to go to the left side attacker, left front quickly moves to a position near the 10-foot line, using slide steps or a three-step crossover. Left front adjusts his or her position to play off the shoulder of the inside blocker. The position is several feet within the sideline or in an intermediate position nearer the block, depending on the ability and tendencies of the attacker. Left front is positioned with his or her back to the side-line, protecting the ball and channeling it inside the court. As the set and/or block moves inside—making the angle attack more difficult for the attacker—left front may release to a position under the block to cover the tip, or may slide back deep to play the angle

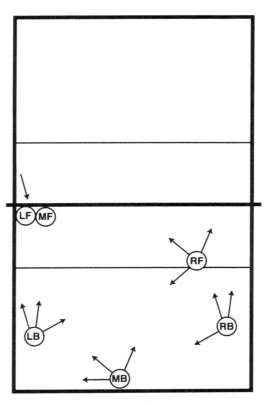

Diagram 8-10A.

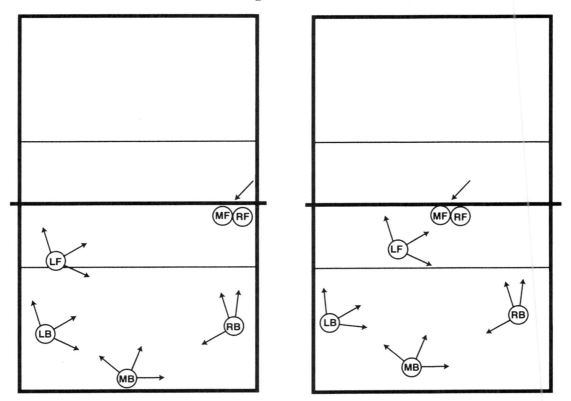

Diagram 8-10B.   Diagram 8-10C.

around the block. Left front plays defense in partnership with left back. They must not reach to play waist-high balls that can be better played by the back row player. As left front moves deeper in the court, left back also moves back to defend a deeper area.

Left back (zone 5). Left back is responsible for the deeper power angle attack. Left back starts in a base position ready for the dump or quick attack. For a high set, left back moves out toward the sideline with his or her back to the line and the body channeled into the middle of the court. Movement is forward toward the net or back as dictated by the attacker and the set.

Left back plays a deeper cross-court angle behind left front, splitting the angle of possible attacks. They are in staggered positions with left front several steps in front of left back. Left back plays a position off the shoulder of the middle blocker with a clear view of the attacker. The more inside the block position, the greater the chance that one of the receivers may be playing in the shadow.

The key is to see the ball around the block. If the defender cannot see the ball, he or she moves forward; or if left front moves farther back into the court, so does left back, to play a deeper position near the corner of the court. In this situation, the possibility exists that left back will be playing in the shadow of the block.

Middle back (zone 6). Middle back is responsible for balls hit deep over or off the block along the endline, as well as power hits through the hole in the block or around a single block.

Middle back starts several feet inside the baseline and in the middle of the court and/or toward the middle hitter's tendency. Middle back remains shallow to play the hole in the block. If the double block is solid, middle back moves back to the endline, playing in the seam or shadow of the block. Generally, middle back is the deepest player on the court—the safety, playing all deep balls.

MAXIM: *Winners don't whine.*

Defending the Middle Attack.   The defense against the middle attack (see Diagram 8-11) is executed from player back base positions and are the same regardless of the defensive system employed with the exception of the middle up (zone 6) defense. (See the middle up defense described later in this section under "Middle back (zone 6) up.")

Single block. Left and right front (zones 2 and 4) back off the net and move inside to play the tip or soft attack. Left back (zone 5) plays the power angle. Right back (zone 1) plays the cut back shot. Middle back (zone 6) plays "deep" at the tendency of the attacker.

Double block. The middle blocker is assisted by either the right or left front blockers (zone 2 or 4).

The secondary blocker is determined by (1) the position of the set and nearness to the blocker, (2) the directional tendencies of the attacker, or (3) the tactical option to protect a specific area of the court. The player nearest the attack sets the block and the remaining blocker closes. The non-blocking front row player covers the angle tip. When the outside blocker participates in the block, the corresponding back row defender releases to cover the tip. The remaining back row players read the direction of the attack and position themselves accordingly.

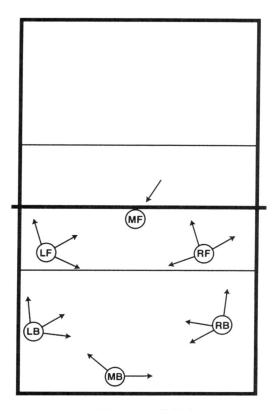

Diagram 8-11A.

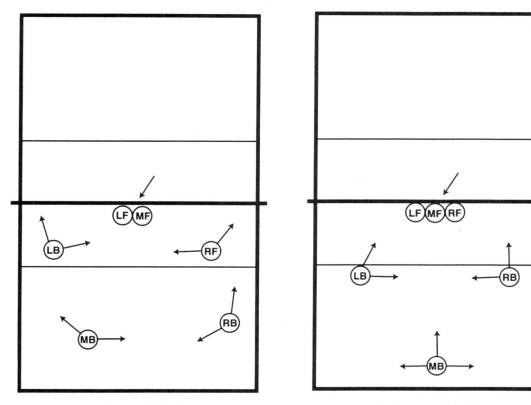

Diagram 8-11B.   **Diagram 8-11C.**

Triple block. Left, middle, and right side players (zones 2, 3, and 4) block the middle attack. Right and left side wings (zones 1 and 5) defend the angle attacks or tips. Middle back (zone 6) reads and defends deep back row.

> **MAXIM:** *If an opponent has found a hole in your defense, plug it up. If an opponent consistently exploits a weakness, make an adjustment.*

Player up Defenses

The up defenses provide tip coverage by one "up" player while the remaining receivers play deep. This system is advantageous against teams with the tendency to tip as well as for strong blocking teams that cover a large area at the net and force the attacker to tip or channel the ball to an area defended by receivers.

Player Across. The player across defense (see Diagram 8-12) utilizes the nonblocking front row player in zone 2 or 4 to move across the court to cover tips behind the block. This leaves three defensive players in the back row. This system is advantageous when the attacker cannot attack the ball to the sharp angle near or inside the 10-foot line. Starting positions are identical to those of the player back system. When the set direction is determined, the nonblocking front row player moves under the block to cover the tip. Back row coverage is also identical to the player back system, but back row receivers have limited tip responsibility.

The disadvantage of this system is the difficulty it presents for the up player to transition from defense to the traditional outside attack position.

Rotation. The rotation defense (see Diagram 8-13) is a combination of both the "deep" and "up" systems. Starting positions are identical to the player back system until the set is directed outside. Then the line player directly in front of the attacker "rotates up" to a position inside the court near the 10-foot line and is responsible for all tips. Middle back (zone 6) rotates to a position near the sideline to play the "line" shot and the back row wing rotates to play middle back. The front row wing player rotates off the net to play a position beyond the 10-foot line.

A variation allows the line player to rotate up while all remaining defenders play in a nonrotation position to receive cross-court hits. No one is defending the line in this situation; but this is a good option if the attacker has difficulty attacking the line. Consideration must always be given to the block. If there is no solid double block, all back row players must hold their deep positions. (See Diagram 8-14.)

Middle Back (Zone 6) Up. The starting base position for the zone 6 up defense (see Diagram 8-15) differs from that of the other options given in that the player "up" begins up. The defender is positioned midcourt near the 12-foot line and, as the double block forms, moves behind the block and has responsibility for all dumps, mishits, roll shots, deflections, and overpasses. Generally, the player up is the setter or secondary setter in the back row.

The front row wing moves behind the 10-foot line and near the sideline to defend the power angle. The two remaining back row players divide the responsibility of back row coverage and "read" and adjust to cover the areas most likely attacked. The weakness of this system is defending the quick attack with only two deep receivers.

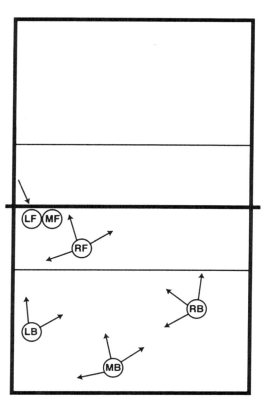

Diagram 8-12A.

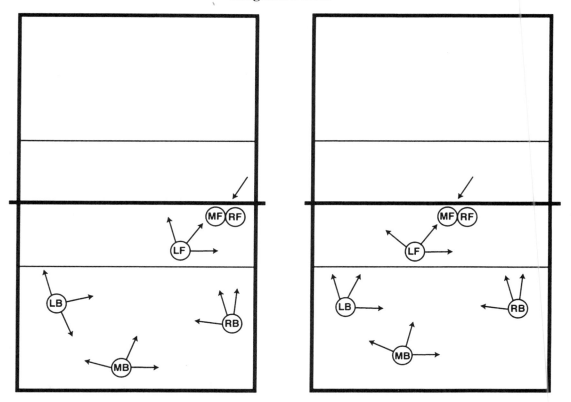

Diagram 8-12B.   **Diagram 8-12C.**

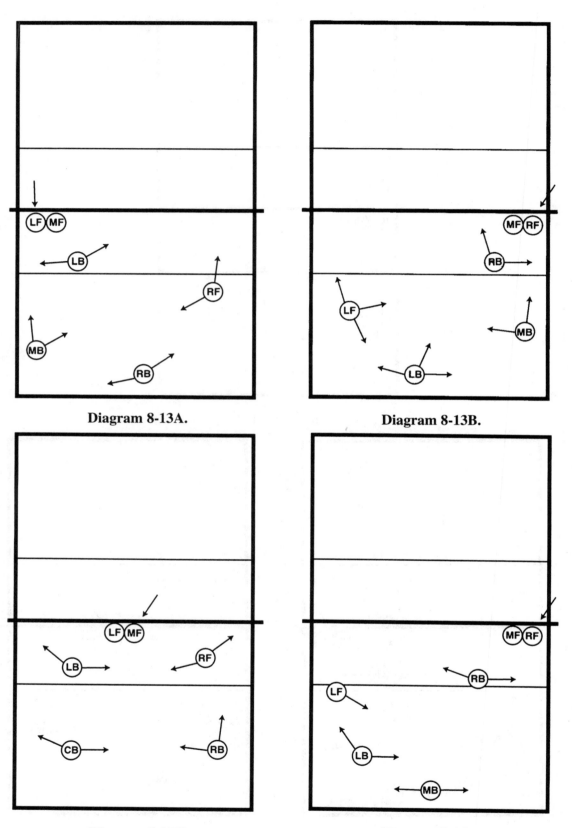

Diagram 8-13A.

Diagram 8-13B.

Diagram 8-13C

Diagram 8-14.

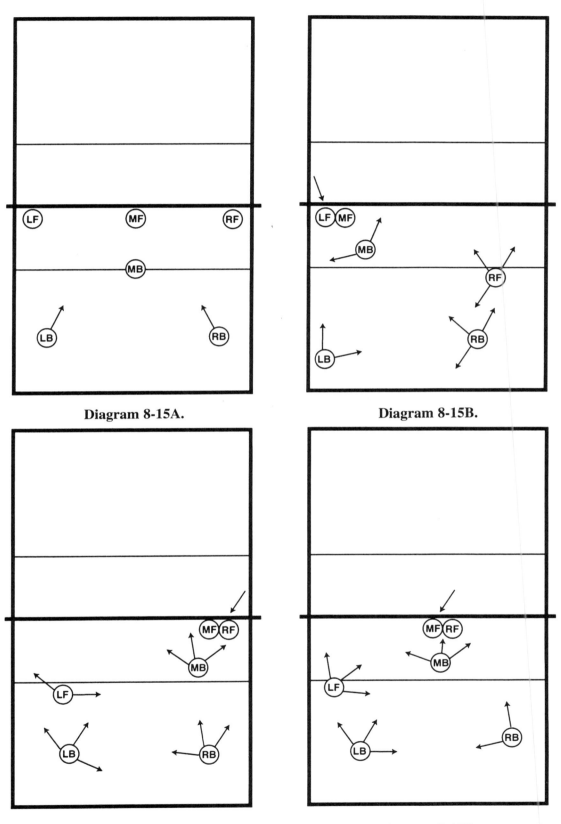

Diagram 8-15A.

Diagram 8-15B.

Diagram 8-15C

Diagram 8-15D.

> *MAXIMS: Defense starts offense. Combine defensive skills*
> *as rapidly as possible with the attack.*

DECISION 4: NO BLOCK/DOWN BALL CALL

Not all attacks warrant a block. The "no block" call is made on a weak attacker or on a poor set that does not allow a powerful attack. Simultaneously with the no block call, blockers quickly back off the net and have responsibility to play balls within the 10-foot line. Back row players adjust forward or back according to the position of the set and the ability of the attacker. All back row defensive players are positioned straight across, rather than in a staggered formation. (See Diagram 8-16.)

> *MAXIM: Create point-making opportunities through tough, aggressive, and smart play.*

DECISION 5: FREE BALL CALL

The defensive team calls a free ball when the opponent must underhand or overhand pass the ball over the net. The free ball is very important to winning volleyball games, as it is an opportunity to run the offense off an easy pass. Repeated success from the free ball forces the opponent to attempt more difficult plays that could generate errors.

It is the responsibility of all players to identify and call the free ball. Simultaneous with the free ball call, players move from their defensive position into a receiving pattern for the standard 4-2, international 4-2, or 6-2 system and the setter releases to the target area to await the pass. (See Diagram 8-17.) Back row players have primary pass responsibility allowing front row hitters to prepare for the attack. The overhand pass is preferred for all passes, but especially for short distances.

Returning a Free Ball to Opponents

When a player must pass the ball over the net to the opponents rather than attack it, the player should consider the following.

- Send the ball to zone 1, the spot left vacant by the back row setter in the 6-2 system.
- Pass the ball to a front row attacker, especially a quick hitter, to disrupt the offense.
- Place the ball to zone 2 to make transition to set the middle attacker more difficult.
- Pass the ball high to allow teammates to reorganize and return to their defensive positions.
- Pass the ball deep to zone 6 between two back row defenders.

> *MAXIM: If you want to get more out of volleyball, put more in.*

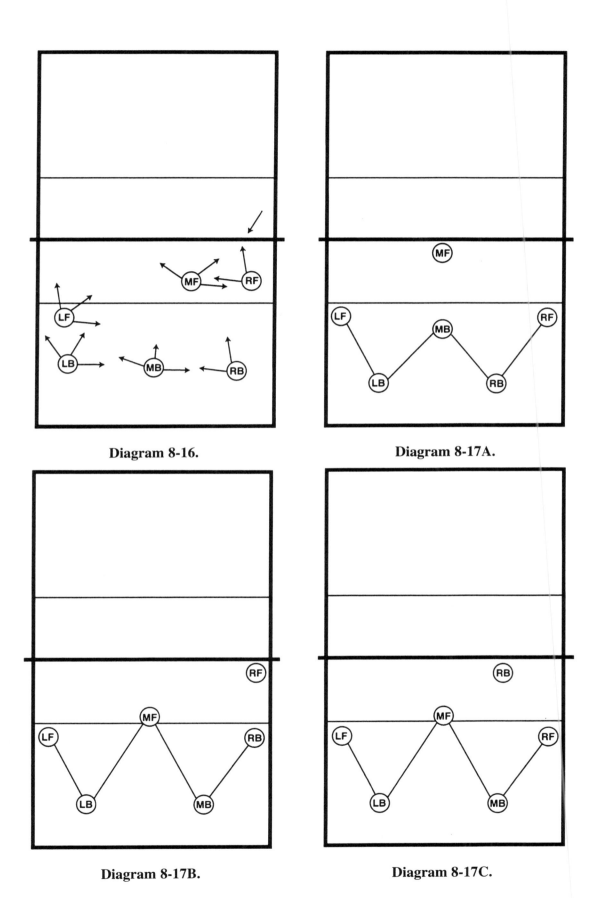

Diagram 8-16.

Diagram 8-17A.

Diagram 8-17B.

Diagram 8-17C.

DECISION 6: PLAYING BALLS IN THE GAP (TWEENERS)

Who's ball is it? It is fairly easy to determine whose ball it *was* after the ball drops, but there is not sufficient information to determine prior to this who *should* make the play. It is the responsibility of both players to go for balls in the seam, one moving in front and one moving behind in a crossing pattern. Staggered positions by adjacent players help facilitate this movement; when in doubt, however, both players should go after the ball rather than backing off and letting it drop. Whose ball was it? If no one went for the ball, the answer is . . . it was ours! (See Diagram 8-18.)

The player in the better position should take the ball when two players make a simultaneous call. Generally this is the person farther away with the best angle to the target, as well as the best view of the whole court. Call the ball again and make the play. The second player should respond with a "yours" or "okay" to indicate he or she will not take it.

DECISION 7: ATTACK COVERAGE

All players should "cover" the attacker in preparation to receive the ball if it is deflected back by the block. Players assume a low ready position to cover with the weight forward and the arms

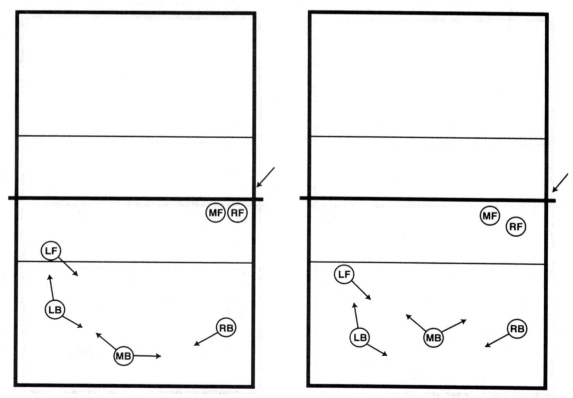

Diagram 8-18A.   **Diagram 8-18B.**

apart. On the close cover, one hand is up and one hand is down to anticipate either a high or low returned ball. The eyes are focused on the hands of the opponent's block rather than on the ball or on the attacker.

Players must evaluate the rebound angle of the ball according to the angle and penetration of the block, and the position and depth of the set. The ball will be blocked down rather than deep on tight sets. Players must be low, ready, and stopped as the attacker contacts the ball.

> **MAXIM:** *Do not give up second-chance opportunities. Cover the attacker.*

Attack Cover Formations

Cover formations are generally referred to as a 3-2 or 2-3 cup surrounding the hitter. The first number refers to the number of players in the "close" cover position one to three feet behind the attacker, and the second number refers to the players in a "deep" cover position.

4-2 System Coverage. The close cover for the outside attacker in the 4-2 system is formed with the front row setter, the middle blocker, and the back row player directly behind the attacker. The deep cover is formed with the nonattacking front row player and the back row player diagonally opposite the attacker. (See Diagram 8-19.)

6-2 System Coverage. The close cover position for the outside attack in the 6-2 system is formed with the setter, the quick hitter, and the back row player directly behind the attacker. The setter follows the set and is the middle person in the cup while the quick hitter lands from the "fake" and turns to cover from a position near the net. The deep cover is formed with the nonattacking front row attacker and the back row player diagonally opposite the attacker. (See Diagram 8-20.)

Differences Between 4-2 and 6-2 Coverage. In the 6-2 system, the setter has released from the back row to the front row to set, leaving only two players in the back row. They divide the court and play right and left back positions. The back row player directly behind the attacker moves up the line to participate in the close cover, and the remaining defender plays diagonally opposite the attacker in the deep coverage position.

In the 4-2 system, middle back participates in the close cover, while in the 6-2 the quick attacker fulfills this role.

> **MAXIM:** *Do not hope to win points on opponents' errors; rather, win them*
> *the old-fashioned way—by earning them!*

ATTACK COVERAGE CHECKLIST

✓ Precise cover positions are not always possible for first- and second-tempo sets and/or when players are pulled out of position.

✓ Focus on being "stopped and ready" when it is not possible to establish precise cover positions.

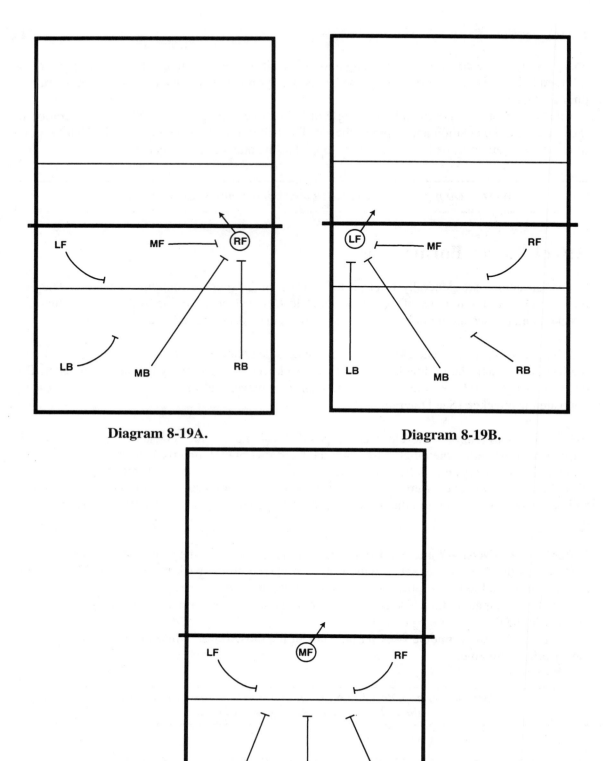

Diagram 8-19A.

Diagram 8-19B.

Diagram 8-19C.

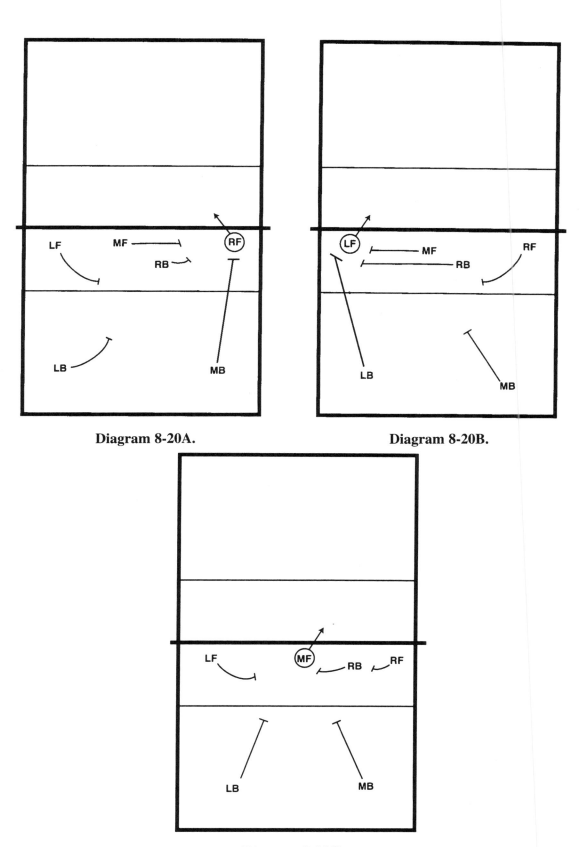

Diagram 8-20A.

Diagram 8-20B.

Diagram 8-20C.

✓ The setter offers primary coverage on quick sets, and all other players assume a ready position wherever they are on the court.
✓ Be flexible to fill in open spots whenever possible.
✓ Expect the ball to be blocked back and cover!
✓ The only person not expecting to get blocked is the attacker.
✓ A good cover is like an offensive rebound in basketball—it offers a second opportunity to score.
✓ A good cover gives the attacker confidence to swing.
✓ Know what plays have been called and be prepared to cover.
✓ Coverage for the back row attacker is in front of him or her.

> **MAXIM:** *Give the ball to a teammate in better shape than you received it! Better the ball!*

SAMPLE DEFENSE GUIDELINES

General

Rule 1.   We will use a perimeter or "read" defense. Players have the responsibility to "read" the play and select the best defensive position based on the attacker's ability, tendencies and position of the set. Each player has movement responsibilities and freedoms, but in relation to the rest of the team.

The court will not necessarily be balanced. We will cover the most probable areas of attack.

We will be aware of teammates' defensive positions and adjust and fill in as necessary on defense and the cover.

Rule 2.   All players must learn all positions so when it is tactically prudent, we will be able to match up specific diggers and blockers to attackers.

We will utilize the strengths of individual players to assume more or less court responsibility.

Rule 3.   Blockers start in a ready position at the net (pinched in or wide depending on our tactics) with the arms extended high. Blockers look through the net and indicate the eligible attackers. Left back and right back wings are positioned up and inside for the quick attack and/or the dump. Middle back is positioned deep middle and/or at the tendency of the quick attacker.

Rule 4.   Until a hitter proves that he or she can hurt us on the line, we will block strong angle and remain back to dig the line.

Rule 5.   We will option to rotate up on tight sets, after a player has been blocked, in a long rally, or in critical points in the match when we cannot afford to give up a tip.

Rule 6.   We will block line and rotate up on individuals who consistently hurt us with the tip.

Rule 7.   We will rotate up on inside sets, high center sets, or play sets when the blocker in front of you is involved in the block.

Rule 8.   We will double release with the line player and the front row nonblocker when the opponent tips or off-speeds frequently.

Rule 9.   We will not rotate up automatically when the attacker is hitting over a smaller block.

Rule 10.   We will triple block the outside attacker occasionally. Back row wings will release to cover the tip and the sharp cross-court angle (single release). Both wings will release (double) to cover tips when necessary.

Defense vs. Front Row Setter

The defense generally has the advantage in the three rotations when the opponent's setter is front row because there are three blockers to defend against two attackers and a setter.

Rule 1.   We will prioritize who is most important to defend against, and overload our best blockers on their best and most probable hitters.

Rule 2.   We will determine if it is necessary to block the front row setter on a good pass or if it is more important for the left front blocker to commit on the quick attacker.

Rule 3.   We will determine if it is more appropriate for the middle blocker to "read" the quick attack and double block with the left front blocker, or release immediately to the outside hitter leaving the left front blocker in charge of stopping the quick attacker.

Rule 4.   On a good/tight pass with an effective setter, left front blocks the setter and middle blocker takes the quick attacker.

Rule 5.   When the attackers are split and the pass is good/tight, the middle blocker takes the dump.

Rule 6.   On passes zero to four feet off the net, left front commits on the quick attacker and middle blocker "reads" the quick attack or releases to the outside.

Rule 7.   Do not block the setter when he or she is back row.

Rule 8.   Learn which hand the setter prefers to attack with and his or her directional tendencies.

Rule 9.   Once the ball (dump) passes the block, primary responsibility rests with left back to pick it up.

Rule 10.   The dump becomes the responsibility of right back only when it crosses well beyond the center of the court.

Blocking the Quick Attack

Rule 1. All players are responsible to block the quick hitter in their area. If you have no other block responsibility in your zone, commit with the quick hitter.

Rule 2. We will double block against a quick attacker who poses a threat of repeated kills.

Rule 3. We will double block the quick hitter on sets toward an outside blocker.

Rule 4. Right front is the primary blocker on the inside shoot (3), and middle blocker assists. Right back covers tips and middle back plays the seam. (Also see Chapter 9.)

Rule 5. Left front assists the middle blocker on the quick set (1) and is the primary blocker on the back 1. Left back covers the tip and middle back plays the seam. (Also see Chapter 9.)

Rule 6. We will single block the quick hitter (1) when the attacker is weak and/or when the pass is at least five feet from the net, (2) when the quick hitter scores primarily on tips or miss hits, and (3) when we become disadvantaged on the outside block.

Rule 7. Front row players not involved in the block are responsible for tips and missed hits. Step off the net and get low!

Rule 8. We will double or triple block second tempo (2) on attackers who pose a threat. The middle blocker is the primary blocker and right or left front assists. (Also see Chapter 9.)

Rule 9. We will rotate up on quick sets when the outside blocker in front of you is involved in the block.

MAXIM: *Successful defensive players combine solid techniques with good reading skills and an attitude that every ball is playable.*

CHAPTER 9

TEAM OFFENSE

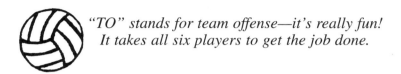

"TO" stands for team offense—it's really fun!
It takes all six players to get the job done.

Most coaches choose a system and adapt their players to fit the system. Although this is the easiest choice, the real challenge is to design a system that meets the needs of your specific team. Evaluate the individual athlete's mental and physical strengths and weaknesses and utilize a system that is appropriate for the athletes' skill and experience level. Use a system that will help players excel technically and tactically.

MAJOR QUESTIONS IN CHOOSING AN OFFENSE

- What do we need to do to win and what are we capable of doing?
- How can we maximize our strengths and minimize our weaknesses?
- What will be fun, challenging, and developmental?
- How much practice time is available to prepare the team?

DECISION 1: NUMBER OF SETTERS

Carefully consider the number of setters available as well as those athletes who might have the potential to become setters. Consider the effectiveness of these setters as attackers or of attackers as setters. Just because a player is a great hitter should not rule out the possibility that he or she also could develop into a great setter/hitter.

> **MAXIM:** *Do not just find setters; train them.*

4-2 System

The 4-2 system (4 hitters/2 front row setters) is effective for inexperienced teams because it is easy to learn and makes the most of simple plays. (See Diagram 9-1.) The setters in the 4-2 are placed opposite one another in the rotation so that one setter is always in the front row while the other is in the back. The front row setter has primary setting responsibilities.

Standard 4-2.   The setter in the standard 4-2 system (see Diagram 9-2) is a front row player and sets from the middle of the court (zone 3). When the front row setter is not already in this position, he or she switches to middle front immediately after the server contacts the ball. The attackers position themselves right and left front near opposite sidelines. The setter sets high outside to one of the attackers, forcing the opponent's middle blocker to cover the entire length of the court in order to execute a double block.

This system is utilized by teams that do not possess strong passing and/or setting skills because, in this system, the accuracy of the pass is less critical as well as the timing and placement of the set.

International 4-2.   The front row setter switches to the right front position (zone 2) and sets from this position, which allows a stronger blocker to play in the middle (zone 3). (See Diagram 9-3.) The international 4-2 is an advanced system and is used during three rotations in the 5-1 when the setter is front row.

6-2 System

The 6-2 system (6 hitters/2 back row setters) is an advanced system utilizing all players as attackers and two of these players with the dual role of setting and hitting. (See Diagram 9-4.) It is an effective developmental system where young players have the opportunity and are encouraged to learn both attacking and setting skills.

The two setters are positioned opposite one another in the rotation so that, as in the 4-2, one setter is in the front row while the other is in the back row. The back row setter in this system has primary setting responsibilities, and the front row setter becomes an attacker. This system is utilized when the two best setters are also effective attackers. The advantage of this system is that the setter has the option of setting three front row attackers, one of which is the front row "secondary" setter.

In the side-out portion of the game, the back row setter releases to the pass target area, right of center front (between zones 2 and 3), immediately after the serve has been "contacted," and awaits to set the second ball. In the transition portion of the game, the setter remains back row to play defense. If the setter does not dig the ball, he or she releases to the target area to set.

6-3 Triangle System

In the 6-3 system (6 hitters/3 setters) three setters are placed in a triangle formation in the rotation. (See Diagram 9-5.) The system can be used with a front row setter similar to the 4-2 or a back row setter as in the 6-2.

6-3 Front Row Setter.   The 6-3 front row setter option gives each setter/attacker setting responsibility two times and attack responsibility once. When the setter rotates to the center and right front positions, he or she switches to the center to set. Although the 4-2 is generally accepted as the initial system for beginners, it limits player development. The 6-3 triangle with the front row setter option maintains the simplicity of the 4-2 while affording players the opportunity to learn and improve all fundamental skills prior to exposure to a more advanced system of play. It is recommended as a progression toward a more advanced system.

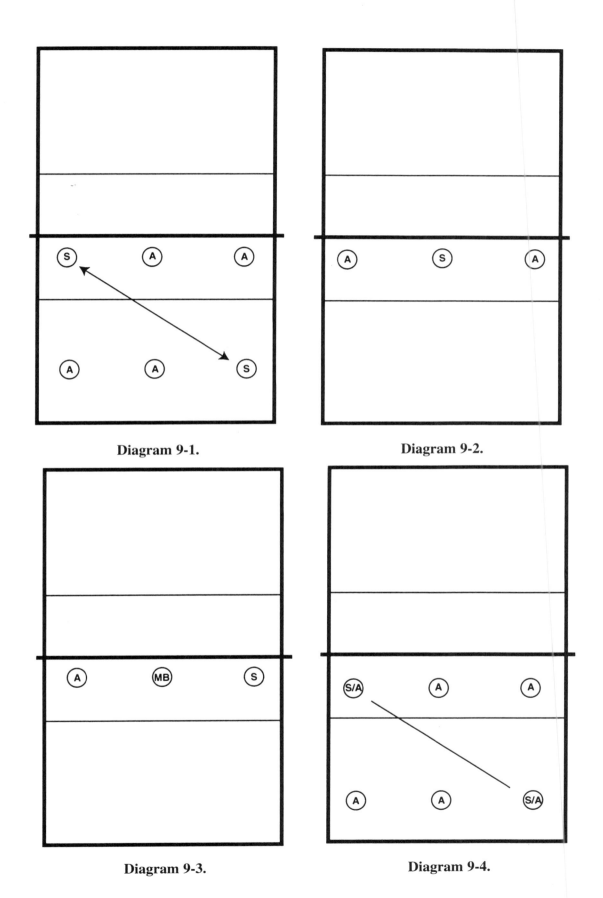

Diagram 9-1.

Diagram 9-2.

Diagram 9-3.

Diagram 9-4.

6-3 Back Row Setter.   In the 6-3 back row setter option, the setter/attacker sets when he or she is in the right and center back position, allowing for an easy transition to the front row. This modification of the 6-2 system is intended to give more players an opportunity to develop as back row setters, but it is also intended only as a progression to the 6-2 or 5-1 system.

5-1 System

The 5-1 system (5 hitters/1 setter) is a combination of the international 4-2 and the 6-2, with one setter having primary set responsibility both in the front and back rows. (See Diagram 9-6.) This system is best employed when the team has only one capable setter and/or when the coach wants to take advantage of one setter who is extremely talented. If your best setter is also your best hitter, consider the 6-2, which allows your setter to hit when he or she is in the front row.

Advantages of the 5-1 include efficient practices where players need only focus on their specific role as hitters or setters, and consistency in setting and leadership, in that the attackers have only one setter to adjust to. It is a demanding role for the setter—both physically and mentally—and a very specific role where the setter generally does not have the opportunity to practice hitting.

The 5-1 system can be used as a primary system or learned as a back-up system for the 6-2 when no substitute setters are available.

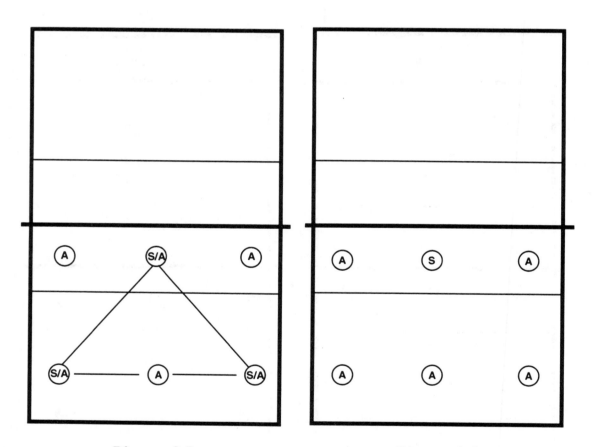

Diagram 9-5.   **Diagram 9-6.**

DECISION 2: DEGREE OF POSITIONAL SPECIALIZATION

All sports specialize. It would be uncommon to see football, baseball, or basketball players playing every position on the field or on the court. Specialization maximizes team efficiency by placing players in positions offensively and defensively where they will be most effective, and giving them the opportunity to practice those specific skills. Players identify with a position and become confident in their team role.

Players are categorized in general terms as setters and attackers. Attackers are classified more specifically as outside or middle hitters and/or as outside and middle blockers. There are also various categories of specialists; for example, defensive or serving specialists.

The international numbering system further delineates the positions by dividing the volleyball court into six zones or areas, beginning with right back as zone 1, right front as zone 2, and continuing in rotation order through zone 6. Each zone has offensive and defensive responsibilities relating specifically to the team's system and tactics. (See Diagram 9-7.)

Very few switches are needed in the beginning stages of the 4-2 system. The front row setter switches to zone 3 and sets the ball either forward or back to an outside hitter (standard 4-2). In the more advanced international 4-2, a strong blocker switches to zone 3 and the front row setter occupies zone 2.

Another form of specialization is the utilization of tactical switches that strengthen the team by matching-up players against specific opponents. *For example:* (1) A primary attacker can switch to hit against a weaker blocker, (2) the best blocker can switch to block against the opponent's best attacker, and (3) the best defensive player can defend the position most likely attacked.

Although specialization is essential for proper execution of the game's systems and tactics, it is equally important that players learn a variety of skills and positions to give the team tactical flexibility and options. Middle blockers should learn the outside attacker position and be competent attacking both high and quick sets. Outside attackers should be capable of playing on both

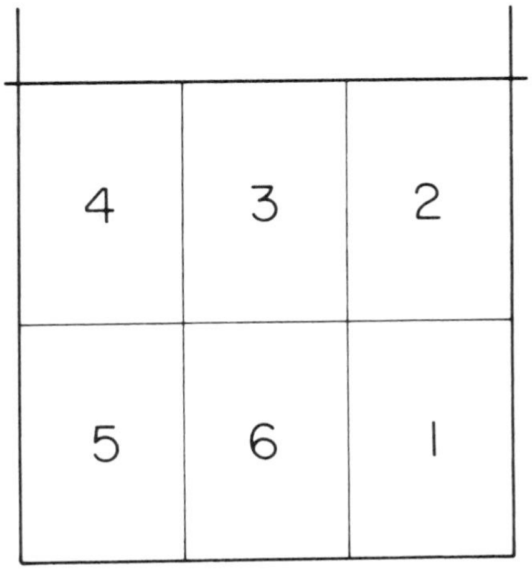

Diagram 9-7.

right and left front. All players should learn to block high and quick sets. All players should be competent setters—this is a big advantage for the overall offense. The best teams use specialization, but at the same time, good players are versatile enough to play more than one position.

Traditional Zone Characteristics and Job Descriptions

Zone 1: Right Back.   The setter or secondary setter traditionally occupies zone 1 in the 6-2 and 5-1 systems. This position requires good setting and defensive skills. Defensive responsibilities come first; then, if the setter does not dig the first ball, he or she releases to the front row to set.

Zone 2: Right Front.   The setter or the secondary setter traditionally occupies zone 2 in the 6-2 and 5-1 systems. In addition to good setting skills, the setter needs good blocking ability to defend against the opponent's power attacker. If the player is a setter/attacker, he or she should possess good right side attacking skills. Left-handers have some advantages because the ball does not have to cross their body prior to contact, as is the case for right-handers attacking from the left side.

Zone 3: Middle Front.   The setter occupies zone 3 in the 4-2 system, whereas the middle blocker plays this position in the 6-2 and 5-1. Defensively, the middle blocker needs to be aggressive, quick, mobile, and with good jumping ability to block all attackers along the net. It also helps to have good "reading" skills to utilize the cues from the opponent's setter to determine early the direction of the set. Offensively, the middle blocker must be mobile and quick to transition from defense to the attack.

Zone 4: Left Front.   The left front player is the primary attacker in all systems. This player needs to be powerful and/or consistent, attacking with a variety of options. He or she also needs to be smart. This position receives the highest percentage of sets, especially on bad passes, so this attacker needs to be able to hit the good as well as the imperfect set. The attacker must be smart to understand when to go for the kill and when it is best to just keep the ball in play.

Zone 5: Left Back.   This player must possess good defensive skills, because this position receives the majority of attacks from the opponent's power hitter.

Zone 6: Middle Back.   Zone 6 players need good lateral movement to cover the deep area of the court. If there is a double block, they play in the shadow of the double block. These defenders are the deepest in the court and must recover all deep balls not received by teammates. They need to be experienced and quick to read the direction of the play because their position is a little more flexible.

Switching Procedures.   All players must begin each point in their proper rotational order. Switches to a player's specialized position are allowed immediately after contact is made on the serve. This is most easily accomplished when your team is serving. Players position themselves on the court prior to the serve in order to be ready to make an easy switch to their defensive positions.

When receiving serve, back row switches are generally made after the pass, set and hitter coverage responsibilities have been met, and the ball has crossed the net to the opponent's side. Front row players may switch positions during the pass while in route to their attack positions or after the ball crosses the net.

It is the responsibility of all players to call the "switch," or to call it off by calling "stay" if there is not sufficient time during the rally to make the change. It is important to follow the movement of the ball as the switch is being made, and to remember to return to the original position in the rotation prior to each serve.

DECISION 3: COMPLEXITY OF THE OFFENSE

> ***MAXIM:*** *The success of the offense does not correlate with complexity; rather, on good execution.*

The high set is used as the primary offense in beginning volleyball as well as playing a major role in the advanced game. The high set is the foundation of the game (the "meat and potatoes") and is used by itself or in combination with the quick attack (the "dessert"). Passes cannot always be accurate even with the best teams; thus, success depends to a large degree on the ability to successfully attack high sets.

All attackers—regardless of their position—need to practice and become proficient at hitting high sets. Training should progress from simple to complex, teaching third-tempo high sets first and then progressing to second-tempo play sets and, finally, first-tempo quick sets.

The more complex and diverse the offense, the higher level of passing, setting, and attacking skills is necessary. It is fun, developmental, and motivational for athletes to strive to improve their skills so they will be able to effectively utilize a quick offense. The more proficient the passing and setting, the more quick and combination plays can be integrated into the system. Sufficient practice time is necessary to develop the offense and train the technical and tactical skills necessary for proper execution.

DECISION 4: OFFENSIVE OPTIONS
AND LANGUAGE

The Jim Coleman system of terminology has been a popular method in the United States to describe the offense, both for theoretical use in the classroom, as well as in the game. The basic terminology used in this style system to indicate set location and height is very specific.

The net is divided into nine zones, 1-meter wide with the numbers 1 through 9 beginning from left to right. The setter occupies zone 6. Two numbers are used to describe a set: The first number indicates the zone and the second indicates the height and speed of the set. A "51," for example, would indicate a quick set 1-foot high positioned directly in front of the setter. For sets above nine feet, the digit "O" is used. A "10," then, would be a high outside set to the zone 4 attacker. Back row sets can be given a third number; for example, 14-4 would signify a 14 set, set four feet off the net. (See Diagram 9-8.)

A second system style, less specific, that is often used to call plays and sets in the game employs a type of "shorthand" that is clear, quick, and simple. The attack zone, height, and depth of

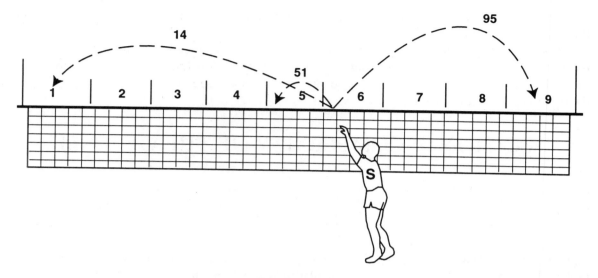

Diagram 9-8.

the set in this system is indicated by a single digit number, letter, or a one-syllable word. (See Diagram 9-9.)

Individual Attack Options

The following names, numbers, and letters represent examples of how sets can be identified. (Refer to Diagram 9-9.) Coaches are encouraged to create their own system language.

High Set, Third Tempo (5).   The high set is a high arching set either forward or back, 10 to 15 feet above the net, that should descend near the sideline and allow the attacker to hit line or the angle. The ball should be set back from the net, allowing the hitter a comfortable margin in which to contact the ball and work around the block.

Outside Shoot Set, Second Tempo (4).   The basic shoot is set to the sideline, three to six feet above the net and one to two feet off the net. The set may have various arcs and speeds depending on the abilities and preferences of the attacker. The attacker begins the approach just after the ball leaves the setter's hands. The goal of the shoot is to create a gap between the right side blocker and the middle blocker where the attack can be directed. This set is effective because it does not require pinpoint precision and, if the middle blocker remains in the center of the court, it beats the middle blocker to the outside. The set is high enough to leave room for timing errors, but fast enough that it does not give the defense sufficient time to form a solid block.

Play Sets, Second Tempo (2, B, C).   The play set is a ball set two to five feet above the net, in front of the setter (2) or behind the setter (B/C), and is utilized by itself or in combination with first-tempo sets to create time differentials. The height and placement of the "2" varies with the preference of the attacker. It can be close to the setter (2 in) or wide (2 out). The "2" behind the setter can be set close to the setter (B) or the setter can loop it out to the antennae (C).

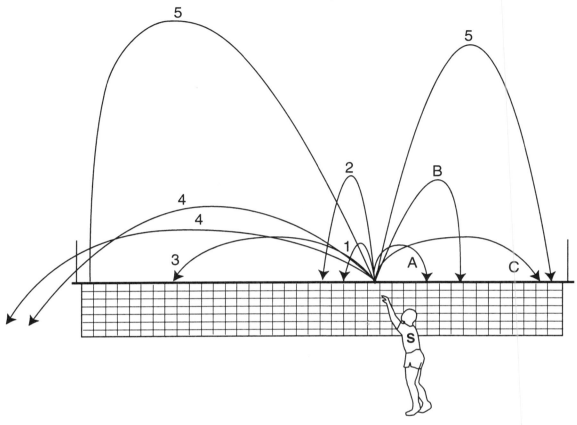

Diagram 9-9.

Quick Front Set, First Tempo (1).   The quick front set is a ball set one to two feet in front of the setter at the height of the attacker's reach. The attacker in the "quick–quick" is in the air prior to the set, and the hitter in the "slow–quick" lifts off the floor as the ball is being set. The setter determines the timing and often the direction of the attack according to the position of the set.

Quick Back Set, First Tempo (A).   The quick back set is similar to the quick front set with the set going tight behind the setter.

Inside Shoot, First Tempo (3).   The inside shoot is a ball set quick and low along the net three to five feet from the setter and set to the height of the attacker's reach. The attacker is in the air just prior to the set. The goal, as in the outside shoot, is to create and hit through the gap created by the outside and middle blockers.

Slide (One-Foot Take-off), First or Second Tempo (Slide A/C).   The slide is used frequently in the women's game by both the middle and right side attackers. The slide is generally set behind the setter for right-handers (back slide) and in front of the setter for left-handers (front slide). The attacker uses an approach pattern that is more along the net than diagonal. The take-off is off one leg and the attacker broad jumps from one spot along the net to another, making it more difficult for the defender to select a blocking position.

The slide is used both as a first- and second-tempo set and can be run tight behind the setter (slide A), wide out to the antennae (slide C), or to the attacker's preference anywhere in between.

In the first-tempo slide, as in other quick attacks, the attacker is past the setter and in the air ready to hit when the setter contacts the ball. The ball is set one to two feet high in the first-tempo slide and the attacker runs to catch up with it, moving laterally in the air parallel with the ball. The best jumpers have the opportunity to evaluate the position of the block and choose the best moment to hit through an opening or catch the blockers reaching.

Fade, First Tempo.   Men primarily use the fade option. It is a quick set where the attacker approaches straight in for a first-tempo set, jumps, and plants with both feet, but instead of going straight up, broad jumps laterally to hit the ball in a slightly different position. The attacker "fades" or "slides" along the net, moving away from the blocker and causing the blocker to reach to block the ball rather than establishing good position in front of the hitter. The attacker "fades" along the net either in front (front fade) or behind (back fade) the setter. The advantage of the two-foot take-off fade is that both front and back fades can be utilized equally by right- and left-handers.

To use the fade successfully, the attacker must first establish an effective "vertical" first-tempo attack that holds the blocker to the position directly in front of the take-off position. Once the blocker is conditioned to assume this position, the attacker can approach and plant in front of the blocker and "fade" or drift sideways away from the setter and the opposing blocker, causing the blocker to lean and reach to block the ball.

Double Pump, Second Tempo.   The pump is a movement where the attacker approaches for the quick hit and plants, but does not jump. The attacker hopes to draw the blocker into the air and then jump to hit a slightly later set, creating a time differential with one person.

Pump Step-Out, Second Tempo.   The pump step-out is similar in timing to the double pump, while also stepping away from the initial plant position to attack the ball at a different location away from the blocker. *For example:* the attacker approaches hard and fast to hit a "3," stops on the plant, and jumps laterally with a step-out move on the take-off to the "1" quick-hitting position to hit a slightly higher set. The attacker also can approach and plant in the "1" position and "step out" on the take-off behind the setter for the back "1."

To use the pump successfully, the attacker must establish the standard first-tempo quick hit options. The blocker must be convinced that, without going up with the attacker, there will be no chance of stopping the opponent from scoring. Once the blocker begins to commit with the quick hitter, the attacker must approach convincingly enough not to give away the intention to pump or step-out.

Back Row Attack, Second or Third Tempo.   The back row attack plays an important role in the men's game and is developing into a successful tactic in the women's game as well. Originally, the back row hit was used most frequently when the setter was front row to help equalize the number of attackers facing the blockers. Today, its role has expanded to utilize the best attackers regardless of their position in the rotation. The offense has the ability to come at the defense with up to five attackers and there are more aggressive, offensive options in bad pass or out-of-system pass situations.

The men's back row set differs from the women's set in that it is lower and closer to the net, allowing a more aggressive attack. Strong jumpers can take off from behind the 10-foot line and contact the ball in a position near the net, similar to a regular front row set. It is most effective to place the back row set in an open zone against the flow of the front row offense, or directly behind the quick attacker as a play set.

> *MAXIM: Master the basics first! Progress from third-tempo sets to second to first.*
> *Perfect the front row offense before adding the back row attack.*

Combination Attack Options

The concept of combination plays is to move two attackers toward one blocker in order to create an overload situation. The first attacker approaches for a first-tempo set, followed closely by a second attacker who is ready to hit a slightly higher second-tempo set (play set) to the side of the setter and/or quick attacker, or directly behind (tandem) the first attacker. The blocker cannot block both attackers and, thus, the blocker must make a decision as to which of the two attackers to block.

The key to effective combination plays is a quick attacker who will score if the middle blocker does not commit with the set. If the middle blocker commits with the quick attacker, the second attacker can be set and vice versa. Each attacker in this situation is hitting against a single block or a weak double block. The object is to capture the attention of the middle blocker and hold him or her to this block position. At the least, the quick attacker must cause the blocker to hesitate, waiting to see if he or she will receive the ball. This makes it difficult for the blockers to put up a solid block on the play set attacker.

Combinations may be run straight in or with two players whose paths cross in an "X" formation. Situations where players' paths cross force blockers to change their assignments or switch their player-to-player coverage in order to cover both attackers. It is very difficult to defend against this maneuver if the offense is executed effectively.

Right Side "X" and "Fake X".   The quick attacker in the right side "X" approaches for a first-tempo front or back set, and the right side player crosses behind to the middle of the court to hit a second-tempo play set. Once the defense has adjusted by switching blocking assignments, the offense readjusts by faking the cross and cutting back to attack on the right side. (See Diagram 9-10.)

Left Side "X" and "Fake X".   The quick attacker in the left side "X" approaches for the inside shoot (3) with the left side player crossing behind the middle attacker into the middle of the court, to attack a second-tempo set between the setter and the middle hitter (left–in). As in the right side "X," the blockers must switch assignments in order to stop this play from succeeding. Once the blockers change assignments, the left side attacker fakes the "X" and moves left to hit off the outside shoulder of the first-tempo hitter. (See Diagram 9-11.)

Slide 4-2 Combinations.   The slide is an effective option for the zone 3 attacker, especially when in the front row with the setter. The concept is to first establish an effective quick middle attack that forces the opponent's left side blocker to move inside to help block the quick set. Once the left side blocker moves to this inside position, the middle hitter can "slide" outside. The "slide" attacker has the edge of beating the blocker to the outside position, thereby forcing the

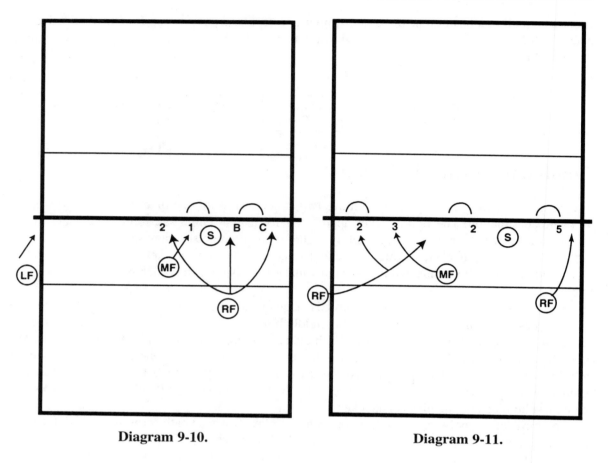

Diagram 9-10.   Diagram 9-11.

blocker to reach to block the ball. If the left side blocker remains near the sideline, the slide can be run tight behind the setter, forcing the blocker to reach inside. The attacker must be aware of the blocker's start position and move to an open spot for the slide to be effective. (See Diagram 9-12.)

Slide 6-2 Combinations.   The slide is also used effectively in combination with the right side attacker. If the right side (zone 2 player) is left-handed, the middle attacker can hit quick in front of the setter or move toward the right side for a tight or wide slide. The right side attacker crosses in front of the setter to hit a front slide toward the middle of the court. If the zone 2 player is right-handed, the middle attacker calls for a first-tempo front set and the right side attacker hits a back slide behind the setter, moving toward the right sideline. (See Diagram 9-13.)

Tactical Admonitions for Effective Combinations

Keep It Simple.   More is not always better. Utilize three to four plays and work to execute this well. Experiment in the preseason and then select the most effective sets and play options.

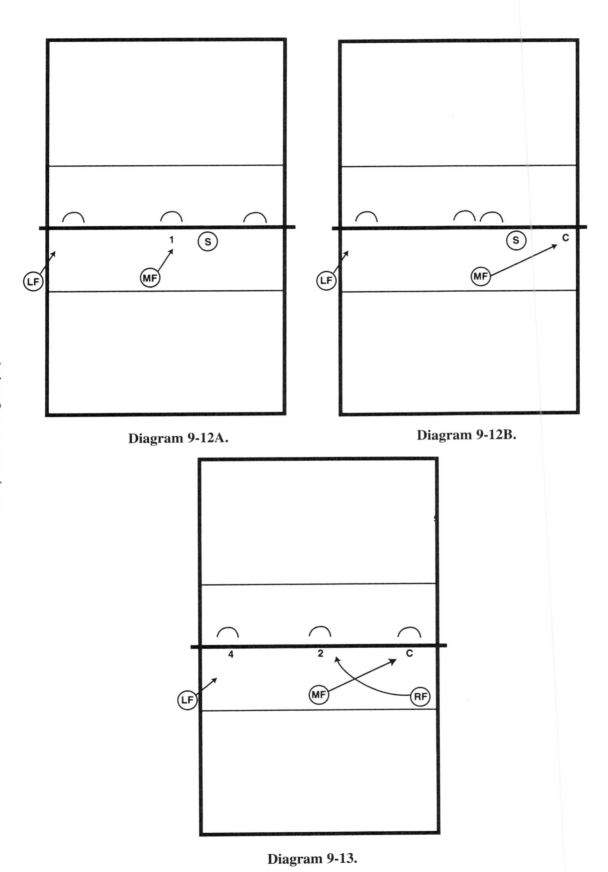

Diagram 9-12A.

Diagram 9-12B.

Diagram 9-13.

Establish an Effective First-Tempo Middle Attack.   Quick sets are designed to hold or delay the middle blocker and commit blockers and receivers to incorrect positions. Once the quick attacker poses a threat to score on every good pass, combination plays can be built around it. If the first-tempo set is not effective, the overall success of the combination play is greatly reduced.

Force Blockers to Make Decisions on Whom to Block.   Once the first-tempo attacker is effective, the middle blocker must make a conscious choice to block or not block this attack. If the player does not block, the probability is high that the quick attacker will be successful.

Avoid Setting the Second-Tempo Set Too High.   It is important to set the play set attacker low enough so that the attacker is going up to hit as the quick attacker and middle blocker are coming down, allowing the attacker to hit with no block or a late-formed blocked. A play set that is too-high gives blockers time to go up with the quick attacker and recover, and go up a second time to block the play set attacker.

Create Deception in the Play with the Attacker.   The second-tempo attacker must be in the same relative position when the setter releases the ball, then break to a position in front or behind the setter just after the quick attacker commits to lift-off and the setter contacts the ball. The play set attacker should hit the ball about the time the quick attacker lands.

Create Deception in the Play with the Setter.   The setter must avoid setting the second-tempo play set attacker before establishing the first-tempo attack. The middle blocker must commit to the first-tempo attacker before the play set hitter is set. Once the middle blocker commits with the first-tempo attacker, the setter counters by setting the play set attacker.

Isolate the Best Attacker.   Run the quick attacker away from the best outside attacker. If the quick hitter is effective, the middle blocker must defend him or her first, causing the blocker to be late to reach sets to the best outside attacker. *For example:* If the quick attacker calls a "3," it can open up a second-tempo set to the right side attacker. If the quick hitter goes for the front or back "1," the left side hitter will be open for the "4."

Spread the Offense.   Force middle blockers to move sideline to sideline by separating the attackers as far as possible. Greater movement makes it more difficult to double block the middle and outside sets. *For example:* The quick attacker approaches for a first-tempo set in the middle of the court, and the outside attackers run a second . . . or third . . . tempo near their respective sidelines. It is especially effective when the outside blockers' starting position is pinched inside the court and/or the middle blocker is slow to reach the sidelines. The spread offense is simple to execute and, if executed properly, can be very effective.

Call Attack Options Based on the Block.   Train setters and attackers to "see, evaluate, and respond" to the opponent. Attackers must be aware of the positioning, abilities, and tendencies of the blockers. Is the block spread out to the antennae or pinched in toward the middle of the court? Is the middle blocker tall, short, slow, or quick? Who are the weakest blockers?
   For example: The play set hitter bases his or her call for an "X" or "fake X" on the starting position of the outside blocker observed prior to or during the pass. If the outside blocker is positioned near the sideline, the play set attacker breaks inside for the "X." If the outside blocker is

© 2001 by Parker Publishing Company

pinched inside to help defend the "1" or "X," the play set attacker fakes inside and moves outside to attack near the sideline.

Set in Predictable Patterns to Program Blockers. Program blockers to position themselves to block predictable patterns of sets in specific zones. Once they do, counter with another pattern. Here are several examples.

- Program the middle blocker to position him- or herself for the first-tempo "1" attack by setting it successfully a series of times. Then, from the same initial start position, the middle attacker goes for a "3" or an "A" set to catch the middle blocker off guard.
- Program the outside blocker to position him- or herself inside to help defend the "X" with a successful series of plays. Counter with the play set hitter calling the "fake X" toward the sidelines.
- Program the middle and outside blockers to pinch inside to block the tight slide directly behind the setter. Once the blockers move inside, counter with a slide wide to the antennae.
- Avoid changing an effective set or combination play before the defense has made an adjustment and/or has been able to stop it.

DECISION 5: CALLING THE PLAYS

Plays can be called by the setter or attacker, either verbally or by hand signals, before the rally begins or as an audible. It is most common to use a combination of systems, giving the most responsibility to those experienced players who best understand the game tactics.

The hitter has the major decision-making responsibility in the attacker-oriented system. The hitter communicates the play to the setter before the serve (predetermined) and/or calls it as an audible while the ball is in the air between the passer and the setter. The audible call allows more flexibility in the offense and gives the attacker the opportunity to evaluate the pass and the block and make situational and tactical adjustments. Each attacker, within his or her zone, has a variety of set options he or she may call. The primary attacker in each rotation is given the largest zone and the most options. These attackers call their option first and the secondary attackers make a complimentary call.

In the setter-oriented system, the setter has the responsibility to call the plays. This system can be used only in the side-out phase of the game. The setter calls the plays verbally or by hand signals prior to the serve. A single number is given that indicates the play for all attackers, or the setter signals each attacker separately to indicate his or her specific set.

Regardless of the system, setters and hitters must constantly work together and communicate what plays they feel will be most successful.

DECISION 6: PASS TARGET

> MAXIM: The offense is dependent on the quality of the pass.
> The more consistent the pass, the greater the offensive options.

The coach defines the desired height and location of the pass. Traditionally, the pass target is based on the system of offense. The target is in zone 3 in the standard 4-2 system; it is between zones 2 and 3 for the international 4-2, 5-1, and 6-2 systems. (See Diagram 9-14.)

The setter releases immediately to the target area as the server contacts the ball to await the pass. The setter assumes a ready position that allows him or her to see both the server and his or her own team. Setters generally face the direction of the best front row attacker in the 4-2 system; but the setter squares off to face the left side and middle attackers in the 5-1 and 6-2. The setter is positioned nearer the right side line, within the target area, so movement can be made forward to set the ball, giving the setter a wider field of vision.

It is important for players to learn to distinguish between good, average, and poor passes in

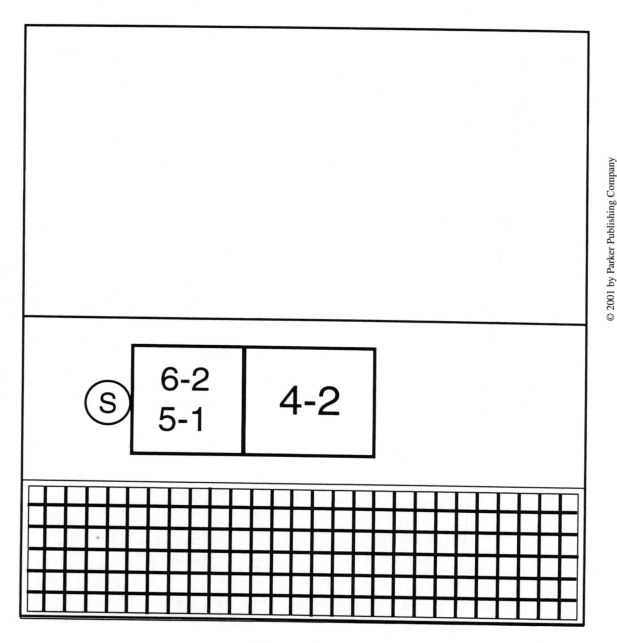

Diagram 9-14.

© 2001 by Parker Publishing Company

order to call the appropriate attack option. A good pass allows the team to run all desired options. An average pass allows the offense to attack the ball, but the options are limited. A poor pass dictates a high set only with few or no options. A bad pass forces the offense to give the opponents a free ball or, worse, results in an immediate loss of a point.

DECISION 7: FREE BALL OFFENSE

The free ball offense is a counterattack from a nonattacked ball (pass or set) received from the opponent. This ball should result in an accurate pass to the target. Traditionally, the free ball play is predetermined, but it can be called as an audible as the ball passes over to the offensive side.

The free ball may be received with an overhand or underhand pass, depending on one's individual skills. As a general rule, it is best to use the overhand pass on balls received close to the net and either the underhand or overhand pass on those balls received deep in the court. Whenever possible, back row passers should receive the free ball allowing front row players to concentrate on the attack. The overhand pass is stressed when utilizing a fast offense, because it gets the ball to the setter more quickly.

DECISION 8: TRANSITION OFFENSE

The transition offense is a counterattack from the dig to the attack. In transition, plays are generally called as audibles by the attackers because the position of the pass is unpredictable. The attackers evaluate the pass and make an appropriate call according to the situation. Each hitter is given attack options within a specific zone, with the primary attacker generally given the greater variety of options.

Establish who sets the second ball when the primary setter digs the first one. The secondary setter generally has priority in handling the ball, but it can also be based on the team's personnel, court position, and/or position of ball. Preference may be given to a back row player allowing the front row players to attack. On balls passed close to the net, the attacker should be given the freedom to hit on the second contact.

DECISION 9: SIDE-OUT OFFENSE

The serve receive phase of the game is referred to as the side-out offense. Plays are traditionally "pre-determined" and called prior to the serve by the setter or the hitters.

Serve Receive Formation Options

The offensive potential of a team is based on its ability to consistently and accurately receive serve. Utilize the following information as a guideline for designing a system that optimizes the team's chance for success.

• Identify, through drills and statistics, the team's best passers and those areas from which they are most effective.

- Place the best passers in primary pass positions and hide or reduce the area that weaker passers need to cover.
- Identify the best attackers and enable them to transition easily to an attack position.
- Enable the setter to transition easily to the target position.
- Allow quick attackers in the front row to concentrate primarily on the attack.
- Design options by rotations based on individual strengths and weaknesses.
- Provide for system adjustments in each formation when the team or an individual is having difficulties. Change the system, alter the positions of the players within the formation, or have a player who is having difficulty passing move out of the pattern and be replaced by another. System adjustments instill confidence in the team as well as force the server to alter his or her tactics.
- Teach all players applications of the overlap rule so they can utilize all system adjustments.

5-Player "W" Formation.   Receiving with five players offers the best coverage with the least court responsibility per player. Players are capable of positioning themselves behind any ball to pass without a great deal of movement. This formation can be advantageous for young players who lack the experience to judge the flight of the serve and to position themselves correctly for the pass.

A disadvantage of this system can be that while this shared passing responsibility makes it easier to physically cover the court, it can create zones of confusion. Players often hesitate and question who should take the ball.

Also, the 5-player formation gives all players equal responsibility to pass the ball, but "all receivers are not equal." If serves are directed to the weak passers, the team cannot utilize the strengths of those who have the ability to pass more effectively.

5-player "W" Pattern in the 4-2 System. The "W" pattern is formed with the two front row receivers positioned about midcourt and toward their respective sidelines. Traditional positioning places the center front, player in the right side receiving position when the setter begins right front, and in a left side receiving position when on the left. Right and left side back row receivers are positioned to the inside of the front row receivers and about four feet from the endline. Center back forms the point of the "W."

The front row setter assumes a sideways position near the net facing both the server and the receiving team. As the ball is contacted on the serve, the setter immediately moves to the center front position to receive the pass. (See Diagram 9-15.)

5-player "W" Formation in the 6-2 System. The "W" pattern is identical to the 4-2 with the exception that the middle front forms the top of the "W" and is positioned just behind the 10-foot line. Right and left front receivers are positioned midcourt and near their respective sidelines. The back row setter is positioned behind his or her corresponding front row player with the remaining two back row receivers splitting the remaining area. The setter immediately releases to the target area as the serve is contacted. (See Diagram 9-16.)

5-player "W" Formation in the 6-3 System. The "W" pattern is identical to the 4-2 or 6-2 pattern with the exception that the setter sets two rather than three times. The setter sets in the 4-2 when he or she is positioned right and middle front, and sets in the 6-2 when he or she is positioned right and middle back.

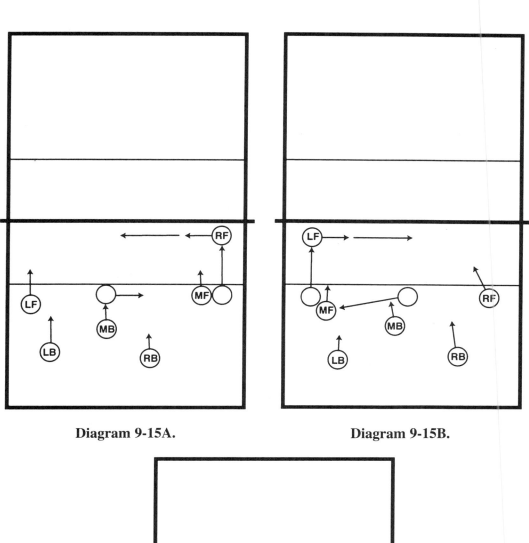

Diagram 9-15A.   **Diagram 9-15B.**

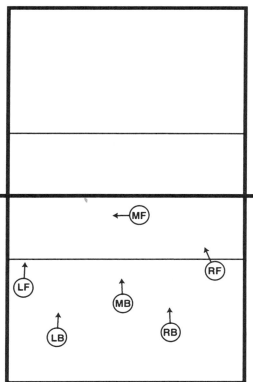

Diagram 9-15C.

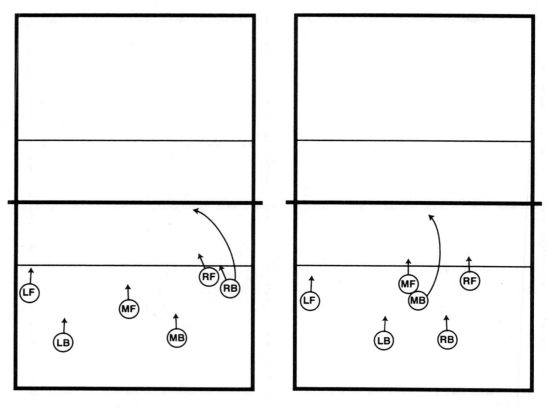

Diagram 9-16A.

Diagram 9-16B.

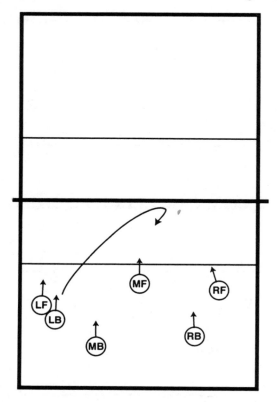

Diagram 9-16C.

4-player "U" Formation. The "U" pattern is formed with the two front row players positioned about midcourt and toward their respective sidelines, and two back row receivers positioned deep and more to the inside. This pattern offers good front and back row coverage while eliminating one zone of confusion—the player at the top of the "W." It also permits the team to hide a poor passer, to eliminate an attacker from passing responsibility, and/or give the setter an easier route to the target area. (See Diagram 9-17.)

2- and 3-player Formations. Passing with two or three players places the best receivers on the court in their most advantageous passing positions, and eliminates the weaker receivers. The "zones of confusion" are reduced and the serve receive roles are clear. Although it appears that receiving with two or three players leaves the court very susceptible, there is better passing in this system by experienced, confident, and aggressive players. In a three-player pass system, the best passer should play in the middle because this position receives the most passes. Practice time can be well utilized because all players need not be in every passing drill. (See Diagram 9-18.)

Swing Option. The swing option is often utilized with the two- and three-player serve receive formations. It allows for more flexibility in the offense.

Generally the left side attackers function as swing hitters in the two-player pass pattern, with responsibility to both pass and hit. These same two players receive every serve whether they are in the front or the back row. Either player may receive from the right or left side in any rotation (review overlap rule), and the front row attacker swings to hit at any position along the net.

Generally three outside attackers share pass responsibilities with the best receiver and/or hitter positioned midcourt in the three-player pass pattern. This middle player is the swing hitter and has the option to hit in the middle of the court or swing to the right or left. (See Diagram 9-19.)

The advantage of the swing option is that regardless of players' starting rotational positions, they have the option of receiving from any position on the court and they have the freedom to transition to hit at any location along the net. Attackers move to positions where they feel they have the best opportunity to score, based on their own preference and/or to exploit a weakness in the block. The destination of the attackers is less predictable, making it more difficult for the blockers to match-up or overload a key attacker.

Swing Hitter Characteristics

- Excellent passer technically.
- Tough mentally to handle the pressure and responsibility of passing and hitting.
- Good movement to cover the court to pass and to transition to the attack.
- Good jumping skills and body control to take off from various body positions and angles, and to be able to equally hit the ball in any direction with power.
- Ability to make long approaches and in an inside–out pattern.

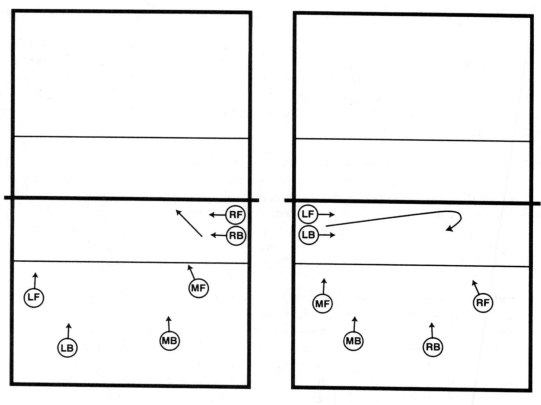

Diagram 9-17A.

Diagram 9-17B.

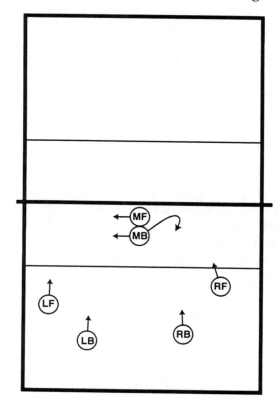

Diagram 9-17C.

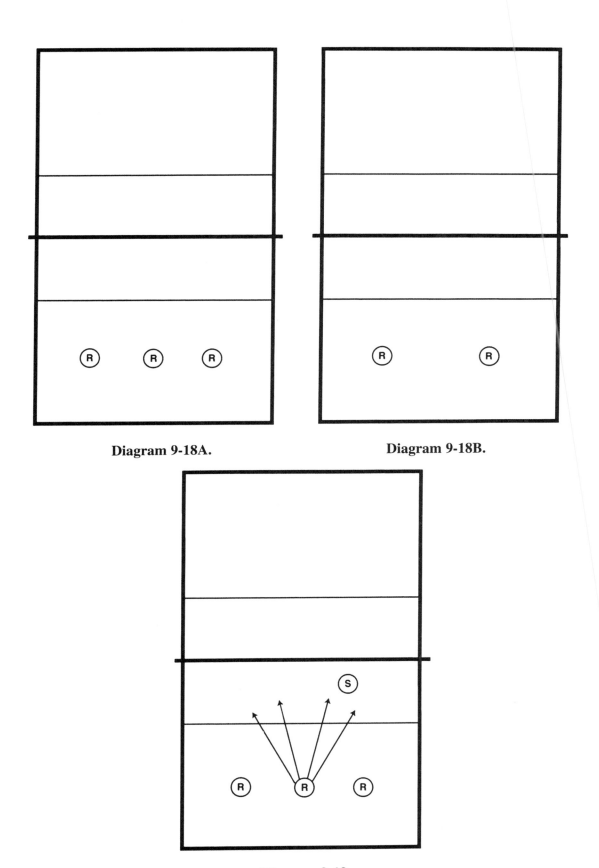

Diagram 9-18A.

Diagram 9-18B.

Diagram 9-19.

CHAPTER 10

THE MATCH

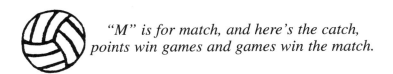

*"M" is for match, and here's the catch,
points win games and games win the match.*

SELECTING THE STARTING LINEUP

Many factors must be taken into consideration when selecting the starting six. No one skill should automatically qualify the athlete for a starting role. Evaluate the total package that each player has to offer the team.

Technical

The foundation of the game is built on solid fundamental skills. Those players with the best individual skills should form the base of the team.

Tactical

It is important to have good technical skills, but to be effective they must be used correctly in a tactical sense. The athlete must have the ability to make good choices, especially in critical moments in the game.

Consistency

Flashy players catch the eyes of the fans and coaches, but the occasional spectacular play should not be confused with consistency of performance. Some players do not appear to be so strong as teammates because there is no one area where they excel, but these players can be deceiving. Consistency plays a big role in winning.

Desire

The biggest intangible to success is heart and desire. The best players physically are not always the most successful because they do not always direct their energy to the game.

Team Dynamics

Every good team has positive chemistry among the players, but this does not have to mean that all team members need to be alike or even like each other. Good team dynamics translates into shared goals, good communication, and respect for each other. Just as it takes a combination of physical talents to meet the positional requirements of the team, often times a combination of personalities (analytical, instinctive, intense, easy-going, quiet, and talkative) helps create a more effective team.

Potential

Consideration must be given to the athlete's potential. If it appears that the athlete will surpass his or her teammates in the future, it might be a good strategy to place that player in the starting lineup from the beginning.

Closers

It is just as important who finishes the game as who starts it. Flashy and/or inexperienced players can start the game and, if successful, they can remain; but it is important to have those players with the most consistency and experience in the closing moments.

COURT PLACEMENT OF THE STARTING SIX

6-2 System

In the traditional lineup for the 6-2 system, the best setter, middle attacker, and outside attacker form a triangle, permitting the best setter to set the best hitters two of three rotations in the front row. If these players are not the team's best attackers, it might be necessary to place two best hitters next to each other. An effort should be made to have a balanced triangle of hitters in order to minimize weak rotations and allow for an equal distribution of sets. (See Diagram 10-1.)

5-1 System

In the 5-1 system, traditionally the lineup is built around the setter, whose starting position is based generally on his or her blocking skills. The setter is usually surrounded by the best middle and outside attackers. This formation places the two best attackers in the front row with the setter. The advantage of this alignment is that although there are two rather than three attackers in the front row, one or two of the attackers are the team's strongest. (See Diagram 10-2.) The middle or outside attacker can lead the setter. Each option presents different player alignments in the receiving patterns.

Rotational Order

The specific order of who serves first must be determined once the basic lineup has been established. Every effort should be made to place players in their position of strength at the beginning

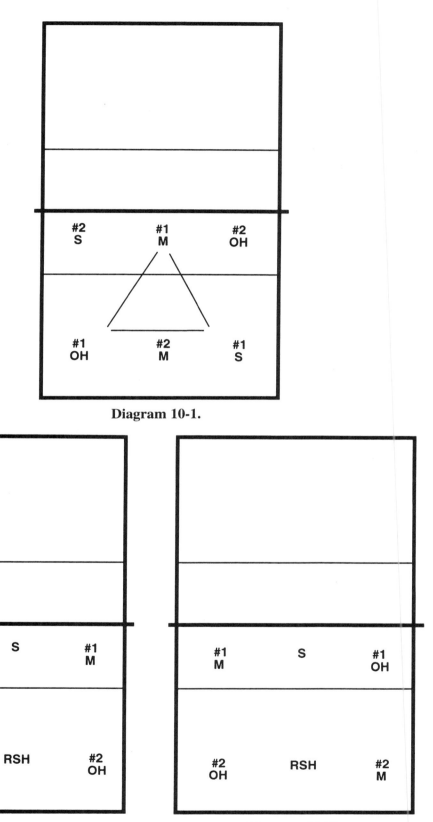

Diagram 10-1.

Diagram 10-2A.

Diagram 10-2B.

© 2001 by Parker Publishing Company

of the game. One of the team's best attackers should start in the left front position and one of the best passers should be in a primary pass position. If serving is a priority, the best servers should have the opportunity to serve early in the rotation. If substitutions are used on a consistent basis—for example, a defensive specialist always plays in the back row for the middle attacker—their placement on the court should most effectively utilize the maximum number of rotations and substitutions according to the association's specific rules.

Rotational Balance

Every effort must be made to balance strengths and weaknesses in each rotation, not only for attacking, but also for blocking and defensive play. Although some rotations will be stronger and more effective than others, at the least, some consideration has been given to a minimum amount of balance that hopefully will reduce the chances of the opponents scoring a run of points in any one specific rotation.

Match-Ups

Consider creating match-ups by altering the lineup completely. Change the personnel or the positions of players in relation to each other or begin the game in a different rotation.

Lineup Adjustments

Scouting or past results against opponents should be considered when making future lineup decisions, as well as game results during a current match. The score sheet can be utilized after each match to record points won and lost in each rotation. This information is used to strengthen weak rotations in practice and for lineup changes in future matches.

THE GAME PLAN

First determine how much emphasis to place on scouting opponents. Know your players well enough to assist those who can handle more information and know those who cannot. The primary game plan focuses on execution on your side of the net. The more advanced the team, the more focus can be placed on making adjustments specific to the opponent.

Plan ahead for all "what if" situations. Know your options for adjustments due to injury or poor play technically, tactically, or emotionally. There is little time to vacillate over decisions once the match begins. The more you analyze the options prior to the game, the easier it will be to make good decisions.

Before the day of the match, provide the team with essential information about the opponent even if it is very basic. It gives players time to adjust, at least psychologically, to teams that appear very strong or very weak. Practice and review game tactics on the court as well as in written and diagrammed form.

ON GAME DAY

Have a specific routine on game day for players to follow from the time they enter the gym until the match begins. This routine helps players eliminate distractions and directs their focus to the important issues.

Pre-Match Meeting

Emotional

- Set the emotional tone for the match through your enthusiasm and excitement for the game.
- Be conscious of the need to increase the players' motivation or calm them down.
- Be careful not to create overconfidence when playing a weaker team or build the opponent's strengths so high the team feels it has no chance to win.
- Respect all opponents, knowing that either team can win.
- Insure the team that it has trained hard and is prepared to compete.
- Take the emphasis off winning and place it more on performing well.
- Make any necessary comments about the officials' tendencies so it does not come as a surprise to the athletes once the game starts.

Tactical

- Be honest about the situation and confident about what the team must do to be successful.
- Always give players the most positive scenario. No matter how good the opponents are, focus more on what "we" can and must do tactically.
- Confirm and/or announce the starting lineup and major substitutions.
- Review the game plans and tactical adjustments for probable situations.
- Speak specifically to players regarding their individual responsibilities.
- Keep it simple. Too much information can be detrimental.

> **MAXIM:** *Making adjustments is what all great players do.*

Match Goals. Success should not be judged only by the score, but on performance. Establish statistical and observable match goals other than winning. If these goals are met, the match will be considered a success whether or not the team won. *For example:*

- Attack 30 percent as a team and keep the opponent's attack percentage to 20 percent.
- Recover all balls blocked back to our side by the opponent.
- Transition to attack off opponent's attacked balls 50 percent of the time and convert successfully 80 percent of all free balls.
- Keep unforced errors to less than three per game as a team.
- Give 100 percent effort as a team. Do not let one ball hit the floor without making an effort to dig it.
- Demonstrate a positive attitude regardless of the score. Force spectators to look at the scoreboard to see whether we are winning or losing.

Wrap-Up

- End the session with a story or motto to give the players a final focus.
- Give players two to three minutes of personal time to visualize the match and review their goals and responsibilities.

Pregame Warm-Up

- Monitor the warm-up. Players must warm up with the same intensity and attention to detail that they want to have in the game.
- This is the time to prepare—both mentally and physically—for the match.
- The warm-up should last no more than one hour and less if the gym is extremely hot. It is better that the athletes save their energy for the match.
- Avoid lengthy warm-ups. A player cannot "cram" right before the match to correct faulty mechanics or relearn the game.
- Have players familiarize themselves at away matches with the court environment: lines, lighting, floor surface, ceiling heights, net tension, obstructions, visual keys, and so on.
- The coach can have direct involvement in the warm-up by hitting and tossing balls to players, or the athletes can warm up on their own.
- Take time to have some personal contact with each player, reminding them of their specific game responsibilities as well as instilling confidence in them.

> **MAXIM:** *Self-involvement is counterproductive to the team effort.*

Timeouts/Between Games

Timeout Procedures for Players

- Substitutes hustle onto the court to ballhandle.
- Court players hustle to the bench to towel off and take water.
- Establish specific positions on the bench for the setters, middle blockers, and outside attackers. Information can be more efficiently delivered to players in similar role positions.
- Water is important, but it can be a big distraction. Players must learn to drink and listen at the same time.
- Insist on eye contact. You may lose them altogether if you lose eye contact with athletes.
- Do not allow competing conversations. Insist that no one else talk when you are speaking, except to ask or answer questions. Player discussions can follow if time remains.
- Bring the team together to conclude the timeout. Huddle, touching hands, united again in the team's efforts.

Timeout Procedures for Coaches

- Be prepared before the timeout is called. Know what you want to say. Take notes, if necessary, to help remember and organize your thoughts.
- Utilize all coaches to give important information to players. *For example:* One coach could speak to the setter while another coach speaks to the group or another individual.

- The best communication is one on one. Stress individual corrections and suggestions. Speak to individuals rather than the whole group.
- Say one thing to one person rather than five generalities to the group.

Be Positive

- Always maintain a hopeful outlook.
- Provide reinforcement and encouragement to players.
- Emphasize the solution rather than reemphasizing the problem.
- Have an adjustment in mind or some helpful comments.
- Be decisive. Tell the players what they need to do to be competitive.
- Avoid stating the obvious. "None of you can pass the ball to the target. If we don't start passing, we'll lose."
- Even though there may be many reasons why you may not be successful, emphasize how you *can* succeed.
- Do not discourage the team. Sell the team on the possibilities rather than the probability.
- Never give up on the team. Your expectations have a very powerful influence on players.
- Stay in control emotionally. This is the only way to think clearly and make good decisions.
- Trust your instincts in making decisions. Do what you think is best regardless of the statistics or the opinions of others.

MAXIM: *The next play is more important because you have some control over it.*

Technical and Tactical Information

- Give statistical information to the appropriate players.
- Indicate to the setter the set distribution and who is "hot and who it not."
- Indicate to the middle blockers the opponent's set patterns and successful attackers.
- Predict the opponent's next attack off serve receive and in transition and tell athletes how to defend it.
- Point out weaknesses in the opponent's defense and where to direct our attacks.
- Indicate who to serve to and make serve receive, block, and defensive positioning adjustments all based on statistics.
- Continually emphasize what you want players to do. Do more of this and less of that.
- Reinforce what players are doing right and make adjustments in those ineffective areas.
- Keep changes to a minimum.
- Do not ask players to do something they have not practiced.
- Do not ask players to do something they have not executed successfully on a consistent basis in practice.
- Make changes early to know if they will be useful later in the match.

MAXIM: *Do not worry so much on what the opponent does that you cannot concentrate on what you need to do.*

Keep It Simple

- Make the message simple and almost impossible to misunderstand.
- Simplify players' responsibilities and keep them focused on what they need to do.
- Prioritize information and confine your comments to one or two major points. Then repeat them!
- It is better for players to be able to repeat the message word for word than not hear it at all.
- Assume nothing. Clarify everything.
- Make your last words really count. They will be the most memorable.

When to Call Timeouts

- When the team is visibly upset.
- To stop the momentum when the opponent becomes three to four points ahead.
- Early enough when there is still time to pull out of a difficult situation.
- Avoid calling timeouts too early and having no way to "slow the game down" at the end when the game is on the line.
- Avoid calling timeouts too late, for example, when the opponent has 14 points and your score is very low. Even at best, it will be very difficult to come back to win.
- Avoid calling timeouts too quickly. Give the team a few points to settle down. Try to distinguish between a run of points and a runaway.
- Save timeouts by sending a message in through a substitute or giving signals from the bench.

Substitutions

All players deserve an opportunity to play and will be very disappointed if they do not get on the court. Unfortunately, only six players can be on the court at one time. Players may not like their role as a substitute, but they must accept it or choose not to participate as a member of the team. Listed are examples of substitute policies:

- Substitutes must maintain a positive and encouraging attitude.
- Substitutes must be physically and mentally ready to enter the game.
- Substitutes who are not "involved" in the game mentally and encouraging their teammates do not deserve to get into the game or future games.
- Substitutes must alternate standing, stretching, and doing light jumping movements in place with sitting on the bench. Substitutes ballhandle and hit (if permissible) on the court during timeouts or between games.
- Substitutes do three tuck jumps (or other form of exercise) on every point scored by the opponents.
- Substitutes do five sit-ups and five push-ups on every missed serve by our team.
- Substitutes stand to acknowledge a teammate's good plays and give a "standing" high-five when a teammate comes out of the game.
- Substitutes do not "fool around" on the bench, criticize teammates, or complain about not being in the game.
- Substitutes who will not have an opportunity to play in the match are given statistical assignments to help the team.

Take a look at the coach's and the players' commandments for substitutions.

MAXIM: Do not let what you cannot do interfere with what you can do. John Wooden

COACH'S COMMANDMENTS
FOR SUBSTITUTIONS

- *You shall* explain to the subs their role and what is expected of them in the game and on the bench, so they will feel like important and contributing members of the team.
- *You shall* know that you can never fully satisfy subs, short of making them starters. This is normal!
- *You shall* explain to subs why they are not starting and what they must do to earn a spot on the court.
- *You shall* strive to give playing time to everyone on the team. This keeps players motivated to practice hard and maintain a positive attitude.
- *You shall* train substitutes in all the positions they will likely play in the game, so that when it is game time, they will be prepared.
- *You shall* understand that some tactical substitutions are arranged; whereas others are spontaneous, addressing a specific and immediate need.
- *You shall* not automatically sub to give young players an opportunity to play when the team is winning easily. Changes in personnel can alter the momentum in a negative way.
- *You shall* judge not only technique and tactics, but also attitude and spirit.
- *You shall* give subs an opportunity to help when the team is playing poorly. *You shall* give everyone an opportunity to contribute to the loss.
- *You shall* demand that all players perform at their highest levels all the time. A substitution is made if players drop below this level.
- *You shall* sub for a player who is not hustling or has a bad attitude.
- *You shall* consider which players are better as starters and which ones come off the bench effectively.
- *You shall* know that it is not always necessary to start the best team, but you want the best team to finish the match.
- *You shall* sub early, especially if a long match is expected, to rest starters (if necessary) and to see which substitutes might be effective.
- *You shall* not expect subs to perform in the fifth game after sitting for two hours. *You shall* make an attempt to give subs some playing time earlier.
- *You shall* make subs toward the end of the game, when being beaten badly, so the subs will be warm for the start of the next game.
- *You shall* sub to break the momentum of a successful opponent.
- *You shall* consider subbing to change the flow of the match before it is necessary to use a timeout.
- *You shall* sub a player who is not mentally and physically in the match. *You shall* try someone else.
- *You shall* sub to strengthen the team. Narrow the substitutes' role, if necessary, but don't expect them to do something they can't do.
- *You shall* not always sub in games where the team is winning by a big margin. The starting team also deserves to play and needs experience working together.
- *You shall* remember momentum changes quickly and it is best to avoid changing a winning combination.
- *You shall* not sub to give a player experience unless that player can contribute something positive to the team.
- *You shall* sub to bring in new tactical information.
- *You shall* sub in case of injury.

© 2001 by Parker Publishing Company

- *You shall* sub to rest a player.
- *You shall* give subs an opportunity to prepare to enter the game whenever possible.
- *You shall* never embarrass or ignore a player when he or she is subbed out.
- *You shall* explain, as soon as possible, why a player was replaced.
- *You shall* find something good that the sub did rather than dwell on his or her weaknesses.
- *You shall* give everyone an opportunity through practice to become a starter.
- *You shall* make it a general rule that no one is above being subbed.
- *You shall* never be afraid to sub.
- *You shall* explain to everyone that being subbed is nothing to be ashamed of.
- *You shall* give subs a chance to show their worth once in the game, *and shall* never sub a player after a single error.
- *You shall* not let players' occasional errors obscure the total value of their play.
- *You shall* make the subs feel that this is not their only chance. There will be others.
- *You shall* interact with subs on the bench frequently during the match.
- *You shall* explain that an important obligation of a sub is providing team support.
- *You shall* include starters in the sub category. Players work hardest when they know they must push themselves to maintain their position.

PLAYER'S COMMANDMENTS
FOR SUBSTITUTIONS

- *You shall* understand that subs are an important part of a team's overall strength and essential to winning.
- *You shall* realize that every winning team must have quality subs.
- *You shall* strive to understand and trust the coaches and know they have the team's best interest in mind.
- *You shall* acknowledge the total team concept and understand and accept your role.
- *You shall* keep things in perspective. There are twelve players on the squad, but only six can be on the court.
- *You shall* communicate with the coach. If the coach doesn't tell you, then you must ask.
- *You shall* always give your best effort. No attitude!
- *You shall* never consider yourself above being subbed.
- *You shall* know that there is no shame in being a sub or being subbed. It is part of the game.
- *You shall* always be mentally and physically prepared to enter the game.
- *You shall* stay warm during the game and utilize all opportunities to ballhandle and hit.
- *You shall* not sulk, pout, or criticize those on the court.
- *You shall* save gripes for after the game so as not to distract the coach and teammates.
- *You shall* be considerate of teammates' feelings. *You shall* first be a member of the team and, second, an individual.
- *You shall* understand that the bench aids in squad morale and one must be positive and supportive—both visually and verbally.
- *You shall* always look ready to play so the coach wants to put you in.
- *You shall* study the game and learn from the bench. Analyze the opponent's offense, defense, and tendencies. *You shall* share this information with teammates and utilize it when subbed.
- *You shall* be aware of the rotation in which you enter the game (if it has been determined that it will be automatic).
- *You shall* not be a martyr. Ask to be subbed if injured.
- *You shall* enter the game with spirit and confidence.
- *You shall* know that a finisher is as important as a starter.
- *You shall* exit the game with the same fighting spirit with which you entered.
- *You shall* encourage your replacement and the rest of the team.
- *You shall* sit close to the coach if an immediate explanation is desired about the substitution.
- *You shall* strive to be a valuable part of the team.
- *You shall* cooperate with the coaches in whatever assignments they give, such as, shagging balls, or filling water bottles.
- *You shall* know when you become a starter. You must help new subs adjust to their role. *You shall* give subs a boost when necessary.
- *You shall* visualize yourself going in and making the big plays.
- *You shall* have absolute faith in yourself.
- *You shall* work hard in practice to earn a starting spot.
- *You shall* understand that the coach makes the decision as to who plays in the best interest of the team and it's nothing personal.

- *You shall* earn playing time by working hard in practice and consistently doing a better job than the people playing ahead of you.
- *You shall* understand your role as a substitute has the possibility of changing through daily efforts and achievements in practice.
- *You shall* understand that you must have recurrent good performances in the game to become a starter. One "hot" game does not justify an immediate change.

Post-Match Meeting

- Find a quiet and private place in the gym, in a classroom, or outside.
- Keep the meeting brief and team oriented.
- Players and coaches need time to cool off and evaluate the game on their own.
- Congratulate a winning effort and let the players enjoy the victory.
- Be supportive after a loss and direct the team's attention to the positives, what worked, and the goals that were achieved.
- Have each player, when time permits, give an example of a great play he or she remembers about a teammate's play.
- Begin to look to the next game.
- Save the negatives and/or explanations for practice and focus on making the necessary improvements.

Post-Match Evaluation

- Coaches meet as soon as possible after the match to evaluate and analyze the team's performance.
- What were the reasons for the win or loss?
- What did we do well and what do we need to improve?
- What worked and what must be changed?
- Base evaluations on statistical information as well as subjective analysis.
- Use the score sheet to evaluate points scored by "us" and "them" in each rotation and the net gain in each.
- Regardless of who won or lost, what is the game plan for the next time we meet this opponent?
- How did I do emotionally? Was I in control?
- Did I react properly after controversial calls by the official?
- How did I handle difficult moments in the match?
- How did I handle player errors?
- Did I support and show confidence in the team?
- Did I give the players sufficient information in the game?
- Did I give them too much information?
- Was my behavior professional?
- What did I learn new about the opponent or an individual player?
- What must we do in practice to prepare for the next match?

COACH'S TACTICAL MATCH CHECKLIST

General

- ❏ Be a detective. See how quickly you can discover the opponent's tendencies.
- ❏ Every time the ball goes to the opponent's side, how does the opponent respond to it?
- ❏ Keep a notebook of information about opponents. Add to the information after every match.

❑ Study the opponent's coach to learn his or her tendencies and preferences. Players change from year to year, but the coach's overall tactics often are very similar.

❑ Learn styles of the officials. How do they call the game—tight or loose? Do they call unnecessary overlaps or nets? Do they differ in calling the game from other officials?

Starting Lineup

❑ Note the opponent's starting rotation and positional placements.

❑ Indicate the middle blockers, right and left side attackers, and setter(s).

❑ Indicate each player's height and years of experience.

❑ Indicate key players offensively and defensively.

❑ Consider your starting lineup and what the match-ups would be.

❑ Look for opponent lineup changes each game.

Opponent's Back Row Defense

❑ What defensive system(s) are they using?

❑ Do they change the system during the match?

❑ What areas are the receivers defending?

❑ Do they move a player up to cover the tip?

❑ Where are the effective tip spots?

❑ Are they open for the dump? When and to what spot?

❑ Which defenders are weakest reacting to the tip?

❑ To which defenders do we want to direct the hit or tip?

Opponent's Block Patterns

❑ What is the starting position of the outside blockers? Are they pinched in or positioned toward the sideline?

❑ Do the outside blockers help block quick sets?

❑ Do they block line or angle?

❑ Do they overload certain attackers?

❑ Do they use match-up blocking tactics?

❑ What is the starting position of the middle blockers? Do they follow the setter or the middle attacker, or do they remain in the middle of the court?

❑ What are the tendencies of the middle blockers? Do they read or commit on quick sets?

❑ How good is the lateral mobility of the middle blockers? Are they slow or quick to the outside? Do they leave a hole or seam?

❑ Who are the weakest and/or smallest blockers? To which blockers should we direct our attack? Who can we hit over?

❑ Which outside blockers reach out and invite the "wipe-off"?

❑ Who are their best blockers? How high do they get over the net? How far do they penetrate over the net? What are their blocks-per-game statistics?

Our Offense

❏ What do we need to do offensively to be effective?
❏ What attack options do we want to emphasize to exploit the opponent's defensive weaknesses?
❏ Who and what is most effective offensively for us off serve receive and in transition?
❏ What is our set distribution? Are our most effective attackers receiving the most sets?
❏ Indicate to the setter our best attackers and distribution of sets.
❏ In what situations and where should our setter dump the ball?
❏ Which blockers should we set toward and away from?

Opponent's Offense

Setter

❏ What is the ability of their setter? Is the setter accurate with quick sets? High sets?
❏ Is the setter deceptive? Are there any clues that give away the type or direction of a specific set?
❏ How effective is the setter attacking on the second ball?
❏ In what situations does the setter dump?
❏ Does the setter dump with the right hand, left hand, or with both hands?
❏ Does the setter dump from the front and back row?
❏ Which types of sets are most effective for the setter?
❏ Does the setter set in any specific patterns for first-, second-, or third-tempo sets?
❏ Does the setter have difficulty setting quick when the serve is to a particular area?

Opponent's Attackers

❏ Who are their strongest and weakest attackers? What are their attack percentages and kills per game?
❏ Who receives the most sets? Is it different in the side-out or transition offense?
❏ What are their strongest and weakest rotations?
❏ Who are the most effective and weakest attackers in each rotation?
❏ What are the tendencies of the strongest attackers? What are their most effective options and placements? Do they tip, off-speed, hit off the block, attack angle, or line?
❏ Are there any specific attack patterns?
❏ Who do they go to in critical situations?
❏ Who is effective for them in this match?
❏ What is the distribution of quick and high sets?
❏ When is the quick set used?
❏ Who are their weakest attackers? Do they warrant a block?

Our Defense

❏ What do we need to do to defend against their attack? Who do we need to stop?
❏ How do we stop or slow down their most effective attackers?

❑ Do we commit or read, single or double block the quick attack?

❑ On which attackers do we block line, angle, commit, read, or release?

❑ Are there attackers we do not need to block?

❑ Do we want to "overload" their most effective attacker?

❑ Do we want to match up our strongest blocker on their most effective attacker?

❑ Are there attackers we should only single block?

❑ Do we want to commit a blocker to the setter's attack?

Opponent's Service

❑ Who are their most effective servers? What type(s) of serve do they use and to which zones do they direct it?

❑ Are there any effective jump servers?

Opponent's Serve Reception

❑ What serve reception formations do they use?

❑ Who are their weakest passers and in what positions?

❑ Who and where do we want to serve to disrupt their offense?

QUICK TACTICAL GAME CHECKLIST

Maintain a continuous "evaluative" self-dialogue.

❑ How are points being won and lost for "us," that is, serve, attack, block, unforced errors, and opponent errors?

❑ How are points being won and lost for "them"?

❑ Which tactics are working best for us?

❑ Which tactics are working best for them?

❑ How are they hurting us?

❑ How are we hurting them?

❑ How do we need to play them to be successful?

❑ What weaknesses do we need to exploit?

❑ How can we reduce their effectiveness?

❑ Do we need to make any adjustments?

A TIMEOUT POEM

We've just 30 seconds so jog to the side
this timeout will turn the tide.
Dig it, block it, serve it, score it,
your friends in the stand will just adore it.

Serve deep down the line, tip to spots 1 or 3,
go quick in the middle, it'll sting like a bee.
Play the defense up and block the line,
on those confusing balls, always call mine.

Just relax and have confidence in you,
mental toughness will pull you through.
Think out there and use your head,
remember all the things I've said.

Go all out, put yourself to the test,
know that win or lose, you did your best!

SERIOUS MATCH CRIMES CHECKLIST

✓ Dwelling on a previous error.
✓ Not encouraging a teammate.
✓ Not responding to the "support" of a teammate.
✓ Missing a serve after a previous serve error by the opponent or teammate.
✓ Bumping the ball when it should have been attacked.
✓ Bump setting the ball when it should have been set overhand.
✓ A ball touching the floor and no one making an attempt for it.
✓ Standing and watching a player play a ball close to a line and not helping with a "good" or "out" call.
✓ Waiting for someone else to play the ball when you could have played it.
✓ Letting a teammate take the blame for your mistake.
✓ Missing an easy ball after a teammate makes a fantastic get.
✓ Quitting on any point before the play is over.
✓ Discussing the problem and not the solution.
✓ Giving up!
✓ Not putting out your best effort.
✓ Pointing a finger at someone else.
✓ Not thinking.
✓ Letting a teammate out-hustle you.
✓ Not being fired up to play.

MATCH SETUP CHECKLIST

Secure Personnel

❏ Setup and takedown crew
❏ Referee and umpire (2)
❏ Official scorer
❏ Linespeople (2)
❏ Ball shaggers (3–5)
❏ Scoreboard operator
❏ Announcer
❏ Statisticians
❏ Ticket sellers
❏ Ticket takers
❏ Athletic trainer
❏ Photographer
❏ Troubleshooter

Arrival Time

❏ Report to the gym by two hours before the match.
❏ Secure towels from the laundry room before reporting.

❏ *Linespeople:* Arrive 15 minutes prior to the game.
❏ Wear dark slacks and a white collar polo shirt.

Before the Match

Court Setup

❏ Game net set up with antennae by one hour prior to the match
❏ Measuring stick to measure correct height of net
❏ Gym floor swept
❏ Referee stand set up
❏ Safety pads for standards
❏ All basketball hoops up
❏ Bleachers out, locked with side rails
❏ Wipe bleacher seats with wet towel
❏ Warm-up balls (old)/two carts (15 each)
❏ Towels (25 total): each bench (3), at each side of net (1), visiting team showers (15), scorers' table for ball shaggers (2)
❏ Chairs (15) for each team bench
❏ Water coolers, water, ice, cups, plastic bags for ice

General Setup

❏ Portable booth for ticket sales
❏ Table for selling team products, T-shirts, programs
❏ VCR set up and blank tapes (label with match and date)

Scorers' and Statisticians' Table

❏ Team protocol outline
❏ Score sheets and pencils (4 black, 4 red) [see sample score sheet, Figure 10-1]
❏ Statistics forms and pencils (5)
❏ Line up and roster cards [see sample line up sheet, Figure 10-2]
❏ Flags for linespeople
❏ Officials' checks or pay cards
❏ Game balls for ball rotation (4)
❏ Scoreboard, PA microphone, and cassette recorder connected
❏ Cassettes for warm-up music and national anthem

Game Time

❏ Lock up warm-up balls and carts.
❏ Turn on VCR.

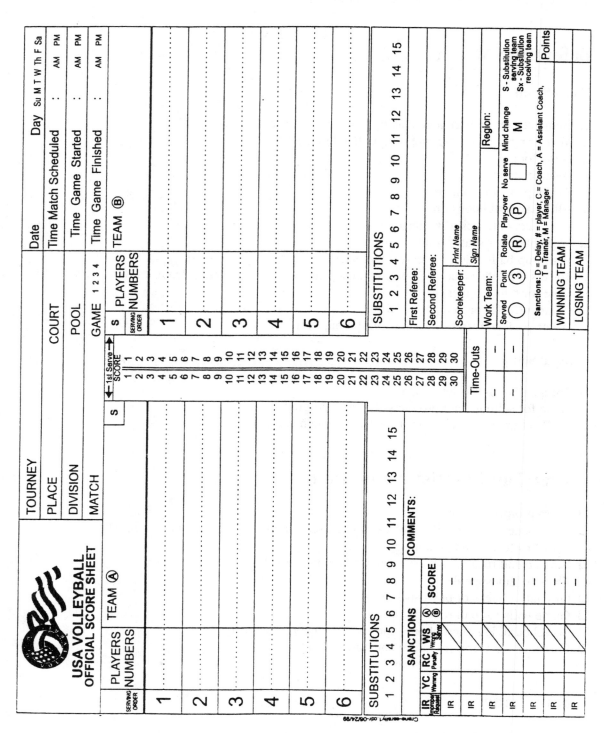

Figure 10-1.
Reprinted with permission from USA Volleyball.

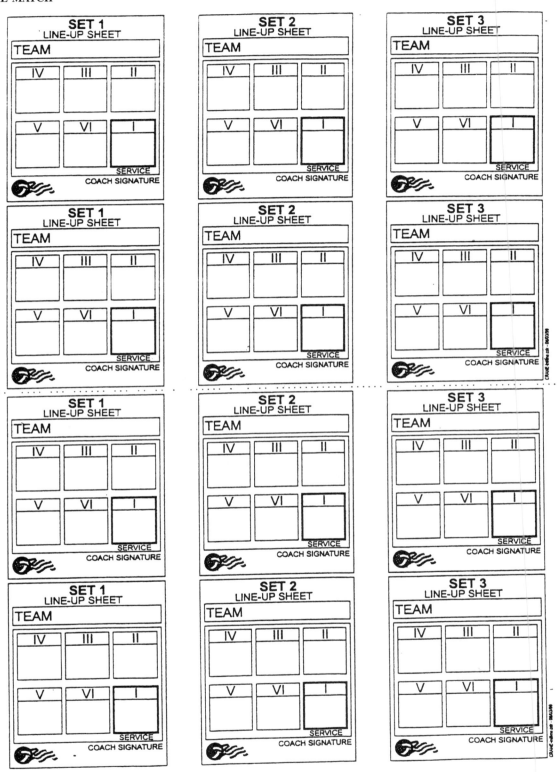

Figure 10-2.
Reprinted with permission from USA Volleyball.

Postgame

❏ Lock up game balls.
❏ Provide towels to visiting team.
❏ Clear score table of score sheets, pencils, and statistics.
❏ Return towels to laundry room.
❏ Clean bleachers and under bleachers. Lock them.
❏ Clear gym, turn off lights, lock doors, and secure building.

CHAPTER 11

STATISTICS

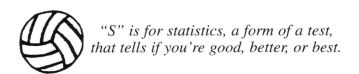

"S" is for statistics, a form of a test,
that tells if you're good, better, or best.

The purpose of this chapter is to provide a summary of the basic statistical options that can be used for beginning and advanced levels of play. These statistics are not to be thought of as complete, but to serve as a foundation and a steppingstone to further study in the area.

Statistics can be compiled on every aspect of the game, but the most relevant in the early stages of the game are individual mistakes committed, serve receive and attack efficiency, and a shot chart on the opponent's attackers to determine proper defensive positioning.

Statistics are a valuable coaching tool and should be a part of the overall plan. This objective data, however, must be combined with a subjective evaluation of the athlete and the team to be the most beneficial. Statistics are not only valuable to the coaches and players, but to the media and fans as well.

THE VALUE OF STATISTICS

Game Promotion

Use statistics to promote the game. Along with reporting match results to the media, utilize statistics to publicize and give recognition to top individual and team performances.

Game Education

Use statistics to teach the game of volleyball and make it interesting and attractive to the public. Help sportswriters and fans understand the game by speaking through statistics, the common language of sports. Spectators can have a greater appreciation of all aspects of the game if you highlight many statistical categories.

Player Evaluation

Use statistics to evaluate individual performances and, later, as a tool to assist in the decision-making process regarding player positions, starting lineups, substitute roles, as well as cuts. Although statistics give objective information, final decisions should be based on a variety of objective and subjective factors, not excluding the coach's intuition, experience, and general knowledge of game.

Match Adjustments

Use statistics during the match to make immediate adjustments through substitutions, lineup changes, and/or changes in tactics. Decisions, again, should be based both on subjective and objective evaluation of individual and team play.

Scouting

Use statistics to evaluate the opponent's performances against your team as well as other teams to make future game plans.

Objective Feedback

Use statistics to provide athletes with specific and objective feedback on their strengths and weaknesses and the "numbers" or standards they must achieve to be successful.

Player Motivation

Use statistics to help motivate athletes to improve their numbers and, in doing so, their performance by working hard in practice and the game.

Practice Enhancement

Use statistical evaluations of individual and team performances in games to assist in planning practice content in subsequent training sessions. Also use statistics in practice drills to help motivate athletes to maintain game-level efforts. Statistics hold the athlete responsible for every contact.

STATISTICAL ADMONITIONS

Keep Statistics Meaningful

Use statistics that will be helpful and meaningful to the team. It is not necessary to take statistics if the information is not going to be utilized to publicize, motivate, and/or improve the team.

Make Statistics Valid

Statistics should be related to winning. They should be interpreted to indicate to coaches and players strengths and weaknesses in relation to what is necessary to be successful.

Monitor Statistical Information

Statistics can be a positive or negative influence on individuals. Some players become so absorbed and concerned with their statistics that they lose sight of the game and their teammates. Monitor the amount of information given to athletes during and after the game. Educate athletes to the benefits and proper use of statistics.

Teach "How" to Take Statistics

Statisticians must know the game and the regulations associated with their specific statistic. They must be serious and attentive while performing their job; otherwise, the statistics will be inaccurate and potentially harmful. For consistency, it is best to use the same person for each statistic.

Record the Basics

Statisticians must write the date, opponent, and place of the match on the statistics form before the match begins. The final game score is recorded immediately following each game. Information not recorded at game time can be very difficult, if not impossible, to secure at a later date.

Keep It Consistent

Keep all statistical information as consistent as possible. *For example:* Place player names in the same order on the statistics sheet to assist in compilation of all statistical totals.

STATISTICAL OPTIONS

Running Systems

Running statistics show the result of each rally and how the point or side-out was won or lost for each team. It is easy to determine the positive and negative point-ending plays for each team at the end of the match. An example of a running statistic places your team on one side of the form and the opponent on the other. The final result of each play is indicated with a team's positives or its opponent's errors under the point or side-out section or point section only in rally score. (See Figures 11-1, 11-2, and 11-3 for sample forms.)

Plus, Zero, Minus System

The plus, zero, minus system evaluates the performance of an individual in a particular phase of the game, not just the end result. A plus (+) indicates a point or side-out. A zero (0) indicates a keep in play and a minus (−) indicates an error that results in the loss of a point or side-out. This statistic can be used to evaluate all skills, or those deemed most important to the individual or team. Individual forms can be used for each category of skills or "Statistics in a Box." See Figure 11.6 for a sample form.

POINT / SIDEOUT STATISTIC **

DATE: SITE: SCORE:

TEAM: TEAM:

POINTS	SIDEOUTS
1.	1.
2.	2.
3.	3.
4.	4.
5.	5.
6.	6.
7.	7.
8.	8.
9.	9.
10.	10.
11.	11.
12.	12.
13.	13.
14.	14.
15.	15.
16.	16.
17.	17.
18.	18.
19.	19.
20.	20.
21.	21.
22.	22.
23.	23.
24.	24.
25.	25.
26.	26.
27.	27.
28.	28.
29.	29.
30.	30.
31.	31.
32.	32.
33.	33.
34.	34.

TOTALS
Aces: _____
Kills: _____
Blocks: _____
Opp Errors: _____

POINTS	SIDEOUTS
1.	1.
2.	2.
3.	3.
4.	4.
5.	5.
6.	6.
7.	7.
8.	8.
9.	9.
10.	10.
11.	11.
12.	12.
13.	13.
14.	14.
15.	15.
16.	16.
17.	17.
18.	18.
19.	19.
20.	20.
21.	21.
22.	22.
23.	23.
24.	24.
25.	25.
26.	26.
27.	27.
28.	28.
29.	29.
30.	30.
31.	31.
32.	32.
33.	33.
34.	34.

TOTALS
Aces: _____
Kills: _____
Blocks: _____
Opp Errors: _____

© 2001 by Parker Publishing Company

** Record ending plays for each rally. On each team's side, indicate their positive actions or the opponent's errors.

Figure 11-1.

POINT / SIDEOUT STATISTIC

DATE: OCT 26   **SITE:** USA

SCORE: 15-9

TEAM: UNIVERSITY OF CALIFORNIA

(US)

Ursula	Sandra	Star
3	7	9
14	4	8
Margie	Deb	Jill

TEAM: USA NATIONAL TEAM

(THEM)

7	18	14
6	2	13

POINTS	SIDEOUTS
1. #18 KE	1. URSULA K
2. MARGIE SA	2. " "
3. " "	3. #6 KE
4. #14 KE	4. SAM BS
5. #13 STE	5. #14 BE
6. STAR BS	6. DEBBIE DUMP
7. SANDRA DUMP	7. #7 SE
8. #14 KE	8. MARGIE K
9. SAM KT	9. SAM KT
10. #1 KE	10. #4 SE
11. #1 KE	11. STAR K
12. SAM KWO	12. " "
13. SANDRA-STAR BA	13.
14. #7 KE	14.
15. #18 BHE	15.
16.	16.
17.	17.
18.	18.
19.	19.
20.	20.
21.	21.
22.	22.
23.	23.
24.	24.
25.	25.
26.	26.
27.	27.
28.	28.
29.	29.
30.	30.
31.	31.
32.	32.
33.	33.
34.	34.

POINTS	SIDEOUTS
1. MARGIE BE	1. #7 K
2. STAR BE	2. #7 KWO
3. REGINA KE	3. #7 KT
4. #18 KT	4. #1 K
5. #6 KT	5. #14 KT
6. #6 KWO	6. #18 BS
7. #6 K	7. #5 BS
8. #13 DUMP	8. #6 KT
9. #7 K	9. #6 KWO
10.	10. URSULA SE
11.	11. MARGIE SE
12.	12. #18 K
13.	13.
14.	14.
15.	15.
16.	16.
17.	17.
18.	18.
19.	19.
20.	20.
21.	21.
22.	22.
23.	23.
24.	24.
25.	25.
26.	26.
27.	27.
28.	28.
29.	29.
30.	30.
31.	31.
32.	32.
33.	33.
34.	34.

TOTALS

Aces: 2
Kills: 10
Blocks: 3
Opp Errors: 12 (USA ERRORS)

TOTALS

Aces: 0
Kills: 14
Blocks: 2
Opp Errors: 5 (UC ERRORS)

Figure 11-2.

© 2001 by Parker Publishing Company

POINT STATISTIC **

DATE: **SITE:** _____   **SCORE:** _____

TEAM: _____   **TEAM:** _____

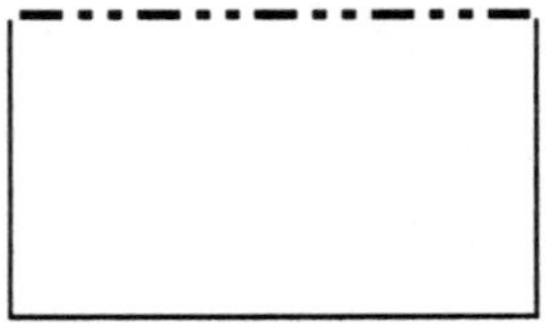

POINTS

1.	35.		1.	35.
2.	36.		2.	36.
3.	37.		3.	37.
4.	38.		4.	38.
5.	39.		5.	39.
6.	40.		6.	40.
7.	41.		7.	41.
8.	42.		8.	42.
9.	43.		9.	43.
10.	44.		10.	44.
11.	45.		11.	45.
12.	46.		12.	46.
13.	47.		13.	47.
14.	48.		14.	48.
15.	49.		15.	49.
16.	50.		16.	50.
17.	51.		17.	51.
18.	52.		18.	52.
19.	53.		19.	53.
20.	54.		20.	54.
21.	55.		21.	55.
22.	56.		22.	56.
23.	57.		23.	57.
24.	58.		24.	58.
25.	59.		25.	59.
26.	60.		26.	60.
27.	61.		27.	61.
28.	62.		28.	62.
29.	63.		29.	63.
30.	64.		30.	64.
31.	65.		31.	65.
32.	66.		32.	66.
33.	67.		33.	67.
34.	68.		34.	68.

TOTALS

Aces: _____
Kills: _____
Blocks: _____
Opp Errors: _____

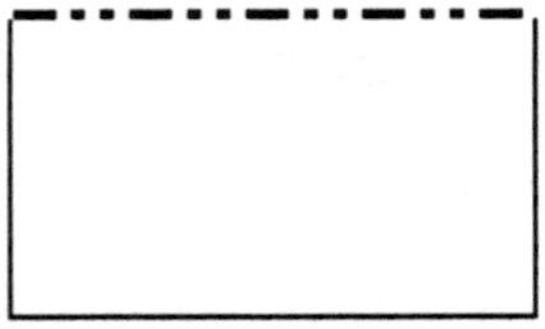

TOTALS

Aces: _____
Kills: _____
Blocks: _____
Opp Errors: _____

** Record ending plays for each rally. On each team's side, indicate their positive actions or the opponent's errors.

Figure 11-3.

© 2001 by Parker Publishing Company

Block

- + = Ball blocked (stuff) to the opponent's side for a point or side-out. More specifically, the block can be indicated as a block solo or block assist when more than one person participates in the successful block.
- 0 = Ball blocked back to the opponent's side that remains in play. Generally blocking statistics are utilized as a rally termination statistic and balls kept in play are not considered in the equation.
- − = Block error (net or line violation) that results in a point or side-out. Poor block technique that might cause an attacker to receive a point is not considered an error, nor are balls deflected off the block that are not playable by the blocking team.

Attack

- + = Attack (kill) that results in a point or side-out.
- 0 = Attacked ball that remains in play.
- − = Attack error that results in a point or side-out.

Serve Reception

- + = Good pass to the target that permits all first-, second-, and third-tempo options.
- 0 = Average pass that permits second- and third-tempo options only.
- − = Poor pass that causes a passing error or forces the receiving team to give the opponents a free ball.

Dig

- + = Dig that permits transition to set for the attack.
- 0 = Dig that is playable, but cannot be set for the attack.
- − = Dig error that causes a point or side-out. An error is categorized as an attack that the receiver was capable of digging but did not due to poor body or court position.

Serve

- + = Ace serve that results in a direct point.
- 0 = Serve that remains in play.
- − = Serve error that results in a point or side-out.

Set (Assist)

- + = Set that results in a positive attack (kill).
- 0 = Set that results in an attack that remains in play.
- − = Mishandled ball called by the official or a ball that is judged as not playable by the attacker.

Point Systems

The point system assigns a number value to each performance of a given skill and should be proportional to the probability of success in the rally. This statistic can be used to evaluate all skills or those deemed most important to the individual or team. Listed are examples of common point system methods of evaluation.

Serve

- 4 = Ace serve that results in an immediate point for the serving team. Equal to a receiving error. Probability of success = 100%.
- 3 = Good serve that results in the opponent's inability to set the ball for an attack. The ball is returned to the serving team with a free ball. Equal to a "1" pass by the receiver. Probability of success = 75%.
- 2 = Average serve that results in opponent's ability to attack with second- or third-tempo sets only. Equal to a "2" pass by the receiver. Probability of success = 50%.
- 1 = Poor serve that results in a perfect pass to the target and allows opponent all first-, second-, and third-tempo attack options. Equal to a "3" pass by the receiver. Probability of success = 25%.
- 0 = Serve error that results in the loss of a point or a side-out. Probability of success = 0%.

Serve Reception

- 3 = Perfect pass to the target that allows all first-, second-, and third-tempo attack options. Equal to a "1" serve.
- 2 = Good pass that allows second- and third-tempo options. Equal to a "2" serve.
- 1 = Poor pass that forces the setter to set with the hands or a forearm set in one direction only and/or forces another player to step in to set. Equal to a "3" serve.
- 0 = Poor pass that forces the receiving team to give a free ball to the serving team. Equal to a "3" serve.
- 0 = Reception error that results in the loss of a point. Equal to a service ace, that is, a "4" serve.

Block. Numbered blocking statistics more effectively focus on blocking than the plus, minus, zero system.
- 4 = Stuff block that results in an immediate point or side-out for the blocking team.
- 3 = Ball that is deflected by the block and results in a free ball for the blocking side.
- 2 = Ball that is deflected by the block and remains in play on either side of the net.
- 1 = Ball that is deflected by the block and results in a free ball on the attacker's side of the net.
- 0 = Block error that results in a point or side-out. This type of error includes line or net violations or balls deflected off the block that are not playable by the blocking team.

STATISTICAL FORMULAS

After all statistics are compiled, individual and team skill averages and efficiencies are calculated.

- Serve reception average (efficiency) = total points earned divided by the total number of attempts.
- Serve average (efficiency) = total points earned divided by the total number of serve attempts.
- Attack percentage (efficiency) = total number of kills minus the errors divided by the total attempts.
- Kills per game = total kills divided by the total games played.
- Blocks per game = total block solos and assists divided by the total games played.
- Assists per game = total assists divided by the total games played.

- Digs per game = total digs divided by the total games played.
- Service aces per game = total aces divided by the total games played.

Various forms are provided that can be utilized with plus, zero, minus, or point system statistics. See Figures 11-4 through 11-7.

STATISTICAL TOTALS

All pertinent individual and team statistics should be compiled on a match summary form. The Official American Volleyball Coaches Association (AVCA) Box Score Form is provided in Figure 11-8.

SCOUTING SYSTEMS

All of the previously listed statistics can be used to discover strengths, weaknesses, and tendencies of the opponent. In addition, side-out and shot charts are commonly used to indicate tendencies, strengths, and weaknesses of individual passers and attackers.

Side-Out Chart

A basic side-out chart consists of six volleyball courts, one for each of the six rotations. (See Figure 11-9.) The team's serve receive formation is drawn exactly as the players appear on the court. The plus, zero, minus system is used to indicate the quality of the pass and the effectiveness of the first attack off serve receive. Arrows are drawn to indicate the approach pattern of the attacker and direction and result of the attack. (See Figures 11-10–11-12 for a sample.) This statistic shows the tendencies of the offense in each of the six side-out rotations.

Shot Chart

Shot charts can be taken on individual attackers to indicate the location, direction, and result of each attack in transition after the initial side-out attack. Patterns develop and defenders can easily see when an attacker primarily hits toward a specific spot. This information helps determine team and individual defensive tactics.

Score Sheet

The score sheet is a valuable source of information. It can be used after the match to calculate points per rotation for the home team as well as for the opponent. Strong and weak rotations can be identified and the lineup can be altered or adjustments made to strengthen the team. Serve efficiency can also be calculated by dividing the number of points won by the number of rotations.

Computer Statistics

There are various types of computer statistical systems. These on-court computer programs record the play-by-play action of the game for immediate use (real time) or are available at the end of the match.

ATTACK STATISTICS WORKSHEET

Site: _____   Date: _____   Team: _____

Name or Number	Attempts (O) Kills (/) Errors (X) Game (])	Game	1	2	3	4	5	T
   Game 1 2 3 4 5	1 2 3 4 5 6 7 8 9 10 11 12 13 14 15 16 17 18 19 20 21 22 23 24 25 26 27 28 29 30 31 32 33 34 35 36 37 38 39 40 41 42 43 44 45 46 47 48 49 50 51 52 53 54 55 56 57 58 59	K= E= A=						
   Game 1 2 3 4 5	1 2 3 4 5 6 7 8 9 10 11 12 13 14 15 16 17 18 19 20 21 22 23 24 25 26 27 28 29 30 31 32 33 34 35 36 37 38 39 40 41 42 43 44 45 46 47 48 49 50 51 52 53 54 55 56 57 58 59	K= E= A=						
   Game 1 2 3 4 5	1 2 3 4 5 6 7 8 9 10 11 12 13 14 15 16 17 18 19 20 21 22 23 24 25 26 27 28 29 30 31 32 33 34 35 36 37 38 39 40 41 42 43 44 45 46 47 48 49 50 51 52 53 54 55 56 57 58 59	K= E= A=						
   Game 1 2 3 4 5	1 2 3 4 5 6 7 8 9 10 11 12 13 14 15 16 17 18 19 20 21 22 23 24 25 26 27 28 29 30 31 32 33 34 35 36 37 38 39 40 41 42 43 44 45 46 47 48 49 50 51 52 53 54 55 56 57 58 59	K= E= A=						
   Game 1 2 3 4 5	1 2 3 4 5 6 7 8 9 10 11 12 13 14 15 16 17 18 19 20 21 22 23 24 25 26 27 28 29 30 31 32 33 34 35 36 37 38 39 40 41 42 43 44 45 46 47 48 49 50 51 52 53 54 55 56 57 58 59	K= E= A=						
   Game 1 2 3 4 5	1 2 3 4 5 6 7 8 9 10 11 12 13 14 15 16 17 18 19 20 21 22 23 24 25 26 27 28 29 30 31 32 33 34 35 36 37 38 39 40 41 42 43 44 45 46 47 48 49 50 51 52 53 54 55 56 57 58 59	K= E= A=						
   Game 1 2 3 4 5	1 2 3 4 5 6 7 8 9 10 11 12 13 14 15 16 17 18 19 20 21 22 23 24 25 26 27 28 29 30 31 32 33 34 35 36 37 38 39 40 41 42 43 44 45 46 47 48 49 50 51 52 53 54 55 56 57 58 59	K= E= A=						
   Game 1 2 3 4 5	1 2 3 4 5 6 7 8 9 10 11 12 13 14 15 16 17 18 19 20 21 22 23 24 25 26 27 28 29 30 31 32 33 34 35 36 37 38 39 40 41 42 43 44 45 46 47 48 49 50 51 52 53 54 55 56 57 58 59	K= E= A=						
   Game 1 2 3 4 5	1 2 3 4 5 6 7 8 9 10 11 12 13 14 15 16 17 18 19 20 21 22 23 24 25 26 27 28 29 30 31 32 33 34 35 36 37 38 39 40 41 42 43 44 45 46 47 48 49 50 51 52 53 54 55 56 57 58 59	K= E= A=						
   Game 1 2 3 4 5	1 2 3 4 5 6 7 8 9 10 11 12 13 14 15 16 17 18 19 20 21 22 23 24 25 26 27 28 29 30 31 32 33 34 35 36 37 38 39 40 41 42 43 44 45 46 47 48 49 50 51 52 53 54 55 56 57 58 59	K= E= A=						
   Game 1 2 3 4 5	1 2 3 4 5 6 7 8 9 10 11 12 13 14 15 16 17 18 19 20 21 22 23 24 25 26 27 28 29 30 31 32 33 34 35 36 37 38 39 40 41 42 43 44 45 46 47 48 49 50 51 52 53 54 55 56 57 58 59	K= E= A=						
   Game 1 2 3 4 5	1 2 3 4 5 6 7 8 9 10 11 12 13 14 15 16 17 18 19 20 21 22 23 24 25 26 27 28 29 30 31 32 33 34 35 36 37 38 39 40 41 42 43 44 45 46 47 48 49 50 51 52 53 54 55 56 57 58 59	K= E= A=						

Figure 11-4.

GENERAL STATISTICAL WORKSHEET

End of Game ()   GP = Games Played   SA = Service Aces   SE = Service Errors
RE = Receive Errors   BS = Block Solo   BA = Block Assists   BE = Block Error
BHE = Ball Handling Error

Player	#	GP	ASSISTS	SA	SE	RE	DIGS	BS	BA	BE	BHE

Figure 11-5.

STATISTICS IN A BOX

Blocks	Kills	0	Errors	Serves
				BHE
Digs	Name			Assists
	Serve Receive			

Blocks	Kills	0	Errors	Serves
				BHE
Digs	Name			Assists
	Serve Receive			

Scores

Blocks	Kills	0	Errors	Serves
				BHE
Digs	Name			Assists
	Serve Receive			

Blocks	Kills	0	Errors	Serves
				BHE
Digs	Name			Assists
	Serve Receive			

Site

Blocks	Kills	0	Errors	Serves
				BHE
Digs	Name			Assists
	Serve Receive			

Blocks	Kills	0	Errors	Serves
				BHE
Digs	Name			Assists
	Serve Receive			

Date

Notes in a Box

Figure 11-6

STATISTICS IN A BOX

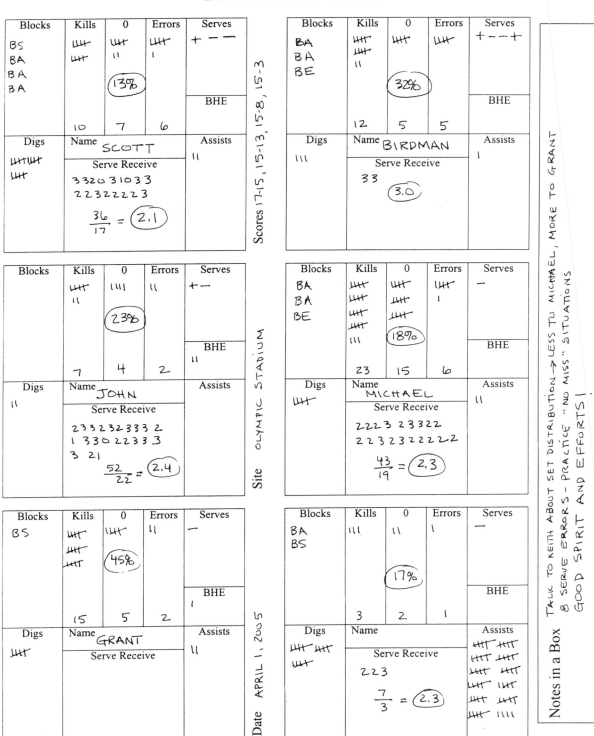

Figure 11-7.

OFFICIAL AVCA BOX SCORE

Site: Date: Attendance:

No.	Player	GP	K	E	TA	PCT.	A	SA	SE	RE	DIG	BS	BA	BE	BHE
TEAM:			ATTACK				SET	SERVE			DEF	BLOCK			GEN
TEAM TOTALS:															

Team Attack Per Game: Team RE: Total Team Blocks:

Gm	K	E	TA	Pct.	Pts	Game Scores	1	2	3	4	5	Team Records
1												
2												
3												
4												
5												

No.	Player	GP	K	E	TA	PCT.	A	SA	SE	RE	DIG	BS	BA	BE	BHE
TEAM:			ATTACK				SET	SERVE			DEF	BLOCK			GEN
TEAM TOTALS:															

Team Attack Per Game: Team RE: Total Team Blocks:

Gm	K	E	TA	Pct.	Pts	
1						Length of Match:
2						First Referee:
3						Second Referee:
4						Notes:
5						

Key:

A = Assists	GP = Games Played	BHE = Ball Handling Errors	SA = Service Ace	Kill Pct = (K - E) / TA
K = Kills	TA = Total Attempts	RE = Receiving Errors	SE = Service Error	D = Digs
E = Errors	Pct = %	SA = Block Solos	Team Blocks = BS + 1/2 BA	BE = Block Errors
		BA = Block Assists	Team RE = RE not assigned to any one player	

Figure 11-8.

SIDE-OUT CHART

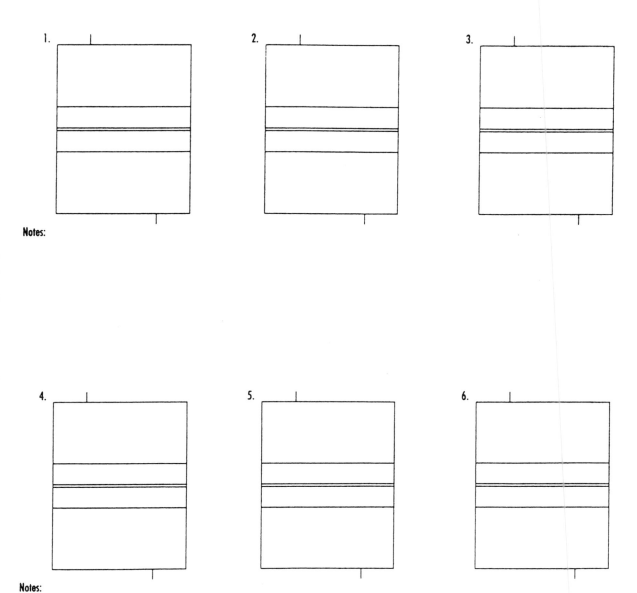

Figure 11-9.

SIDE-OUT CHART

(Switzerland 2000)

1.

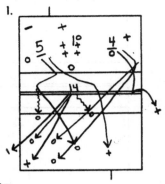

2.

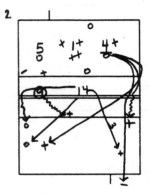

3.

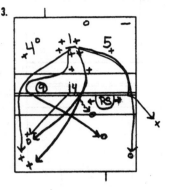

Notes:

STOP #14
Rightside help on "3"
Left side help on "1"
Block #4 cross-court
dig her 1on1

Middle blocker stick
on #14 for "1", "3", "slides"

Right side help on "3"
Left side help on "1"

Go 1on1 with #4

Sideout- right side
start inside to block
The "3" on #14, two
blockers on #1

MB commit on #14
Leftside blocker 1on1
 on #1 on The "slide"
LS_commit on #4 on slide

4.

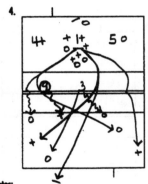

5.

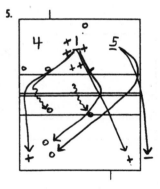

6.

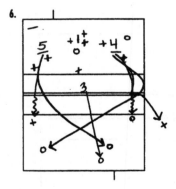

Notes:

Follow #1
Do not block #3

MB follow #1, release to outside
LF, if #1 goes to opposite side
commit on #3 or #9
LF, watch #1 for slide

In transition
LF commit on #3

Block 1on1 on #5
MB release outside
 to #1

overload #4
block cross-court

Figure 11-10.

CODES FOR POINT/SIDE-OUT STATISTICS

© 2001 by Parker Publishing Company

K	Kill. Attack that results in a point or side-out.
KT	Kill with tip. Attacker tips the ball for a kill.
KWO	Kill with wipe-off. Attacker hits the ball off the block for the kill.
E	Error that results in a point or side-out for opponents.
KE	Kill error that results in a point or side-out for the opponent.
KEN	Kill error caused by a net violation.
KEL	Kill error caused by a centerline violation.
KEB	Kill error caused by a back row attacker contacting the ball in front of the 10-foot line.
KET	Kill error on a tip attempt.
BS	Block solo. One player participates in the block for a point or side-out.
BA	Block assist. Two players participate in the block for a point or side-out.
BE	Block error that results in a point or side-out for the opponent.
BEN	Block error caused by a net violation.
BEL	Block error caused by a centerline violation.
BEWO	Block error caused by the attacker. Attacker hits the ball off the block that results in a point or side-out. This is not generally considered a blocking error in most statistics, but is useful information from a coaching standpoint.
SA	Serve ace. Server wins a direct point.
SE	Serve error that results in a point or side-out.
SEN	Serve error caused by a ball hitting the net.
SEO	Serve error caused by a ball landing out of bounds.
ST	Set. Ball set to an attacker.
STE	Set error that results in a point or side-out. A mishandled ball called by the official or a set that does not allow the attacker to play the ball.
A	Assist. A set that results in a kill for the attacker.
SR	Serve reception.
SRE	Serve reception error that results in a direct point for the serving team.
PE	Court position error.
SUB	Substitution.
TO	Timeout.
DE	Defensive error that results in a point or side-out. Incorrect positioning, not going for the ball, or making an incorrect move that results in a negative result.
BHE	Ballhandling error. A violation called by the official that results in a point or side-out.
BOT	Botch. An unforced technical or tactical error.
SOB	Son of a botch. The result of an earlier botch.

Figure 11-11.

USA Men's Volleyball

Team: _____
Date: _____
Location: _____

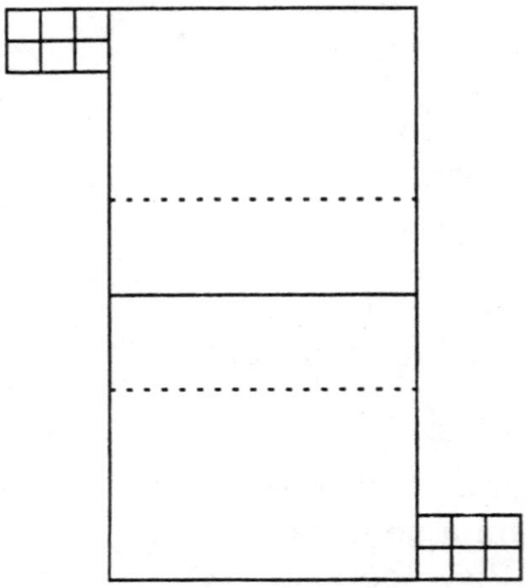

Notes: _____
_____
_____
_____
_____

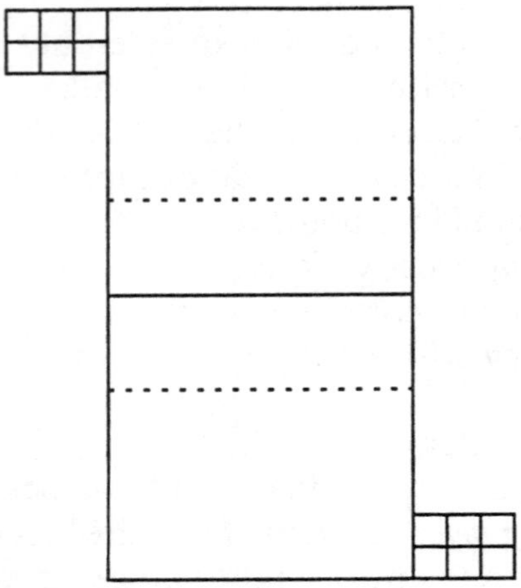

Notes: _____
_____
_____
_____
_____

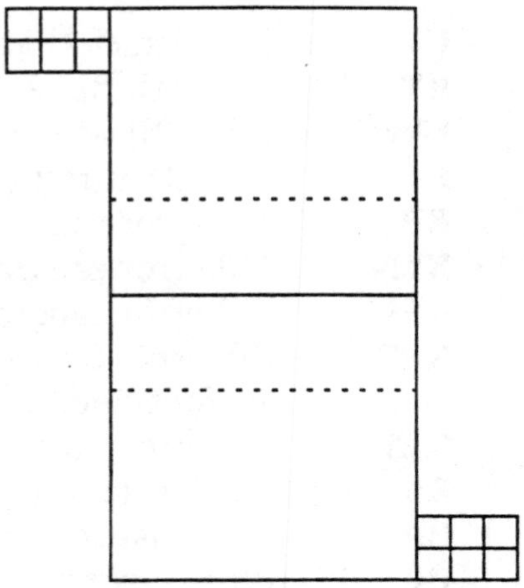

Notes: _____
_____
_____
_____
_____

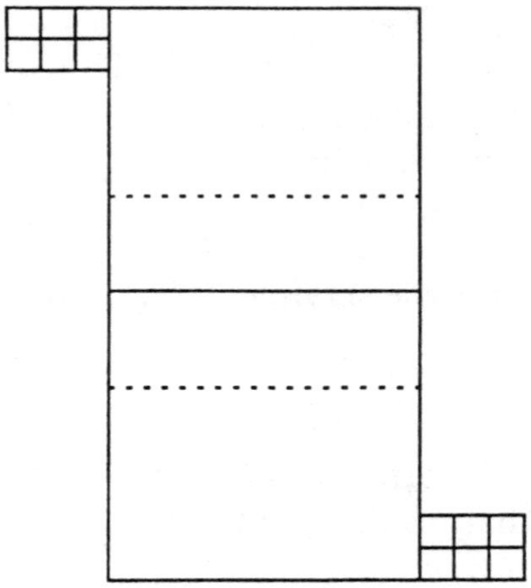

Notes: _____
_____
_____
_____
_____

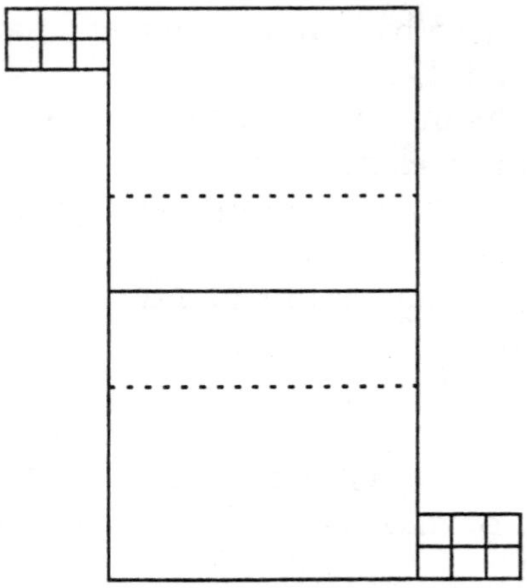

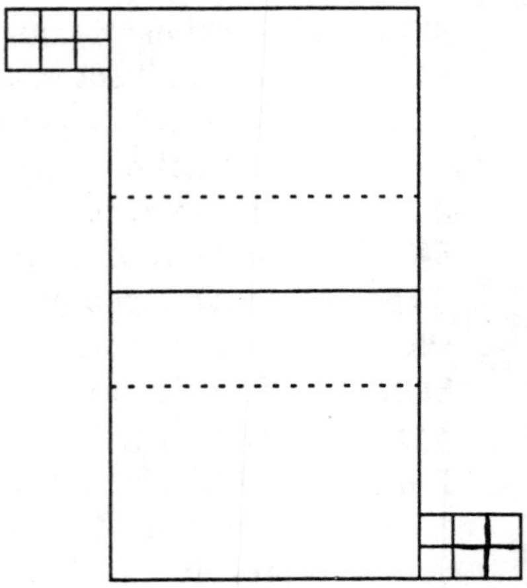

Notes: _____
_____
_____
_____
_____

Notes: _____
_____
_____
_____
_____

Figure 11-12.

RESOURCES

Statistics

- American Volleyball Coaches Association (AVCA) Statistical Manual and Video at *http://www.avca.org*
- *Comprehensive Volleyball Statistics, A Guide for Coaches, Media and Fans* by Stephanie Schleuder (AVCA)
- *Point, Game, Match* by Val Keller (Creative Sports) [Although out of print, this book might be found in your public or school library.]
- "The Relationship Between Serving, Passing, Setting, Attacking and Winning in Men's Volleyball" by James Coleman, Masters of Physical Education, George Williams College, 1975
- "Statistical Analysis of Selected Volleyball Techniques at Three Levels of Women's Intercollegiate Volleyball" by Russell D. Rose, Masters of Physical Education, Lincoln, Nebraska, December 1978
- "A Statistical Evaluation of Selected Volleyball Techniques at the 1974 World Volleyball Championships" by James Coleman, Doctorate of Education, Brigham Young University, 1975.

Software Packages

- Ark Sport Technologies at *http://www.scoutsports.com*
- CompuSTATS CourtSide for Volleyball at *http://www.frontsoft.com*
- Data Volley at *http://www.dataprojectsport.com*
- Sportistics at *http://www.netins.net/showcase/vbstats*
- Stat Crew Software at *http://www.statcrew.com*

Information/Rules

- The Coach Magazine at *http://www.thecoach-online.com*
- Federation Internationale de Volleyball (FIVB) at *http://fivb.ch*
- National Association for Girls and Women's Sports at *http://aahperd.org*
- National Federation of State High School Associations at *http://nfhs.org*
- United States Volleyball Association (USVA) at *http://www.usavolleyball.org*

CHAPTER 12

THE PRACTICE

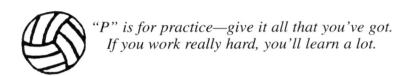

"P" is for practice—give it all that you've got.
If you work really hard, you'll learn a lot.

The six factors of successful practices are preparation, motivation, execution, discipline, learning acquisition, and cooperation. Each one is discussed here in detail.

FACTOR 1: PREPARATION

Successful practices depend on careful planning. Without it, success is a factor of luck. Successful coaches do not "wing it." They have a clear idea about what they want to do and how to do it. They leave nothing to chance and take nothing for granted.

Every team is different. Plans from one year cannot automatically be utilized for an upcoming season. The needs of each team vary with the skill and experience level of the players, as well as the personality of the team. A guideline may be used as a foundation, but adjustments must be made to individualize it. The plans should be constantly reevaluated and adjustments made as necessary.

Develop a Master Plan

Planning the journey begins well before the season. The overall program philosophy and values should be established first, along with requirements and expectations for participation. This is followed by the long- and short-term team goals. Then the current team's strengths and weaknesses technically, tactically, and emotionally are assessed to establish an appropriate starting point.

Together this information is utilized to design an action plan to get the team from where it is to where it wants to be. The first part of the plan is developed in the form of a yearly or seasonal "master plan" calendar. The calendar includes dates of all practices, competitions, holidays, days off, team meetings, and social events. Also included are long- and short-term goals and target dates for completion. The action plan is then divided into monthly blocks of time that coincide with the preseason, season, and postseason.

Preseason

Preseason goals are those things that need to be accomplished to be ready for the first game of the season. The majority of time is invested in developing and/or strengthening athletes' physical condition and their individual technical and tactical skills. Just as important is experimenting and developing team offensive and defensive formations and tactics and establishing player roles and lineup combinations.

Competitive Season

More time is devoted to adjustments and refinements of individual skills and team tactics during the competitive season. Team strengths and weaknesses are evaluated after each competition to determine future practice content. Emphasis is on making technical and tactical corrections, changes, and/or refinements of individual and team play in direct relation to the results of competitions. It is best to avoid making too many big changes once the competitive season has begun. Changes can be counterproductive and shake the confidence of the team. Athletes need to be given a chance to get good at what they are doing.

Postseason

The postseason is an opportunity for athletes to rest and recover from injuries, as well as take a break from volleyball. Athletes are encouraged to stay in shape, but to do so by getting involved in other sports and activities.

Preparation Admonitions

Plan Every Practice.   Practices are most successful when they are carefully structured and planned. Plans must be well thought out to insure that all phases of the game are covered. It is a coaching error if an athlete has to do something in the game that has not been practiced. The players have not been prepared properly.

Spend Quality Time Planning.   Success or failure of the team will be in direct proportion to the quality of the practices. Never wait until the last minute to plan practice and never plan practice in a rush.

> **MAXIM:** *The reason most people fail instead of succeed is that they trade what they want most for what they want at the moment.*

Avoid Planning Practice as a Singular Entity.   Each practice must be an integrated part of the "master plan" and relevant to the goals and needs of the team. Plan four to six practices at one time and then divide what must be done into individual practice sessions. Continuity is achieved when there is a logical progression of practices with each lesson leading smoothly into the next. Continually review and evaluate the overall plan to avoid getting caught up in specific needs or momentary impulses.

Always Come to Practice with a Written Plan.   Outline each individual practice. Include practice objectives, specific activities to accomplish these goals, and the amount of time to spend on each activity. Indicate who does what drill with whom. Assigning players to specific partners and groups is not only an effective and efficient way to organize practice, but it also helps eliminate cliques and brings the team closer together. Assignments can be by position, homogenous by abilities, or balanced by player positions and abilities.

Clearly Present the Lesson Objectives.   Learning is enhanced when the information is meaningful to players and they understand why it is important. Present the objectives of the session prior to practice.

Attempt to Stick to the Original Plan.   A lot of thought goes into the practice plan and a lot of factors are considered. Attempt to stay within the time schedule. If sufficient time was not allocated for a drill, to continue it would mean the elimination of another one or running overtime, which would be counterproductive. It is best to continue on schedule and make adjustments in future practices.

Allow for Some Flexibility.   Be flexible to deal with unexpected events. The best plans on paper do not always meet our expectations in the gym. Be prepared to make some adjustments. *For example:*

- Drills are planned specifically to address the needs of individual players, but these players cannot practice due to injury or illness.
- The drill is completed in less time than calculated.
- Players are physically fatigued and there is concern for injury. The workload must be adjusted.
- The drill is not effective. It is too easy, too hard, or simply does not succeed in accomplishing the desired effect. If the drill is not working, no matter how good an idea it was, consideration must be given to change it or abandon it completely.

> *MAXIM: It's not the amount of time you practice; it's the practice you put into the time.*

Vary Practice Duration to Meet the Team's Needs.   Research concludes that for most effective learning, in terms of maximal returns, more is not always better. Learning occurs best in predominately short practice periods distributed over longer periods of time. The optimal amount of time for the practice session itself is between one and three hours and varies depending on the age and experience level of the players as well as the program goals. Longer practice sessions can be maintained for more mature and skilled players, but in general practices beyond three hours are rarely beneficial: Mentally it is difficult to concentrate, and physically it is hard to maintain a high effort level. The amount of time between practices also varies. Too little rest or too much time off both have equally negative effects. It is a matter of experience and trial and error to make decisions regarding the length and spacing of practices.

Do Not Attempt to Accomplish Too Much at Once.   Create daily objectives for each practice and limit the areas to be covered. Do not attempt to cover everything each session. Break it into manageable chunks. Divide what needs to be done into four to six individual practices. Focus on teaching fewer things in greater depth. Overload one or two skills. Vary the drill, while repeating the skill.

> *MAXIM: The mind is like the stomach; it's not how much you put into it that counts, but how much it digests.* Albert Jay Nock

Prioritize What Is Necessary for Success.   Design an action plan that prioritizes what is most important to be done in each category of the game, such as, individual and team skills, tactics, and conditioning work. Spend the most time on those areas that are perceived as most critical to the team's success, emphasizing strengths as well as working to correct weaknesses.

Balance Hard, Fast-Paced Drills with Drills at a Slower Tempo.   Fast-paced drills are popular with coaches and athletes alike because there are a lot of contacts in a short period of time and because the drill itself creates enthusiasm. The actual game tempo, however, is often slower and, as the tempo slows—at times—so does the enthusiasm. Players have more time to be distracted, to lose their concentration, and worry about errors. Include sufficient drills performed at actual game speeds. Also, maintain a balance between physically strenuous drills and less taxing ones.

Balance Work on Specific Musculature.   Monitor the amount of time spent on each skill with consideration to the areas of the body that are being worked. Be aware of the number of contacts serving, passing, attacking, blocking, and digging by periodically taking this statistic. Keep weekly records on the emphasis of each skill taught, that is, heavy, medium, or light load. Avoid doing too much defense where the athlete is in a very low body position, too much jumping, or too much serving or attacking in one practice or a series of practices. Overemphasis in one area, primarily the shoulders or legs, can lead to injury.

Integrate Drills with Scrimmages.   Use scrimmages and modified games to tie together what has been learned and emphasized in drills. Too much drilling without relating these drills to the game can be detrimental to the learning process; similarly, abandoning drills too early can be of equal harm. Situational scrimmages that emphasize specific aspects of the game are of the most benefit. They help players to focus while providing them with "live" game situations. In unstructured scrimmages, much is left to chance; then old habits often return and players lose sight of their goals.

Avoid Passive Participation of Athletes.   Ensure active participation of the entire team in the majority of practice. Maximize the number of repetitions for each player. Whenever possible, divide the group to avoid situations where players spend a great deal of time waiting to get into a drill. Involve as many players in active participation as possible.

Evaluate Each Practice.   Evaluate every aspect of the workout immediately following each practice. Assess what went well and where improvements can be made for future practices.

> *MAXIM: Even if you have the best skills, you have to keep them polished.*

FACTOR 2: MOTIVATION

There are no secret formulas or magical motivational tricks; rather, it is a shared responsibility of the athlete and coach. Athletes must have some intrinsic motivation to learn and to train or no amount of outside stimulation is going to help. The coach supplements his or her efforts by providing the best program and coaching possible. The coach provides players with the opportunity to learn, but players must accept the offer.

> **MAXIM:** *Motivation is an individual thing and each athlete marches to a different drummer. If you want to motivate them, you've got to find the right music.*

Motivational Admonitions

Have Tough, Structured, and Disciplined Practices. The practice itself is a strong motivational source. It is motivational for athletes to work hard because they know that by doing so they will be well prepared to face the competition. The tougher the practices, the more they feel they not only have the ability to win, but that they *deserve* to win as well.

Give Athletes Your Full Attention. Motivation is heightened when the coach is watching. Attention, both positive and negative, makes athletes work harder than they would on their own. Attention and feedback help players maintain their focus in drills, especially those that require tedious repetitions.

Make Practices Relevant. It is motivational to know that everything being done serves one purpose: to get the team closer to its goals. It is critical that athletes understand the "why" of everything taught and how it fits into the total picture. All players work harder to achieve their goals when they are clear about what is expected of them and why.

Make It Doable. It is motivational to know that success is within reach. Help athletes be successful by keeping the tasks within the range of their abilities. Progress at a speed where successful acquisition can be made.

> **MAXIM:** *If the player catches on quickly, go faster. If the player catches on slowly, slow down the pace.*

Maintain a Balance Between Challenge and Success. Know what the athletes can do and challenge them to do a little more than they can do comfortably. Push them to exceed their previous levels of performance. Do not allow them to settle into a comfort zone, but be careful that the challenge is not so great that it discourages them.

Expect Good Things. It is motivational for athletes to know that you expect them to succeed. Your expectations affect their expectations. If you expect them to do it, the probability is high that they will succeed.

Respect Players' Aspirations. Never underestimate the power of desire. Do not dampen a player's dreams, although you may not feel that these aspirations are realistic. Continue to help players do those things that must be done to reach their goals.

© 2001 by Parker Publishing Company

Make Progress Visible.   Set performance goals for practice, the game, and in the weight room. Keep a record of the results and let players know how they are doing. Display game and practice statistics, as well as weight-room and conditioning achievements. Let the athletes know how they are doing and celebrate each goal that is reached.

Express Appreciation.   Never underestimate the power of an encouraging word. Recognize and reward individual and team contributions, efforts, and achievements. Encourage athletes to want to continue to work hard by catching them doing technical, tactical, or behavioral actions correctly. Constantly look for ways to make players feel like winners. Make sure they know what is expected and reward them when those standards are met. Players need to be noticed, recognized, and appreciated for their efforts. Do it as quickly as possible to the behavior you are trying to encourage.

Sincerely Care About the Athlete.   It is motivational for players to know that you like them. Give each person your attention each day, even if it is just a hello or a smile. Make them feel special. Everyone responds positively to attention. Take every opportunity to talk to players and get to know them. Raise the players' image of themselves and their volleyball skills.

> *MAXIM: An ounce of image is worth a pound of performance.*

Make the Process Fun.   If athletes do not enjoy what they are doing, they will ultimately fail. Every minute of practice cannot be fun, but the overall experience can be. Strive to have practices capture everyone's attention. Boring and monotonous practices are counterproductive. Although some routine work is necessary, give them variety in other areas. Also, help them redefine fun as a process of struggle, discovery, transformation, and change in a way that helps them reach their goals.

Make the Practice Environment Enjoyable.   Be enthusiastic and positive throughout the practice regardless of your mood that day or the difficulties encountered. Maintain a friendly, supportive relationship. Correct errors without dwelling on them. Reward athletes for good efforts as well as good performances. Give them permission to make errors. Tell them to make at least five to ten errors every practice. They probably are already making these errors; if not, they are not challenging themselves enough.

Be Patient.   Give team members sufficient time to absorb new information and learn. Remember that nothing is so easy as it looks, and everything takes longer to learn than you think. As a rule, the first attempts to master a new technique or make changes are unsuccessful. Failure is the part of success that comes first.

Take Advantage of Teaching Moments.   It is motivational for athletes to get "help" when they are in a slump or experiencing difficulties. When the situation arises, take advantage of giving them the information you might have withheld.

Behave the Opposite.   Let players know that you are really serious about what you want. Occasionally, to emphasize a point and command the player's attention, behave in an opposite way from your normal manner. If you are quite verbal, be silent. If you are quiet, be more verbal. A little bit of fear can inspire a positive response in the athlete.

FACTOR 3: EXECUTION

It is your responsibility to instill good work habits. Most athletes must be taught "how" to practice and then "monitored" to ensure that they maintain a high quality of execution. Encourage players to pay attention to details and strive to do the little things extraordinarily well.

> *MAXIM: Practice makes permanent.*

Execution Admonitions

Ensure That Skills and Drills Are Done Properly.   Emphasize the importance of each movement and contact. Discipline team members to execute the skills the same way, *the right way,* every time. Do not allow players to practice improper technique or allow errors to go uncorrected. A skill becomes permanent and ingrained in muscle memory each time it is performed. Repetition is necessary to cement fundamental skills and tactics, but they must be done correctly to be of value.

> *MAXIM: The chains of habit are too small to be felt until they are too strong to be broken.*
> Benjamin R. Dejung

Demand a Full Effort on a Consistent Basis.   Success is dependent on effort. The more effort expended, the greater the chances of success. Make athletes aware of their effort and intensity levels. Very few athletes have the experience to understand what giving an all-out effort means. Many players honestly feel they are giving 100 percent when they are not. Teach them what it means to give their best effort. Teach them to push themselves through difficult practices, fatigue, boredom, moods, and days when they simply do not feel like practicing.

Athletes must understand that giving less than their best or a half-hearted effort is unproductive and unacceptable behavior. Those who are physically or mentally lazy must not be allowed the privilege of practice. They must do it correctly if they want to practice. If not, they can sit and watch, shag for teammates, or—at last resort—be dismissed from practice.

> *MAXIM: Becoming a champion is not a part-time job.*

Mobilize the "Quality Patrol" to Maintain High Standards.   High-quality performance in practice is everyone's responsibility. You must demand it of the athletes; the athletes must demand it of themselves; and teammates must demand it of each other. It is a team effort, and—if one person gives less than 100 percent—it is a disservice to their teammates and diminishes the team's chances of success.

Monitor the Fatigue Level of the Athletes. It is difficult for fatigued players to give their best effort. Train only as hard as their conditioning level allows. Terminate the drill or practice when fatigue results in lack of concentration, incorrect responses, and undisciplined movements. Consider giving an individual athlete, the starters, or the team a day off. It is best to have players rested and mentally fresh.

Enforce Standards with Rules. Establish training rules and consequences that encourage and enforce the standards necessary for success. *For example:*

- If an athlete does not go down for a ball in a defensive drill, the player immediately makes the defensive move that should have been made.
- If a teammate does not go down for a ball in a scoring drill, the group does ten push-ups and their score goes back to zero.
- If too many serves are missed during the game, substitutes do ten push-ups on the spot, and starters do their push-ups after the game or at practice the next day.
- If a ball, in the opinion of the coach, was playable and an athlete did not make a move to play it, everyone sprints.

MAXIM: Working hard does not equate to working well.

FACTOR 4: DISCIPLINE

Success on a consistent basis is dependent on discipline. Anyone can perform well occasionally, but to perform well day after day under all kinds of conditions requires the athlete's full attention mentally, physically, and emotionally. Everyone has the ability to attain success, but he or she must be willing to pay the price. It is a question of discipline.

Discipline Admonitions

Emphasize Focus and Concentration Skills. Practice is the athletes' classroom. Demand their undivided attention to every aspect of practice. *For example:*

- Do not allow visitors to speak to the players or coaches.
- Do not allow conversations between teammates that are unrelated to the specifics of the task.
- Constantly direct and redirect players' attention to specific focal points.
- Help make players aware of their lack of concentration. Ask them what distracted them and bring them back to the correct focus.
- Make players accountable for their actions. Use video, keep statistics, and/or record winners and losers in drills and scrimmages.

Emphasize Continuous Movement. All the athletes have movement responsibilities while the ball is in play. Train them to be involved in every play even though many times they will not actually contact the ball. Emphasize that they should never be simply standing; rather, they should be physically ready and mentally focused, even when it appears that the ball will not come in their direction.

Emphasize Emotional-Control Skills. Success requires an emotional balance. Athletes must learn to handle stressful and frustrating situations. Set up drills to have winners and losers and have the losers do extra conditioning when the drill is over. Purposely make bad calls in scrimmages. Set up situations where players face difficult situations and help them learn to deal with them in a productive way. Do not allow displays of anger, emotional outbursts, pouting, or profanity. A certain amount of anger has the potential to be a motivator for some players, but for most it is a detractor.

Emphasize Listening Skills. All players listen with the ears and the eyes when you speak. Emphasize that they hear it, understand it, and apply it—or they ask for clarification. Everyone listens when a correction is being made for an individual so the same instructions will not have to be repeated when another player is in the same situation. Give explanations *once*. Those who do not pay attention must do some type of physical conditioning. Listen and learn.

Emphasize Thinking Skills. Success at all levels requires thinking. To function independently on the court, athletes must make "thinking" a part of every drill and scrimmage. The game involves constant evaluative and analytical thought. Train team members to make good decisions and solve problems by practicing specific game situations until the correct tactical response is automatic. Make athletes responsible for each decision they make and help them explore the "whys" of each option. Encourage them to explore, think, and express their ideas and opinions.

FACTOR 5: LEARNING ACQUISITION

The biggest responsibility of any coach is to help players learn the game. Use a variety of teaching methods to facilitate learning. No one style is best for all athletes in all situations.

> **MAXIM:** *The best volleyball coaches are not those with the most knowledge, but those who transfer the most knowledge to their athletes.*

Learning Acquisition Admonitions

Use Visuals to Teach. The majority of athletes learn motor skills best through imitation, and this is done most effectively through the use of repeated visuals. Research shows that movement information is retained in the memory in the form of an image and visuals show the athlete these images. In general, images combined with instruction have the greatest influence on learning. Visuals can be used in the form of demonstrations, videos, slides, and pictures. *For example:*

- **Write it down.** Use chalkboards and play books. Writing it down produces better understanding and memorization.
- **Video the athlete's own performance.** Help athletes see for themselves their technical and tactical strengths and weakness. It is especially valuable to show nonbelievers their problem areas. Have athletes view their performances at regular speed and slow motion, and return to visuals of correct performances of other players. Practice the skill and repeat the "recording sessions," focusing on a specific area of concern and correction.

- **Talk less, practice more.** Keep presentations and explanations short and simple. Do not distract them with details. Instruct them, but do not bore them. Doing is more important than listening to someone talk about doing.
- **Show it and let them do it.** Demonstrate the technique or tactic and then get the athletes involved in the activity.
- **Show it and do it again.** Alternate presentations and instruction on one or two keys with practice and feedback. Let players "try it out" and then return for demonstrations and instruction to teach another part of the skill, correct errors, or reemphasize important cues.

MAXIM: When we have to learn to do, we learn by doing. Aristotle

---

- **Show it from different angles.** Demonstrate skills from different angles. Allow the athlete to see the skill performed from the front, side, and back. Each angle will emphasize different aspects of the skill.

MAXIM: I hear and I forget. I see and I remember. I do and I understand. Chinese proverb

---

- **Select demonstrators carefully.** Use skillful demonstrators who model the techniques properly. Whenever possible, use demonstrators who are of the same age and gender of the participants. It is easy for participants to think, "Of course he can do it, he's a guy," or "She's so old, she's had a lot of time to become good, it'll take me forever to reach her level." Coaches should demonstrate only when they are very capable; otherwise, it is best to find another person who can do it.

Avoid Giving the Athlete Too Much Information.   Overloading athletes can slow their rate of skill and tactical development. Vary the quantity of information according to their age, maturity, and experience level. Beginning athletes can process only a limited amount while those at the advanced level can handle more. Regardless, focus each athlete's attention on only a few essential elements at one time.

Focus on Small Steps.   Focus on learning a few things well, rather than partially learning many things. Research indicates that transfer of learning from easy to difficult tasks is most effective when the easy tasks are learned successfully before proceeding to the more difficult ones.

Do Not Rush the Athlete.   Provide sufficient time for athletes to absorb the material before moving to the next stage. They need time to integrate the technique or tactic. Remember to be attentive to the individual athlete's needs; moving too slowly or too rapidly can impede their progress.

Provide Opportunities for Success.   Success enhances an interest in learning and progress is more rapid. The higher the level of intended achievement, the higher the level of performance. Success brings a higher aspiration level.

Reduce the Athlete's Anxiety.   The emotional state of the athlete either facilitates or inhibits performance. Create a positive environment in which players do not feel excessive anxiety. The more positive the environment, the better the learning.

MAXIM: You can observe a lot just by watchin'. Yogi Berra

Observe, Detect, and Correct.   Develop an "eye" for observing technical and tactical performances, and looking for "problem areas." Analyze what is good and what adjustments or changes would enhance individual or team performance. Be alert in detecting and correcting errors early. Each repetition of a skill wears a deeper neuromuscular pathway into the system, and it becomes more and more difficult to change.

- **Avoid showing your anger or frustration.** When giving corrective criticism, your goal should be to motivate the person to make changes, not to blow off steam. Keep your emotions under control and let players know through your actions that you are on their side and want to help them improve.
- **Avoid making corrections after a single observance.** It is most productive to analyze the athlete several times and in different circumstances before making comments. Take sufficient time to see patterns of movements before making an evaluation.
- **Determine what can and should be corrected.** Some technical movements are very difficult to change, if not impossible, depending on the age, ability, and experience of the player. A decision must be made whether it is worthwhile to spend the time making a specific adjustment or improve another area of the athlete's game.
- **Distinguish between an idiosyncrasy and a flaw.** A flaw is detrimental and will have a negative effect on the athlete's present and/or future performance. An idiosyncrasy is an individual adaptation and is the very thing that makes the player unique. A flaw limits the athlete's ability to be successful and must be corrected. Do not worry about an idiosyncrasy.
- **Allow permissible differences.** There is more than one correct method. Avoid insisting that all players conform to one set pattern of skills. Permissible differences exist within a range of correctness. Any technique that is efficient, attains the desired goal, and does not limit future performance should be considered correct. Build upon the foundation of the player's individual game, correcting and improving, but do not attempt to make each athlete fit a specific model.
- **Get them to buy into the change.** It is difficult to change old habit patterns and, even after a change is made, it is easy for players to revert back to old patterns without even recognizing it. Convince them of the benefits of the changes so their commitment to change is strong. Do not assume that the reasons are as obvious to them as they are to you.
- **Be informative without rambling.** Describe the error and how to correct it in simple terms. Focus on the desired change and how to accomplish it. The secret is in the simplicity of the message. Do not require players to process too much information at one time.
- **Make changes incremental.** Avoid asking athletes to make too many changes at once. It can be overwhelming. Point out major mistakes rather than every mistake. Identify and focus on the most inhibiting errors that are essential to continued progress. Start small and build. Before moving to the next correction, athletes should have made the change or at least be moving in that direction.

Give Performance Feedback.   Improvement in performance is related to the amount and quality of feedback. Provide team members with the appropriate knowledge of results, especially in situations where success or failure is not obvious. *For example:* Give feedback on block positioning. The blocker is successful when the ball is channeled to the defender, even though the blocker has not touched the ball.

- **Be a verbally active coach.** Let athletes know what you think and what they need to do. Give them your input and suggestions. Provide praise, encouragement, correction, and guidance.
- **Teach without yelling.** Speak in a firm tone of voice to command attention. Unless players have a hearing problem, it is not necessary to "yell" in order to communicate effectively.
- **Get the athlete's attention.** Tell players something they want to know and hear and combine it with what you want them to know. Get their attention with "encouraging words," and slip in some important "change" while they are still listening.
- **Direct the athlete's attention.** Facilitate learning by focusing athletes' attention on the critical aspects of the technique or tactic. Stress the key points to be learned. They might focus on nonessential elements if left to themselves.
- **Use performance cues.** Performance cues are key words or phrases that describe the entire activity. They direct the athletes' attention to the most essential elements of the skill and help them remember it in a very efficient way. Each coach must determine the performance cues necessary to teach the six volleyball skills.
- **Use positive word corrections.** Say "do this" rather than "don't do that." Ask for what you want rather than what you want to avoid. Focus on the new behavior to replace the old, rather than focusing on the problem.
- **Avoid tentativeness.** Be positive that your suggestion is correct. Say "do this," and sell them on the reason it will work. Don't say "try this," with the connotation that it might not be successful.
- **Say what you mean.** Communicate specifically what you want athletes to know. Avoid backhand compliments or sarcasm. They are often misunderstood.
- **If it needs to be said, say it.** Resist the temptation to hold back criticism for fear of offending players, especially very talented players or friends. Be persistent. Continue repeating the correction until a change has been made.
- **Avoid sounding like a broken record.** Repetitive corrections begin to fall on deaf ears. Search for new ways to say the same things when you have to repeat corrections.
- **Vary the amount of "criticism" or "corrections" for each individual.** Excessive criticism can interfere with learning and motivation. What is considered excessive varies with the individual. Some players can take more criticism and still continue to learn or play well. Give the athlete some breathing room, but after several attempts without a change, restate the correction.
- **Be generous in praise.** Reinforce good technique, tactics attitude, and effort. Learning is enhanced when team members feel good about the experience. Say something positive each day to each player. Give both verbal and nonverbal praise, such as smiles, applause, a pat on the back, or a high five.

MAXIM: Reach down and lift others up. It's the best exercise you can get.

- **Provide frequent feedback about performance and behavior.** Teach players right from wrong technically, tactically, and behaviorally through immediate feedback. Players do best when given feedback about their progress. The younger and less experienced the athlete, the more reinforcement is required.

- **Instructional feedback is more valuable than pure encouragement.** Say "good extension on the spike," rather than "awesome spike." Athletes are motivated by encouraging words, but alone they do not give the information necessary to make improvements in their game.
- **Specific information is more effective than general information.** Say "Your right arm penetrated over the net on the block, but your left arm did not," rather than "Penetrate on the block." Let players know specifically what was good or bad about the action and give them direction on specifically what they must do the next time to perform correctly.
- **Individual feedback is more effective than general information to all athletes.** Group feedback is good, but not at the expense of precise feedback to each individual. One-on-one communication is always the most effective. In a group setting, athletes often are not paying attention to what is being said. When you talk directly to an individual, that player knows that the information is for his or her direct benefit.
- **Immediate reinforcement is more productive than delayed reinforcement.** Give feedback immediately on good or bad performances or behavior. Do not delay the information until a break or after practice.
- **Enhance feedback with "feedforward."** Provide instructional reminders just before the athlete executes the skill. *For example:* Yell out "reach high" in a hitting drill moments before the contact. In this method, players focus at the correct time on a key aspect of performance.
- **Design drills that give players feedback.** Carefully establish drill goals that give immediate feedback to players without the need for the coach to be present. *For example:* Place tape or cones to designate the target area for the attack down the line. Without targets, the zone can be narrow or wide according to the individual's perception. A hard hit at the angle might be very impressive in other circumstances but in this drill would not be considered successful because it did not go down the line within the cones.
- **Check the athlete's "hear-back and see-back."** Check their comprehension of what was taught. Keep it simple at first by asking questions that require only a yes–no, either–or, or correct–incorrect response. Follow these single response questions with multiple options and short answers. Ask players to repeat and/or paraphrase what you have said. Ask them to describe the skill and repeat important verbal cues. Ask them how their technique compared with the demonstration and explanations. Ask them to describe what they are doing technically or tactically and what they need to do. They must be aware of what they are doing in order to learn and/or to make changes.

Other Methodology Considerations

Whole vs. Part (Progressions).   A combination of the whole–part method can be very effective in teaching motor skills. Generally, it is best for players to see, attempt, and explore the technique or tactic first in its entirety before it is broken into parts. The parts may have meaning only if athletes see them as a part of the whole picture. Break the skill down into specific focal points to isolate for corrections or emphasize a point. In situations where there exists an inherent danger—for example, teaching the roll or dive—it might be best to work on the independent parts first, but return as quickly as possible to the whole.

Random vs. Blocked.   Random training that introduces the variables that occur in the game transfers best. Block training is effective for teaching the specifics of each variable, but then you should quickly return to unpredictable patterns. *For example:* Block training would be when you initiate the ball to the setter, and all tosses originate from the same place on the court and are directed to the same target. In random training, you vary the origination position of the toss as well as direct the ball to various locations along and off the net.

Massed vs. Distributed.   Distributed practice tends to be more effective than massed practice. A block of time in massed training is spent on a single skill, whereas, in distributed training, the block includes periods of rest or other skills. *For example:* In mass training players would practice serving for 30 minutes straight. Distributed practice would alternate ten minutes of defense with ten minutes of serving until each skill has been practiced for 30 minutes.

Individual vs. Group.   Individualize practice whenever possible by practicing in small groups of one to four players. Athletes are very motivated in individual sessions because the lesson is specific to their needs and the coach is directly involved. Athletes are able to accomplish a great deal in a short period of time with this individual attention.

Specific vs. General.   Athletes do not always see the relationship between individual practice drills and game situations. Therefore, it is very important to practice skills in relation to their use in the game. The closer the practice simulates the use of the skills technically and tactically in the game, the more meaningful it is to the athletes, and the more often transfer occurs.

FACTOR 6: COOPERATION

Everyone must do his or her part to make practices successful. The better the cooperation, the higher the achievement levels. Successful teams talk in terms of *we* and *us*. They know that success relies on teamwork and that only by working together can they reach their full potential.

It Is Not Coach and Player—It Is a Team

The coach is not a separate entity, but an integral member of the team. Making practice a success is a collective effort. It is your responsibility to plan and manage the practice, and the athlete's responsibility to respond to it positively. The process must be harmonious.

Improvement Is a Shared Responsibility

You and the athletes work together sharing ideas and exploring ways to improve performance. It is your responsibility to teach the techniques, tactics, and behaviors necessary to be successful, and the athletes' responsibility to learn and apply the knowledge in the appropriate situations. It is your responsibility to evaluate and correct performance, and the players' responsibility to do their best to make the changes. It is the athletes' responsibility to hold on to corrections so they do not need to be repeated over and over.

Encourage Athletes to Be Independent Learners

It is the responsibility of athletes to take an active role in their own improvement, that is, to coach themselves and self-correct. Train athletes to analyze their own performance based on the resulting actions. *For example:* The floater serve is performed at a speed where athletes have the ability to easily self-analyze their mechanics. They receive further information from their follow-through and the flight of the ball. Utilizing this information, players can determine what, if any, changes are necessary for a better serve. They should ask themselves questions such as:

- Where did the ball go?
- Did the ball spin? In which direction?
- Is my weight forward or back?
- Did my arm follow-through straight or across my body?

A tactical example is if a player tips the ball and it is recovered. The player should ask him- or herself questions such as:

- Did I tip in the correct location according to the defensive alignment?
- Did they make an exceptional save or did I execute poorly technically or tactically?
- What is a better option tactically?

Your feedback is always important, but athletes who are aware of their own body movements and utilize the results of their action can improve their techniques and tactics at a much faster pace.

Athletes Must Be Willing to Accept Coaching

You can work only with those who want to work with you. Players, no matter how good they are, must be ready to learn or no learning will take place. They cannot assume it will not work or that there is not a better way to do it. They must be receptive to input and have a positive feeling of trust and respect for their coaches. They must believe their coaches can help. If athletes are not willing to cooperate, you are helpless.

> **MAXIM:** *Minds are like parachutes. They function when they are open.* James Dewar

---

Team Members Must Demand the Best from Their Teammates

If players are not giving their best effort, it is the responsibility of coaches and teammates to inform them that it is not acceptable. Players are dependent on one another. One individual's success or failure is based on another's, and only with everyone's support will the team reach its potential. You must let players know when they need to work harder, but—just as important—teammates must insist upon it. Players have an extraordinary influence on each other.

Team Members Must Have Shared Goals and Mutual Respect

Teams perform best when they have shared goals. The goals must be clear and everyone must be committed to them. It is helpful to have good relationships with teammates off the court, but it is not necessary for success. Teammates do not have to like each other, but they must be united in their efforts on the court, interact positively, and respect each other's contributions. You must help blend the egos into a successfully functioning group.

Communication Is a Shared Responsibility

Players and coaches have the obligation and responsibility to bring up important individual and team issues and discuss them openly and honestly. They should share information, exchange ideas, listen to each other, and respond to each other's needs with productive rather than destructive communication habits.

Success Requires Mutual Support and Understanding

All team members must give their unconditional support in both the good and the bad times. It is most critical to stand together during times of adversity when encouragement is most necessary. The true test of the team is during times of conflict.

Success Requires Shared Evaluation

Coaches and athletes together must reflect on practice and game experiences, successes and failures, and analyze what has been learned. If the experiences are not examined, you lose the opportunity to learn from them.

MAXIM: *The will to win is important, but the will to prepare is vital.* Joe Paterno

---

DRILL ADMONITIONS

Have a Purpose for Each Drill

The purpose of drills is to develop and improve the athlete's individual and team skills. Consider specifically what must be accomplished and then select or design drills that address these needs. There are no magical drills, only drills that are effective or not effective for a particular situation.

Make the Purpose Clear

Athletes learn best when they clearly understand the purpose and relevance of the drill. Clearly explain the significance of each drill within the realm of the game. Spend sufficient time explaining its purpose, goals, and focal points the first few times the drill is used. Never assume that the athlete understands the benefits of the activity.

Make Drills Team-Specific

Drills must be specific to the team's personnel, experience level, and desired goals. Utilize drills that are appropriate to your particular team.

Make Drills Game-Specific

Drills that best simulate the game transfer most successfully. Practice with players in their proper court positions, performing the exact movements, sequences, and speeds that are desired in the game. Incorporate all game communciations. (See court talk later in this chapter.) Create game-like emotions through competitive drills with winner and losers.

Train Anaerobic and Aerobic Systems

The action of volleyball is intermittent. An average match lasts one and a half hours but varies from 45 minutes to three hours or more. The average duration of a rally is 7–10 seconds. The average time between rallies lasts about 15–50 seconds depending on the use of the three-ball system. An average game lasts 15–30 minutes. Timeouts are about one minute, substitutions last 20–30 seconds, and time between games is three minutes. Work:rest ratios in the games averages about 1:3.

This information should be incorporated into practices. A guideline would be to have short but very intensive, high-quality exercises with maximum effort for about one minute followed by three to four minutes of rest. Generally there are teams of 12 players and drills can be organized working with three groups of four players or four groups of three to achieve 1:3 or 1:4 work:rest ratios. One group works while the other actively rests while shagging balls for teammates.

Always Use Antennae

A team should never practice without antennae on the net and in the proper location. Players have to become aware of the court boundaries.

Always Use Targets

Incorporate a target into every drill. Players must always strive to direct the ball to the proper location, that is, pass and dig toward the pass target, set toward an attacker, and serve and attack to a specific spot on the court.

Make Drills "Live"

Do less 2's partner drills and more 3's, which offer better game angles. Do more pass, set, and hit drills and less single skills drills. Do more "actual play" drills with 2 vs. 2, 3 vs. 3, 4 vs. 4, 5 vs. 5, or 6 vs. 6, teaching athletes to perform in the context of the game.

Integrate All Game Components into Drills

Integrate the technical, tactical, and emotional aspects of the game into drills and scrimmages. Avoid training the mental and the physical separately. Make tactical training practical rather than theoretical. Incorporate all desired attitudes and habits.

Make Drills Stimulating

Most learning takes place when drills are interesting, fun, and challenging. Repetition is necessary for learning, but monotony is the most common reason for failure. Do not do drills to the point of staleness. Make slower drills interesting through the use of goals and competitions. Vary the drills, the order of drills, and the drill goals to make practices different each day.

Make Most Drills Short

Research indicates that athletes learn most effectively when drills are short and there is sufficient time for rest. There is an optimal time for every drill, but this number varies with each drill and each group. In general terms, a drill lasts between 10–20 minutes. Too little time does not allow learning to take place, and too much leads to fatigue, a lack of concentration, and ineffective repetitions. Keep the activity short and then repeat it with a slight variation. Monitor carefully the athlete's attention span and work levels.

Make Some Drills Long

Provide the athlete with some opportunities to endure longer drills to develop a sustained concentration level and mental toughness. At times, it is critical that the athlete can grind out a drill for the mental skills necessary for a long, tough match.

Maintain Appropriate Tempos

Successful drills maintain tempos that are conducive to the learning level of the athletes. Too fast or too slow and the athlete accomplishes nothing. The majority of drills should be performed at game speeds. A slow tempo is useful in early learning phases. A fast tempo functions as an intense, rapid-fire overload that gives athletes many contacts in a short time with the focus on attitude and effort as much as it is on results. Avoid fast-tempo drills that are done at the expense of the athletes doing the skills correctly.

Do Some Continuous Tempo Drills

Get the most out of the time you have with the athletes. Continuous tempo drills combine game speed with rapid-fire. A drill or scrimmage is made continuous by initiating a new ball immediately after the previous ball is down, giving athletes very little "dead" time and lots of contacts. You (or a player who is not in the drill) can introduce the ball in a variety of ways: with a serve, toss, or hit. You can recreate tactical game situations as well as create stress and fatigue to work through a variety of game difficulties.

Make Drills Efficient

Players learn best when they participate actively. Maximize the number of contacts and repetitions and regulate the work to rest ratio.

- Have a sufficient number of balls. One ball to every two athletes is a minimum, but more is definitely better so that less time is spent collecting them.
- Have a sufficient number of ball carts for ball storage during drills and additional ones for ball retrieval.
- Use as many players as possible in drills rather than rotating players in and out.
- Avoid situations where players are watching others perform while waiting for long periods of time for their opportunity to participate.
- Avoid having players waste time between contacts by walking in drills or collecting balls.
- Divide the team into smaller groups to gain higher contact per minute ratios.
- Avoid lengthy discussions and explanations.
- Avoid disrupting the group to make individual corrections. Call the individual to the side and give suggestions on how to do it better. Stop the game only to make comments that apply to everyone.
- Give drills a descriptive name to reduce the amount of time necessary to introduce the activity.

> **MAXIM:** *Make athletes directly responsible for the outcome of the drill. The larger the group, the less obvious it is who is contributing and who is not.*

Individualize Drills

Players learn best when teaching is "individulized." Consider whether the drill is necessary for the entire team or is more applicable for specific players. Do drills on an individual need basis. Not all individuals or groups need to work on the same drill or have the same goals. Group combinations change depending on the drill emphasis. Individual goals are given to the degree of difficulty that it will be challenging. Stronger players need higher numbers of successful contacts.

Provide Sufficient Repetitions

Break the game down (breakdown drills) into its smaller parts where specifics of the game can be isolated and repeated many times. These segments are more productive than larger group drills or scrimmages because the athlete can focus on a specific skill, situation, or tactic that otherwise might only occur in a scrimmage one or two times, if ever.

> **MAXIM:** *If doing something everyday was all that was needed, everyone's handwriting would be perfect.*

Monitor Drills to Maintain Quality

To develop quality, monitor drills to teach what you want. Stop drills to regain concentration, intensity, and purpose. Modify drills, immediately or by the next practice, that are not working, whether they are too difficult, too easy, or simply are not accomplishing the intended goals. "Kill" drills that are "wasting" the athlete's time.

Make Drills Progressive

Progress from simple to complex. Progress from a single focus of a technique or tactic to a multiple focus. Progress from an easy training situation to more difficult ones.

Require Success

Most learning occurs when the athletes are successful. Drills must be sufficiently challenging to command athletes' attention, but commensurate with their ability. Drill complexity and difficulty should increase as a successful level of consistency is achieved.

Redefine Success

Athletes must concentrate as much on the process as the results. Define success as "effort and heart" striving for the goal. The desired results cannot always be achieved, but the only possibility of reaching these goals is through effort. If athletes do not reach their immediate goals, emphasize what they have gained by striving for them.

Hold Players Responsible to Complete the Assigned Task

When the going gets tough, allow athletes the opportunity to work through their frustration to find a way to be successful. Never say "Okay, that one counts," when it was not a successful contact. Push players physically and mentally to find their limits. It is a disservice to let players off the hook by lessening the intensity of the drill.

Redefine Success in Some Drills in Terms of Attitude and Effort

Drill goals are generally designed to be attainable and guarantee success. In coach-oriented drills, you facilitate these successes through accurate tossing, serving, and spiking at speeds and distances geared to the players' abilities. In the real world, there are no guarantees of success. Train athletes to have a positive fighting spirit. They must be willing to take the risk of giving their all and losing because it is the only chance they have of becoming their best and winning.

MAXIM: Success can only be purchased on the installment plan.

Make Drills Measurable

All drills must have measurable criteria that must be met to complete the drill. These termination points may be based on the following scoring systems:

- **Timed or at the coach's discretion.** The drill is performed for a specific time or as long as you feel it is necessary to accomplish the desired goal. This focuses on skill or tactic development and improvement rather than on performance results. This type of termination point does not have successful performance results built into the drill.
- **Number of contacts or attempts.** The athlete has a specific number of attempts to perform the skill and receives feedback on his or her success rate by recording the number of successful contacts out of the total attempts.
- **Number of successful contacts.** Set the standard for success. Successful contacts build quality into the drill. The athlete's focus is on accumulating a specific number of successful results to complete the drill (get five to get out). Initial goal numbers are selected by trial and error and adjustments are made after a series of drills have been completed. The athlete also can select the goal he or she wants to strive for.
- **Number of consecutive successful contacts.** Consecutive successful contacts help the athlete develop not only quality but also consistency in effort and focus. The athlete needs a series of successful contacts to complete the goal. *For example:* The athlete must attack the ball successfully five times in a row to gain one big point and accumulate a total of two big points.
- **Number of plus–minus successful contacts.** The goal is to complete a successful number of contacts individually or as a group, adding one for a successful contact or subtracting one for an error. The exercise terminates when the goal is reached. Emphasis is placed on successful contacts while reducing errors. *For example:* An individual must serve +5 to the target. One point is scored for each ball to the target and one is subtracted for each serve error. A serve that is in the court but not to the target is considered neutral. Bonus points can be given for jump serves and penalty points can be given for serves that touch the net.
- **Cooperative drills vs. scoring drills.** Cooperative drills encourage working together on one or both sides of the net to achieve a goal. *For example:* 2 with 2 is a drill where both teams work to play the ball back and forth over the net ten times consecutively. Both sides win when the goal is reached. This drill is not the same as 2 vs. 2 where the teams are competing against one another to score points. Cooperative drills empahsize good ball handling and consistency.
- **Competitive drills with winners and losers.** The final score of the drill determines the winner(s) and loser(s) and there are positive and negative consequences of the result. Losers must do some form of "additional conditioning." Players must learn to deal with and be responsible for their individual successes and failures as well as that of the team.
- **Competitive drills with the "wash" concept.** On each play in the "wash" concept, there are three possible options: win, lose, or wash in which no one wins the point. In this system, points are awarded not for a single effort but for consecutive successes. If one player or team receives one point and the opponent(s) receives the other, one success "washes" out the other. No point is scored by either side and the drill begins again. Concentration and effort is rewarded not

always by winning points, but by stopping the opponent from earning one. A consistent high level of performance is demanded for success.

Almost any drill can be adapted and enhanced by utilizing the "wash" concept (created by Bill Neville, former USA National Team Coach). Any number of consecutive points can be utilized. The concept is that a specific number of "little" points must be scored consecutively to earn a "big" point. When a team wins a specific number of "big" points, it wins the game.

For example: It takes two "little" points to win one "big" point and it takes three big points to win the game. One team must win two points consecutively to win a big point. If one team wins the first rally and the opponent wins the second rally, it is a "wash" and no point is scored. The one point "washes" out the other and the rally begins again.

Handicaps can be used to equalize the competition. *For example:* One team must score three points consecutively and the other team only two. Additionally, the coach leading the drill can initiate the ball in a more difficult manner to the winning side or easier to the side that is attempting to catch up. The coach can continue to direct the ball to the losing side, giving it the first opportunity to score.

MAXIM: What we hope to do with ease, we must first learn to do with diligence.

Collect and Organize Drills

- **Acquire drills.** Develop a base of drills from as many resources as possible, copying some and modifying others to fit the team's needs. Then expand upon these drills by creating new ones.
- **Develop a core of drills for each team.** It is not necessary to have hundreds of different drills, but to select a "core" of drills that meet the requirements of the team. Once this core group has been selected, adaptations to these drills can be made by modifying some aspect of the drill and/or varying its goals.
- **Develop a drill file.** Record all drills on 3 by 5 cards and file them for future reference. Give each drill a descriptive or memorable nickname to identify it and utilize this name each time the drill is used in the practice. Indicate the drill purpose, goals, tempo, and measurement. Record any changes made to the drill.

Categorize Drills

- **Movement drills:** Model footwork patterns and skill mechanics without the ball.
- **Ballhandling drills:** Setting and passing work to develop ball control.
- **Individual skill drills:** This includes the serve, pass, set, floor defense, attack, and block.
- **Combination skill drills:** Individual skills performed together in a game sequence.
- **Team system drills:** Side-out offense (serve receive to attack), team defense, and transition offense (attack from the dig, block, free ball, attack coverage, and no block).
- **Position drills:** Specialization work by position for the setter, middle blocker, right and left side attackers, and defensive specialists.
- **Actual play drills:** Ballhandling to competitive games in small groups (2's, 3's, 4's, 5's) or with teams of six.

- **Toughness drills:** Drills that physically, mentally, and/or emotionally overload players, placing them in stressful situations. Train athletes to have the mental discipline needed to play tough games.
- **Comeback drills:** Train players to go after the win even though the obstacles seem insurmountable. Teach them that although a win is not always possible, there is only one way it is possible and that is to fight to the finish.
- **Close-out drills:** Drills that provide athletes with opportunities to close out matches when they are ahead.
- **Conditioning drills:** Drills that physically overload players.

MAXIM: Push athletes, but don't break them.

PRACTICE WORKSHEET GUIDELINES

See the sample worksheets on pages 240 through 244.

Team Meeting (2–3 Minutes)

Begin every practice with a short informational meeting. Make general announcements and give a quick overview of the practice. Indicate specific goals to be accomplished and sell the players on the need for what is being taught and practiced. If the practice follows a match, review game highs and lows and what will be done specifically to address these issues.

MAXIM: The more meaningful the practice is perceived, the more motivated the athlete.

Warm-Up Phase (10–15 Minutes)

The warm-up serves as a transition from the athlete's other activities to volleyball. It is a physical as well as a mental preparation. Focus athletes' attention on volleyball and get them in the proper state of mind to practice.

The content and duration of the warm-up depends on the first main task. If the first activity is serving, only an upper body warm-up is necessary. After serving practice, a more complete warm-up would follow.

The warm-up is progressive, transitioning from nonactivity to maximum effort. It should be short, efficient, and volleyball-specific. (Do not confuse the warm-up with physical conditioning.) Avoid spending more time than necessary warming-up. The majority of time must be spent practicing the actual game skills.

Body Warming (2–5 Minutes). Do some type of nonstop movement progression to increase blood flow to the muscles and increase the core body temperature: low intensity jogging, volleyball movement patterns, or light ballhandling.

Stretching (10 Minutes).   It is critical to raise the core body temperature before stretching. This translates to less chance of injury and more likelihood of increased range of motion.

The goal of stretching is to attain functional flexibility or range of motion (ROM) in a particular joint, so muscles can work at their optimal efficiency. The ROM in each body part is different, and every sport has its own particular requirements for flexibility. Do stretching (functional ROM work) that specifically prepares the athlete for the activity of volleyball.

It is important to stretch the *muscles,* not the tendons and ligaments. Emphasize static rather than ballistic (bouncing) stretching. Also, emphasize a slow and progressive stretch to the limit of movement, *to tension,* but not to the point of pain. Hold 15–30 seconds.

Transition Phase

Many debates exist on the subject of active versus passive stretching and warm-up. A traditional passive stretching/range-of-motion routine is provided. Some coaches prefer to reduce the emphasis on stretching and begin an immediate transition with dynamic movements and work with the ball. More information is available from the National Strength and Conditioning Association at *http://www.nsca-lift.org,* the National Athletic Trainers Association at *http://www.nata.org,* and the Conditioning Press at *http://performancecondition.com.*

Dynamic Movements and Cardiovascular Work.   Incorporate game footwork and movement patterns into the warm-up. Model approach routes and attack, block footwork patterns along the net and blocks, defensive footwork patterns, and emergency moves on the court. Give the athlete the opportunity to work on movement fundamentals and, at the same time, physically prepare for practice.

Work with the Ball.   Ballhandling warm-ups vary from partner passing to actual play. Once athletes warm up the shoulders, it is popular to play a variety of mini-games in 2's, 3's, or 4's. This is not only part of the progression of warm-up, but another opportunity to work on specific fundamentals or game tactics.

Principal Phase (1–2 Hours)

The main part of the practice emphasizes one or more of the following areas.

Individual Skills.   This includes the serve, pass, set, attack, block, and floor defense. Create an attitude for the importance of fundamentals. Basic movement and technique are the backbone of the game at the beginning as well as the advanced levels. Fundamentals win games and, in every drill, emphasis must be placed on sound execution.

> *MAXIM: 'Tis harder to unlearn than learn.* Proverb

Team Skills and Tactics.   This includes the side-out offense (team serve receive to attack) and the transition defense (attack from the dig, from the block, from attack coverage, from the free ball, and from a no block). Team skills can be done in small groups or in 6's.

Position Work. This includes specialization work by position for the setter, middle blocker, outside hitters, and defensive specialists.

Actual Play. Emphasis is on doing drills in "live" situations, in small groups or in 6's.

Conditioning Phase (15 Minutes)

An efficient practice conditions athletes for the game within the drills during the principal phase of the practice. Additional conditioning will augment this and can include a variety of exercises or stations, such as, sprints, sit-ups, push-ups, repetitive defense work, repetitive rapid hitting, hitting or blocking with a weight belt, bench blasts, rope jumping, and so on.

Cool-Down Phase (5–10 Minutes)

It is important to gradually decrease the level of intensity of the workout. The cool-down provides the best opportunity to increase the ROM (flexibility) through stretching and reduce the potential of muscle soreness. Serving can also be used at the end of practice in a progression to slow down from strenuous work.

Closing Phase (3–5 Minutes)

A final team meeting concludes practice with additional announcements, evaluations, visualization work, a team huddle, and cheer. Ask athletes periodically to self-evaluate their effort levels. On a scale of 1–10, with 10 being the highest, ask, "How hard did you practice today?" Only the athletes themselves know if they have given their best. Consistently monitor the effectiveness of practice.

Coach's Evaluation

Immediately following practice, the coaching staff further evaluates the practice by discussing the following questions:

- How effective was the practice plan?
- Did we meet today's technical, tactical, and behavioral goals?
- What was successful and what was not? What can be improved?
- Which drills were successful and which ones should we eliminate or adjust?
- Did the players give 100 percent? If not, how can we motivate them?
- What do individuals and/or the team need to do to continue to improve and reach our goals?
- What future practice suggestions do we have?

Practice Worksheet:
INDIVIDUAL PRACTICE

Date:_____

Time	Activity	Description & Focus

Practice Worksheet:
BLOCK PLAN–QUANTITY

Dates:_____

Indicate focus and quantity of practice: ◯ = Heavy △ = Medium ☐ = Light X = None						
Skills	Practice 1	Practice 2	Practice 3	Practice 4	Practice 5	Practice 6
Serve						
Overhand & Underhand Pass						
Set						
Serve Receive						
Attack						
Block						
Defense						
Side-out Offense						
Transition Offense						
Team Defense						
Conditioning						

Practice Worksheet:
BLOCK PLAN–CONTENT

Focus/Content	Date	Focus/Content	Date	Focus/Content	Date

Focus/Content	Date	Focus/Content	Date	Focus/Content	Date

VOLLEYBALL PRACTICE WORKSHEET

Date:	Time:	Equipment:

ANNOUNCEMENTS

TRAINING EMPHASIS & GOALS

WARM-UP & TRANSITION PHASE

PRINCIPAL PHASE: (individual and team skills)

	Drill name, description, and focus

VOLLEYBALL PRACTICE WORKSHEET
(Continued)

	Drill name, description, and focus

CONDITIONING & COOL-DOWN PHASE

CLOSING COMMENTS & PRACTICE EVALUATION

SAMPLE WARM-UP ROUTINE

Begin range-of-motion exercises only after the body is warm. (See Figure 12-1.) Hold each position to tension, not pain, for a count of 15–30 seconds. Do not bounce. Individuals can perform the exercises at their own pace or the group can work together with an exercise leader.

1. **Lateral dig lunge** (inner thigh). Stretch one leg out to the side and place the knee of the other leg on the floor. Feel the tension on the inner thigh. Hold.

2. **Forward dig lunge** (quad and groin). Lunge forward imitating a giant step to the ball. Place the hands on the ground and hold or place hands and elbows on floor, reaching in a digging motion. Hold.

3. **Side twist lunge** (outer side of the leg and hip). Continue from the forward dig lunge position and twist the body to the side of the bent leg and point the toes and knees outward. Hold.

4. **Spine twist** (lower back and hips). Continue from the side twist lunge directly into the spine twist. Extend one leg forward and step over the opposite knee. Twist the trunk toward the lateral side of the bent knee. Hold.

5. **Quadriceps.** Lie on your side. Grasp the top foot with the same side hand and slowly raise the leg, drawing the heel to the buttocks, not by pulling it, but by pressing it up and back into the hand until a stretch is felt. Hold.

6. **Butterfly** (groin). Sit upright with the soles of the feet together. Place the elbows on the inside portion of the upper legs with the palms over the ankles. Gently press the knees down to the floor and hold.

7. **Modified hurdler** (hamstrings). Sit upright with one leg straight and one leg bent and flat on the floor. The heel of the bent leg touches the inner side of the extended leg. The toes of the straight leg are flexed back toward the body and the hamstrings and quadriceps are engaged. Keep the spine straight and lean forward until tension is felt. Hold.

8. **Hamstrings.** Lie on your back with both knees flexed and the feet flat on the floor. With one hand behind the knee, slowly extend and raise the leg toward the head until a stretch is felt. Hold. For more stretch, move the hands up toward the ankle. *Never lock the knee.*

9. **Knee hugs** (back). Lie on your back with the legs straight. Keep the back of your head on the floor. Pull one knee toward the chest. Hold. Then pull the knee across the body toward the opposite shoulder. Hold. Repeat drawing both legs to the chest. Hold.

10. **Lying spine twist** (lower back, buttocks, and hips). Lie flat on your back with the legs extended and shoulders flat on the floor. Flex one leg 90 degrees and raise it to the chest. Grasp the knee with one hand and pull it across the body and press it toward the floor until tension is felt. Keep the head and shoulders flat on the floor and turn the head to look in the opposite direction. Hold.

11. **Standing V calf stretch.** Position the body with the hands and feet on the floor and the buttocks in the air. Alternate pressing the right and then left heel to the floor, extending and bending the leg respectively.

12. **Shoulder stretch.** In a kneeling position, extend both arms out and place the palms on the floor. Press the shoulders down. Hold. Repeat with one arm at a time, crossing it beyond your midline. Hold.

13. **Arm triad** (arms and shoulders). (A) Flex and raise one arm overhead next to the ear with the hand resting on the shoulder blade. Grasp the elbow with the opposite hand. Gently pull the elbow behind the head. (B) Pull the elbow across to the opposite side. (C) Place the arm in front and gently push the elbow across the chest to the opposite shoulder. Turn the head in the opposite direction of the stretch.

14. **Player's personal favorite.**

Figure 12–1. Warm-Up Routine

SAMPLE COOL-DOWN PARTNER ROUTINE

KEY: Partners' communication is critical to avoid injury.

See Figure 12-2.

1. **Standing quadriceps.** Support your body by balancing yourself with one hand on your partner' shoulder. Hold your foot with the same side hand and slowly raise the leg, not by pulling it, but by pressing it up with the heel toward the buttocks and back into the hand until a stretch is felt.

2. **The heart** (shoulders and back). Place your right foot next to your partner's left foot or vice versa. Grasp your partner's hands and pull away from one another, stretching outward and bending from the side of the body.

3. **The wrestler** (shoulders and back). Place your hands on your partner's shoulders. You and your partner lean forward and gently press down and hold. Repeat turning toward the right and the left.

4. **Trunk twist** (upper back and shoulders). Sit comfortably with the arms clasped behind the head. Your partner stands behind you and reaches under your arms to gently lift and twist your body to the right and left.

5. **Knees in the back** (back and shoulders). Sit comfortably with the arms clasped behind the head. Your partner weaves his or her hands over and under your arms, places his or her own hands on the knees, and gently pushes knees into your back.

6. **Shoulder stretch.** Stand or kneel on the floor with the arms extended behind the body. Your partner is positioned directly behind you, holding your wrists, and gently lifts your arms backward, upward, and crisscross. Hold the stretch.

7. **Back and hamstrings.** Sit with the legs extended with your partner standing behind you. Your partner presses with both hands on the central portion of the back. You bend forward at the waist and allow your partner to assist you in pushing your upper body onto your thighs. Repeat with the legs in a straddle position.

8. **Modified hurdler** (hamstrings). Sit in a modified hurdler position with the extended leg against the partner's flexed leg and interlock hands. Maintain an erect spine, bend forward at the waist, and lower your trunk toward the thigh as your partner leans backward and pulls gently on your hands. Hold the stretch.

Figure 12–2. Cool-Down Routine

PRESEASON PRACTICE CHECKLIST

Complete this checklist prior to the first game of the season.

General

❏ Fill out the necessary form such as player and media information, health histories, insurance, medical release, and eligibility.

❏ Issue team policy, player contracts, and team play books.

❏ Select overall team captain and court captain.

❏ Select exercise leader and give instruction on desired warm-up procedures.

❏ Schedule player session on volleyball rules and rules test.

❏ Schedule written player knowledge test on the team offensive and defensive formations, and individual and team tactics.

❏ Teach how to take and interpret game and practice statistics.

❏ Teach how to officiate and be line judges.

❏ Teach how to talk to the media.

❏ Teach healthy life choices (nutrition, eating disorders, alcohol and drug abuse).

❏ Teach how to tape basic injuries of ankles, fingers, and so on.

❏ Schedule video sessions to see instructional tapes and competitions of top teams.

❏ Teach player communication skills, time management, study skills, dealing with stress, and so on.

❏ Teach players how to prepare individually prior to the match.

❏ Teach game procedures for warm-up, substitutions, timeouts, and regulations for the bench.

❏ Teach how to set up and take down nets, including antennae.

❏ Teach proper behavior and sportsmanship.

❏ Issue practice and game uniforms and kneepads.

❏ Invite local media, boosters, and parents to attend games and observe practices.

❏ Invite parents, boosters, and media to attend a BBQ/chalk talk to promote volleyball and the team.

Conditioning

❏ Evaluate each player's overall aerobic and anaerobic fitness and strength levels.

❏ Goal: All players in necessary condition to compete successfully.

Practice Fundamentals

❏ Teach practice skills for coach-oriented drills.

❏ Teach players how to hand a ball to the coach on the hip.

❏ Teach players how to bounce the ball to the coach so it ends up at waist height.

❏ Teach players how to shag efficiently individually and as a team.

❏ Teach players how to toss two-handed and one-handed.
❏ Teach players practice and game communications.
❏ Teach players how to practice with all-out effort.

Individual Skills Fundamentals

❏ Teach all players all positions to give them a better understanding of the game.
❏ Teach the basics of how to anticipate what will happen in the game based on reading cues.
❏ Teach mechanics and movement patterns for the six basic skills.

Serve

❏ Teach the mechanics of the serve.
❏ Teach placements to the six serving zones.
❏ Teach game signals for zones.
❏ *Goal:* Keep "misses" within the 1-foot error limit, that is, serving deep or wide by one foot.
❏ *Goal:* Serve tough and consistently to at least two targets.

Serve Receive

❏ Teach the technical aspects of the pass for serve reception. Indicate the specific pass target and the height and tempo of the pass.
❏ *Goal:* Reduce the number of "shanks," or opponent's serve aces. Keep the serve in play.
❏ *Goal:* Serve receive to the target with an average of 2.3 or better on a 3.0 scale.

Set

❏ Teach all players to set high, with a "hand set" or forearm set to zones 2 and 4 from various positions on the court.
❏ Teach all players to set high forward or back from zone 3.
❏ Teach the setter to set high and quick set options and when to use each tactical option.
❏ Teach the setter to set hitable balls with few ballhandling errors on any pass within his or her reach.
❏ Teach the setter to set the ball one to two feet off the net on "out of system" passes, allowing the attacker to hit around or off a solid block.

Individual Floor Defense

❏ Teach individual defense movements and mechanics for the run-through, dig, dig variations, and emergency skills.
❏ Teach to focus on "getting the ball up" and to the target.
❏ Teach an aggressive and positive attitude toward defense.
❏ Teach to always make a supreme effort for every ball.

Attack

❏ Teach the mechanics of the attack for high and quick sets.
❏ Teach the footwork patterns and routes for the approach from zones 4, 3, 2, and back row.

❑ Teach how to vertically and horizontally attack with power, off-speed, tip, and off the block.

❑ Teach tactical applications of each option.

❑ Teach attack placements to each zone of the court, or in general terms, angle, line, and corners.

❑ Teach a variety of attack options against a well-formed solid block. Teach the attacker to go after the ball hard, but with a smart option.

❑ *Goal:* Develop at least one consistent attack option that can be successfully placed seven out of ten times to the target with a tossed ball or controlled set.

❑ *Goal:* Work toward a team attack percentage of 25–30 percent.

❑ *Goal:* Good teamwork between the setter and quick attacker on first-tempo attacks.

Block

❑ Teach the mechanics of the block and block footwork, reading the cues, positioning, and tactical block options.

❑ Teach individual and team positioning for first-, second-, and third-tempo sets.

❑ Teach how to set the block and close the block.

❑ *Goal:* Good understanding of basic tactics of positioning, reading, overloading, and committing tactics.

Team Skills

❑ Experiment with offensive and defensive alignments and tactics.

❑ Experiment with player positions and lineups.

❑ Teach switching from original position in the rotation order to specialized positions on offense and defense.

Defense

❑ Teach team back row defense alignments, base positions, individual position responsibilities, and tactical back row adjustments.

❑ Teach team blocking alignments, pinched in or out, setting the block, closing the block, and blocking tactical adjustments.

❑ Teach defense read sequences, movement to and from base positions to dig and block positions.

❑ Teach defense alignments against first-, second-, and third-tempo attacks from zones 2, 3, 4, and back row.

❑ Teach defense alignments against a no block call and free ball.

❑ Teach attack coverage alignments for all positions.

❑ Teach opponent's defense alignments and how to exploit them.

Offense

❑ Clarify height and position of first-, second-, and third-tempo sets.

❑ Teach set language for calling all options.

❑ Clarify offense options and adjustments for in-system and out-of-system passes.

❑ Teach serve receive formations for side-out offense, overlaps, and adjustments.

❑ Teach transition offense options.

❑ Establish preference for receiving the serve and free ball with a "hand" or "forearm" pass.

A PLAYER'S GUIDE TO GETTING THE MOST OUT OF PRACTICE

Formalities

- Inform visitors that they are welcome to attend practices, but are not allowed to talk to or approach the athletes or coaches.
- Do not miss practice or workout sessions. This is *your* and *our* opportunity to improve.
- Do not schedule doctors' appointments or meetings with teachers during practice.

Focus

- Be on time to practice and ready to learn.
- Give your full attention to practice. When the mind wanders, redirect it.
- Do not use practice as a time to socialize. Keep conversations directed to the tasks at hand.

Hustle

- Always hustle. When you do not hustle, expect penalties.
- Do not sit during practice.
- Do not walk in practice. Jog to shag balls, jog to drills, and jog in drills.
- When the coach calls the group to "line up," run to the group meeting place.

Effort

- Play to win in every drill and scrimmage.
- Make effort and results as important to you in practice as in the game.
- Go for every ball. No excuses. No exceptions.
- Make an honest effort for every ball. No token moves.
- Make every moment and every contact count.
- Never compromise. Never do less than your best.
- Demand the best of yourself and your teammates.

Attitude

- No moods or attitudes. Negative attitudes are distracting, waste time, and sap energy.
- Do not show your anger or disappointment by giving half an effort or being moody. If you have a complaint or a suggestion, express it during a break or after practice.
- Challenge yourself to deal with stress and frustration in a positive way. If you cannot take it in practice, you will not be able to take it in the game.
- Avoid negative comments and complaining about practice. Know that *all* training—in the gym, in the weight room, or on the track—will make you a better player.

- Stay enthusiastic no matter the situation. Be positive and motivating to teammates.
- Maintain an attitude that allows you to do your best. Focus on the positive rather than the negative.
- Be enthusiastic. A lot more gets done and it is a lot more fun.
- Contribute to the effort of making each practice a success. If you want to get more out of the practice, put more in.
- At the end of each practice session, ask yourself, "As a result of today's efforts, am I a better player?" If the answer is no, evaluate what changes must be made.
- Believe in yourself and commit yourself to pay the price for success. Strive to be the toughest, the smartest, and the best in every exercise and drill.
- Be patient. It takes time to learn.
- Accept mistakes as part of the learning process. Acknowledge mistakes, learn from them, correct them, and move on.
- Be serious about errors. The times when errors bother you the most are when they are the most important. They should always be important.

Coachable

- Be willing to accept instruction and corrective criticism.
- Take suggestions and criticisms without making excuses.
- Be open to new ideas. The coach cannot change anything that you do not seek to change.
- Do not assume it will not work or it is not a better way to do it.
- Be willing to try anything to make your performance one percent better.
- Push yourself and allow the coaches to push you beyond what is comfortable.
- Listen carefully when the coach talks. Always know what is expected and strive to do it.
- Listen carefully so information is understood and can be applied.
- Listen to corrections given to teammates so that you will not require the same correction.
- Take responsibility for your own improvement. Ask questions and seek information.
- Hold on to corrections so they do not have to be continually repeated.
- Utilize practice to develop a complete game. Do not be satisfied with success in only one or two areas.
- Strive to spend more time working on weaknesses in your game than on the things you do successfully.

Communication

- Communicate with coaches and teammates in a positive way, both visually and verbally.
- Always acknowledge reception of information, both visually or verbally.
- Use game communications in all drills.
- Eliminate the word "can't." "I can't do it because I am not athletic enough." "I can't do it because I am too short."
- Eliminate "I'll try." The statement suggests that it might not work and all that is necessary is a good effort. Don't TRY, DO!
- Think before you speak to avoid thoughtless comments.

GETTING THE MOST
OUT OF YOUR TEAMMATES

Shagging Etiquette

In partner drills, both players shag the ball together. Do not disrupt other teammates' drills by asking them to shag your ball. In group drills, shag with a sense of urgency. Keep the drill safe and keep the drill tempo fast by supplying the coach with balls.

Drill Etiquette

In "live" drills, although it is critical to give teammates your best efforts, it is also important to keep the ball in play to give teammates opportunities to perform. Too many errors slow drill tempo or cause it to stop completely. Focus on not making two errors in a row. If you do, ease up and return to percentage plays and gradually work into tougher performances.

No Coaching, Please!

Do not offer teammates unsolicited advice. You are not the coach and, right or wrong, your teammates may not be interested in your comments. Concentrate on your job and let everyone else concentrate on theirs.

No Demands

Don't tell a teammate, "Give me a pass," or "You've gotta get this serve in." Everyone knows what is necessary and everyone is striving to do his or her best job.

No Negative Messages

"We're playing so bad, if we keep this up we're going to lose . . . they haven't won *yet* . . . we haven't lost *yet* . . ." These messages are annoying and do nothing to make the situation more positive. No "my faults" in obvious situations. Everyone can see who made the error. Do your best not to do it again. In less obvious situations, accept the blame for mistakes that you have made. Do not allow a teammate to take the blame for your error.

Treat Teammates with Respect

Treat teammates as equals, but do not expect them to be exactly like you. Cooperate rather than criticize. Do your part in the effort to maintain a good positive atmosphere. Seek to know and understand teammates and accept and respect their individual differences.

Never Give Up on a Teammate

Never show that you are disappointed or frustrated with a teammate. Getting down on a teammate only makes him or her feel worse and puts more pressure on that player. Take care of teammates emotionally when they are down. Generally, compliment teammates on good plays and give them words of encouragement or a pat on the back on errors. Concentrate on making your teammates better.

Elevate Teammates' Spirits

Pay attention to teammates' verbal and nonverbal signals and learn how your responses can help or detract from their play. Ask teammates how you can help when they are having difficulties. How should you react when they are angry, lose their temper, or are playing poorly? Do they want to be left alone or do they want some encouragement? Think about teammates first; you, second.

Accept Support from Teammates

Always accept support from teammates when you are down and acknowledge their help. Tell teammates how you prefer being treated on the court. If you make an error, how do you want a teammate to respond? Make it easy for teammates to be on the court with you. Create a positive environment around yourself even when you are not playing well.

Call "Mine"

Make it obvious that you will play the ball by calling and moving aggressively to play it. Once you make a move for the ball, go for it. Avoid calling "it's yours." This comment is often misinterpreted and should be utilized only by advanced players who have the experience and understanding of the game to know when it is appropriate.

Stay Connected Between Points

The majority of actual game time is consumed between points. Communicate positively with teammates by reconnecting after each point. Turn toward teammates and say, for example, "Let's go," and/or communicate nonverbally with positive body language, gestures, and eye contact. Do not isolate yourself in your own world. This is a team sport.

Handle Conflict Positively

Small problems grow when allowed to fester under the guise of confidential complaints to close friends. Resolve the problem by talking directly to the teammate involved and do so before it becomes too big to handle.

Push Teammates to Be Their Best

Encourage teammates positively during drills and motivate each other to work hard by giving your best effort. You are not doing your teammate a favor by serving easier so that he or she can finish a receiving drill, or attacking the ball directly to him or her so he or she is able to dig it.

Elevate Teammates' Play

Encourage teammates positively during drills, scrimmages, and games. Acknowledge good plays and good efforts. At the least, the attacker acknowledges the setter and the setter acknowledges the passer. Let them know their efforts are appreciated: "Great dig" or "Way to go after the hit." Make your teammates feel like champions.

Play with and for Teammates

Interact positively with teammates, support them, accept them, challenge them, and forgive them. It's easy to be positive when everything is going well. Work hard through difficult situations.

"COURT TALK" CHECKLIST

All Players

✓ Focus on positive communication, both visually and verbally.

✓ Focus on positive postures and gestures.

✓ Focus on helpful, supportive, and encouraging court talk.

✓ Focus on continuous talk throughout the rally, not just between points.

✓ Avoid negatives, blank stares, and nonsupportive postures, gestures and communication. These do not help.

✓ Accompany high or low fives with eye contact.

✓ Call "mine" every time you are going to touch the ball.

✓ When you and a teammate call "mine" simultaneously, one backs off, saying "okay" or "yours" to confirm the decision to let the teammate take the ball.

✓ On all balls close to the line, the closest player(s) who is not playing the ball calls "in," "out," or "good."

✓ Call "cover" and "free ball."

✓ Share knowledge of opponent's tendencies, such as: "she serves short . . . she can only hit angle, move the block in . . . she hits high seam, stay deep . . . she likes to dump on tight passes."

✓ Share information about opponent's offensive scheme, such as: "they're in rotation one . . . they usually run the right side cross, I'll take the second tempo attacker . . . watch number one, she's the primary attacker . . ."

✓ Help the attacker by indicating the number(s) of blockers up. Call out "one," "two," or "three up."

✓ Give directional suggestions to attackers, such as: "line" (consider the position of the ball), "angle," "hole" (anticipate time of closure), "seam," or "tip."

✓ Remind attackers of weakness in the block.

✓ Acknowledge a teammate's good play and good efforts.

✓ Avoid coaching teammates or giving unsolicited advice. If they want your advice, they will ask for it.

✓ Only the captain talks to the officials, and only in a courteous manner.

✓ All communication on the bench is positive and supportive.

✓ When the blocker has touched the ball and it is "hovering" above them, a teammate points upward and yells out "up" so the blocker can look up and find the ball.

Blocker(s)

✓ Communicate the eligible front row attackers and their position, such as: "hitters split," "overload right," "overload left."

✓ Communicate when the setter is front row.

✓ Communicate about attackers moving into or out of your zone.

✓ Communicate play-sets and crosses.

✓ Call out your intention not to block an attacker, such as: "no block."

✓ Communicate your block position, such as: "inside," "outside," "right here."

✓ Communicate the timing for the jump, such as: "wait," "delay," "now."

Setter(s)

✓ Call "tight," "off," "inside," "outside," "low" to help the attacker evaluate the set more quickly.

✓ Call out the name of the attacker if the ball is set between two players.

✓ Set every second ball unless you call for "help." Only in an emergency should you request that another player set.

✓ When you dig the first ball, you call the name of the player who should set the second ball.

✓ Make the call for adjustments in the serve receive formation.

✓ Call the side-out play, either verbally and/or by hand signal to each attacker, before the serve.

Attacker(s)

✓ In the side-out offense, call and confirm the set verbally. In the case of an out-of-system pass, make an alternate call.

✓ In transition, call for the set according to the options allowed by the pass.

✓ Call for the set while the ball is in the air between the passer and the setter.

✓ Call for the set loudly, aggressively, and early.

✓ Call for the set often enough to convince the setter you want the ball, and convince the opponent's blockers that you will receive it.

CHAPTER 13

TRAINING BY POSITION

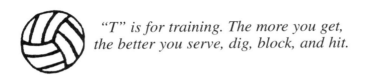

"T" is for training. The more you get,
the better you serve, dig, block, and hit.

Although it is important that players learn all the basic volleyball skills, they should also specialize as middle blockers, setters, and/or outside attackers. The following information is to be used as a guideline to indicate important aspects of each position illustrated through drills. Each drill is presented in its most basic form and must be modified to meet each individual athlete's needs. These are "position drills" and are generally intended for one to four players.

MOVEMENT CONCEPTS

Movement training is an important part of the overall skills training for all players, but it is especially important in volleyball because contact with the ball is limited. To improve mechanics and consistently execute skills technically at a high level, athletes must hurry with the feet to get to the ball and establish a good pre-contact position.

Proper movement also allows athletes to reach more balls. Fortunately, no matter how fast or slow an athlete is, foot speed can be improved with good technique.

For some athletes, good footwork is natural, but for many it is not and it must be trained. As the athlete's footwork improves, so does the rest of his or her game.

> **MAXIM:** *Why wear volleyball shoes if you are not going to move your feet.*

Keys to Good Movement

Good Ready Position.   Train players to initiate every skill from a ready position. It is the most effective and efficient way to move. The center of gravity is forward and the muscles are fired to allow a quick first step in any direction. Like a sprinter, athletes should burst out of their ready position toward the ball, whether it is to pass, set, dig, block, or attack.

Good Reading Skills.   Good movement requires an active ready position with the eyes as well as the feet. Train players to recognize the cues that indicate where the ball will be directed and its trajectory and speed. Train them to respond simultaneously to what they see. Their focus should be constantly switching from the ball to the cues and back to the ball.

Good First Step.   Players are only as fast as their first step. Train athletes to drive off the far foot and move the core of the body toward the ball. To cover the most distance and gain the most consistency in control, it is best when the legs and the body move together. When athletes lead with the head and shoulders first and do not move their legs, the legs always are trying to catch up with the top half.

Athletes must also receive good feedback about "false steps." A common error is to step back with the lead foot. When this occurs, it delays the time it takes to reach the ball, and sometimes it is too late.

Movement into a Pre-Contact Position.   Train players to move to the ball with shuffle/slide steps forward, back, and side to side to cover short distances. Train them to use crossover steps to the right and left to cover average distances, and running steps to cover long distances.

Crossover steps allow athletes to cover twice the distance in half the number of steps as compared with shuffle/slide steps. Slide steps limit players in the distance they can cover because one foot can slide only as far as the other foot. With crossover steps, players can double the distance one foot can travel while still keeping their eyes forward on the opponent.

Movement from the Defensive Ready Position.   Train athletes on defense to make positional adjustments and then stop just as the opponent is about to contact the ball. It is critical that receivers stop as soon as the attacker's arm is in the air and starts its movement forward. If the receiver stops at the same moment as the attacker makes contact with the ball, rather than before, there is often not sufficient time to move to react to the ball's direction.

Train defenders to stop by using a split step, that is, a small hop, widening the base and dropping into a low balanced position, with the weight evenly distributed on the balls of the feet. This position enables the receiver to move instantly toward the ball when its direction is determined.

Good Stopping Skills.   Train players to stop from movements made forward, back, and laterally and to regain their balance on the ground as often as possible before executing a skill. Good body control and balance allow for explosive movements to the ball and power in all sequences of the pre-contact and contact movements.

Good Orientation Movements.   Train players how to position the body in relation to the ball, the court, the net, and the target. It is important not to go directly to the ball; rather, they go behind and under it. Successful contacts are those made in front of the athlete.

> MAXIM: *The only time the athlete does not have a movement responsibility is when he or she is on the bench.*

Good Linking Actions.   Train continuous movement throughout the rally. Each action is linked together in a chain of movements, beginning with players in their initial base position. Simultaneously with reading the cues and following the ball, athletes dance into position, recover, and return to their base position to begin the process again. Athletes move from one skill to another, contacting the ball or supporting a contact of a teammate, that is, covering an attacker or backing up the passer. The sequence ends when the ball is whistled dead at the conclusion of the rally.

Train players to keep their feet moving between contacts. They must never stop, stand flat-footed, or let their feet fall asleep. Even if the athlete is not making the contact, he or she has a movement responsibility when the ball is in play.

> *MAXIM: Be involved in every play! Do not think that just because a teammate is contacting the ball that there is nothing else to do.*

Good Modeling Skills.   Train players to model each skill with perfect technique. If they cannot mimic the action without the ball, they will not be able to do it more successfully with the ball. Emphasis is on proper technical execution and elimination of unnecessary movements.

Good Movement in Drills.   Train movement in all drills. The ball rarely comes directly to players; they must move to reach it. Static skills work does not transfer to game situations. Train how to move and how to minimize the amount of steps needed to get into the proper position.

Good Reaction Time Related to Decisions.   Train players to recognize and react to game situations. Train decision making in both single- and multiple-response scenarios. Movement is fastest when there is only one possible response. The reaction time is longer when the athlete is faced with multiple decisions. Through training, reaction time related to decisions is improved in speed and quality.

> *MAXIM: When athletes stop moving their feet, their game suffers.*

TRAINING THE SETTER
(Zones 1, 2, or 3)

Attributes of a Successful Setter

The success of the team is to a large degree based on the ability of the setter. (See Chapter 3.) Coaches must seek out those players who have the necessary attributes to be successful and be willing to train them whether or not they have had previous setting experience.

Setter development requires more time than it does for attackers; therefore, you must provide setters with additional training sessions separate from the team.

Setter Skills

Beginning Setter

- Train second- and third-tempo "hand" sets forward and back.
- Train forearm sets on low balls when it is not possible to set with the hands.
- Train to attack the second ball with the left, right, and both hands.

- Train setters to expand the range of third-tempo sets forward and back to zones 2 and 4 from anywhere on the court on good and poor passes.

Advanced Setter

- Train the side set facing the net, with the back to the net, and when positioned off the net to set the zone 2 attacker.
- Train the two-hand jump set.
- Train the one-hand jump set on a tight pass.
- Train a variety of first-, second-, and third-tempo sets.

> **MAXIM:** *Setting from the floor position only makes half a setter. The consummate setter is able to set from the ground and in the air.*

Movement Training

"Readiness."   Train the setter to be in an active ready position in the target area. The hands are held at chest level ready to move up into a setting position or to aid in sprinting to an inaccurate pass. The setter reads the pass off his or her teammate's arms for clues as to the direction and trajectory of the pass.

Movement to the Target Area.   Train movements from the setter's initial start positions on serve receive, defense, and the block to the setter target area near the net.

Movement from the Target Area to the Ball.   Train quickness to the ball from the target area along the net and away from the net. Train the setter to have the hands up in a position to set on arrival to the ball. The setter is stopped and balanced prior to the set. The hands and feet are in place.

Movement to Cover the Attacker.   Train the setter to move to cover the attacker immediately after the set. After coverage responsibilities have been met, the setter returns to his or her defensive position.

Drills

Drills are performed generally with one to three setters and/or right side players.

Zigzag Shadow Drill.   The setter sprints to the target area, stops, models the set, and runs to the 10-foot line to model the set again. The setter continues this zigzag movement pattern to and away from the net in the direction of zone 4, alternately stopping to model the set near the net and near the 10-foot line. (See Diagram 13-1.)

Emphasis is on quick movement to the ball, squaring the shoulders to the zone 4 target, and being balanced when executing the set. The setter should have the ability to set forward or back on every contact.

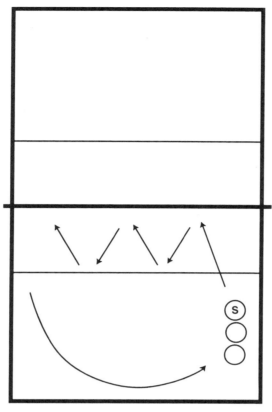

Diagram 13-1.

Repeat the movement pattern, changing the setter's initial start position from each of the team's serve receive and defensive base positions. (See Diagram 13-2.)

Setting Off Coach Toss 0–5 Feet Along the Net. The setter is positioned in the target area and moves to front or back set balls tossed by the coach zero to five feet along the net. The setter hustles back to his or her base position in the target area after each set, tags up by touching the net, and awaits the next toss. The setter sets 10–15 balls and a new setter switches in, or rest is given to the setter before he or she repeats the drill. (See Diagram 13-3.)

Repeat the drill with emphasis on the following training goals.

- **Train movement and set technique.** Sound fundamentals insure continual improvement and consistency of performance. Feedback is based on technique and not the result of the set. Emphasis is on technically proper execution and on correction of improper movements. Setters accumulate points on proper technical performance, that is, balanced set position, square to the target, hands up early, proper follow-through. You are the judge and indicate when a point is awarded. Repeat with front and back sets, side sets, jump sets, and so on.
- **Train accuracy.** The setter accumulates points for accurate sets. Use volleyball carts or players as targets. Target players stand in the target area and cannot move more than one step to catch a ball for the setter to earn a point.

   KEY: Establish a "zone of success" for setters. They must know the expected degree of accuracy. Pinpoint accuracy is not the intention. It is better to set the ball too high rather than too low, too far off the net rather than too tight, and too far inside the antennae rather than outside.

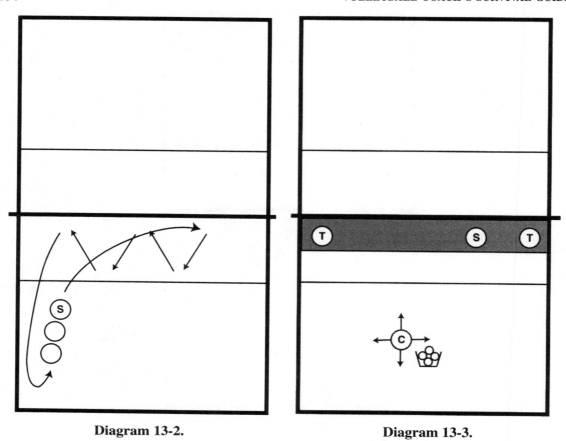

Diagram 13-2.   **Diagram 13-3.**

- **Train deception.** The setter accumulates points based on a good neutral body position in the pre-contact phase that allows both front or back sets on each contact. You control the training by giving a late verbal command, just prior to setter contact, that is, front or back and the setter sets the ball in that direction. You award points based on accuracy of the set and deception.

    KEY: Emphasize all sets being similar until the moment of release in order to conceal the direction of the set. Emphasize making the final decision where to direct the ball at the last possible moment. It is impossible for the middle blocker to determine the direction of the set ahead of time if the setter has not made his or her decision.

- **Train tactics.** The setter accumulates points setting the proper direction based on the position of the pass. You toss the ball to various positions along the net. When you toss to the right of center, the setter sets to the left front attacker. The setter directs the ball back to the right front attacker on passes to the left. (See Diagram 13-4.)

    KEY: Emphasize that on every contact, setters assume a body position that allows the ball to be delivered to all attackers. The setter should have the option to make the best set tactically, rather than the easiest set by virtue of the pass or his or her body position.

- **Train setter response to attacker's visual cues.** A player/target in zone 4 holds one hand on his or her chest in an open or closed position just after you toss the ball to the setter. The setter evaluates the toss from you, and then takes his or her eyes off the ball prior to the set to see the signal of the zone 4 player. The setter calls out "open or closed" and sets to zone 4. Repeat with the setter setting forward or back based on the hand signal. The setter accumulates points with proper responses and accurate sets. (Refer to Diagram 13-4.)

> **KEY:** The "eye check" assists setters in evaluating their court position in relation to the sidelines, the antennae, and the net. This check provides cues to where the ball needs to be directed and, at the same time, gives setters information on the readiness and position of the attackers.

- **Train setter response to blocker's visual cues.** The setter accumulates points for proper responses to blocker movement. You toss the ball to the setter and, prior to set, the setter takes a quick look across net to evaluate the middle blocker's position. The middle blocker steps to the right or left during the pass, and the setter sets in the opposite direction of the blocker's movement. (See Diagram 13-5.)

> **KEY:** Train the setter to see beyond the ball to the antennae, and within this field, the outside and middle attackers and the opponent's middle blocker.

- **Train setter attack technique.** The setter is positioned in zone 2 and models the block. Just before the blocker lands, you toss the ball along the net for the second contact attack. The setter jumps and attacks with a tip with the right and/or left hand. The setter accumulates points for good technical attack execution. (See Diagram 13-6.)

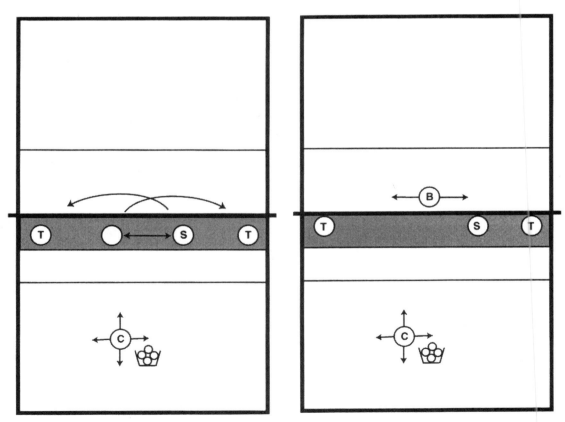

Diagram 13-4.   **Diagram 13-5.**

- **Train setter attack placement.** Continuing the above drill, the setter accumulates points on proper attack placements to the designated targets, front, middle, and back over the setter's head to the short corner. Use towels or cones for targets. Use the right and left hands and add a blocker to train the setter to see and attack over or around it to the targets. (See Diagram 13-7.)
- **Train setter response to coach commands: jump set or attack.** You toss the ball to the setter and, just prior to contact, call out "jump" to set the left side attacker or "tip." The setter accumulates points with proper responses and good technical execution. (Refer to Diagram 13-7.)

    KEY: Emphasis is on disguising the attack by jump setting every ball near the net. The setter should pose a threat to attack on every contact. The ball should be contacted as high as possible (above the net) on the set and the attack.

- **Train setter response to blocker visual cues.** The setter models the block in zone 2, lands, and receives the pass from you. The setter sets or attacks based on the blocker's cues. If the blocker jumps with the setter, the setter sets to the left front attacker. If the blocker remains on the ground, the setter attacks. The setter accumulates points with proper responses to blocker's cues and good execution. (See Diagram 13-8.)
- **Train setter deception (setter–middle blocker challenge).** The setter is positioned in the target area, with a right and left side player/target or cart. A middle blocker is on the opposite side of the net. The coach/player initiates the rally with a toss to the setter. The setter has the

© 2001 by Parker Publishing Company

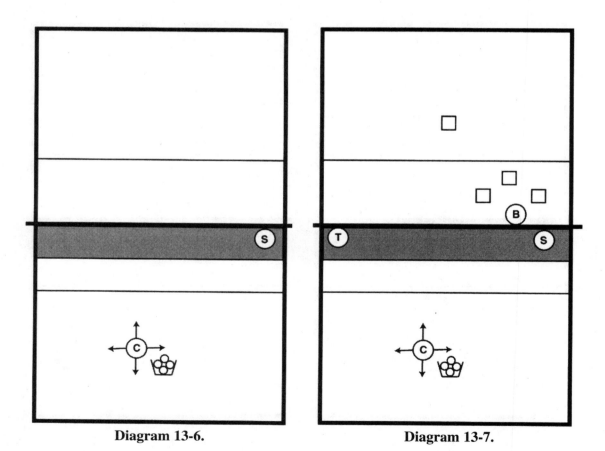

Diagram 13-6.   **Diagram 13-7.**

option to set forward, back, or attack. If the middle blocker moves in the correct direction and executes a block, the blocker scores 1. If the middle blocker does not go, or executes a weak movement, the setter scores 3. First to reach 10 wins. Emphasis is on setter deception causing the middle blocker to be late arriving to the attack point. (See Diagram 13-9.)

- **Train setter response to back row base positions.** Just prior to your toss, the setter looks to the defense side to evaluate the defensive initial start positions. If the receiver is pinched inside for the setter attack, the setter sets primarily outside. If the defender is wide toward the sidelines, the setter attacks. In situations where the receiver is pinched inside, the setter on occasion can attack other placements. Setters accumulate points with proper responses to the visual cues and good technical execution. (See Diagram 13-10.)
- **Train the setter in a game-like situation.** The offense (setter and left side attacker) competes against the defense (one blocker and two back row defenders). Additional blockers and/or defensive players can be added for advanced players. You toss the ball to the setter, who has the option to attack or set the left side hitter. Points are awarded for successful attacks by the offense and good transition by the defense. (See Diagram 13-11.)

> **KEYS:** Train setters to see more than the ball. Train them to look to the opponent's side prior to the pass to see the opponent's base block and back row positions to determine open areas or weaknesses that might be exploited with the second contact attack.

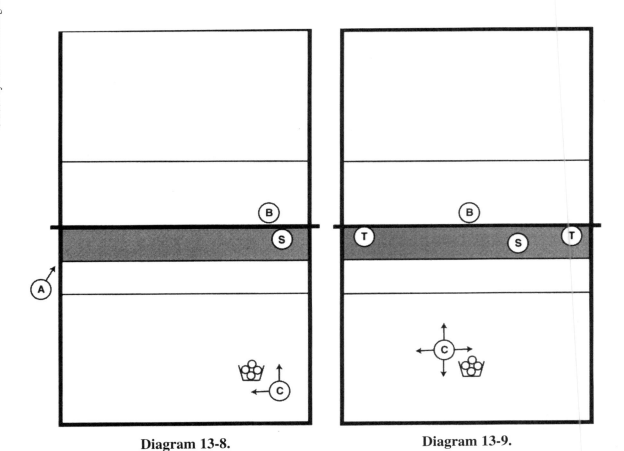

Diagram 13-8.   **Diagram 13-9.**

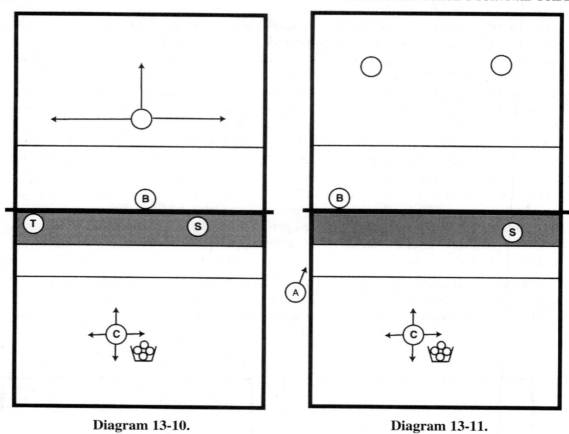

Diagram 13-10.   **Diagram 13-11.**

Advanced setters can also take a quick glance at the opponent's defense just before the pass reaches them. Train setters to look to the opponent's side just after the set, but before the attack, to see the position of the defense in order to help attackers exploit weaknesses.

Setting Off Coach Toss 5–15 Feet Off the Net. The setter is positioned in the target area and moves to set balls tossed 5–15 feet off the net. The setter hustles back to his or her base position in the target area after each set, tags up by touching the net, and awaits the next toss. The setter sets 10–15 balls and a new setter switches in, or rest is given to the setter before he or she repeats the drill.

Repeat the drill with emphasis on the following training goals.

- **Train setter attack placement with two hands 5–12 feet off the net.** The setter models the block in zone 2, moves off the net to receive the pass, and sends the ball to the opponent's side with a two-handed pass over the net. The two-handed attack is effective for setters in the front and back rows on passes off the net. The setter accumulates points on good technical execution and accuracy to the designated targets. (See Diagram 13-12.)
- **Train sets to the left side attacker from out of system passes 10–15 feet off the net.** The setter is positioned in the pass target area and must sprint off the net to receive a toss from you and sets to the left side attacker. The setter returns to the pass target area after the set. The setter accumulates points on good technical execution and accuracy. Emphasis is on squaring the shoulders to the zone 4 target and setting from a two-foot balanced base or using the one-foot spin movement. (See Diagram 13-13.)

- **Train side sets to the right side attacker from passes 4–12 feet off the net.** The setter is positioned in the pass target and moves off the net to receive a toss from you and side sets to zone 2. The setter returns to the base target area after the set. The setter accumulates points on good technical execution and accuracy. Emphasis is on squaring off to the zone 4 target and pivoting to side set to the right side attacker. The side set allows the setter to see the target on contact and aids in accuracy. (See Diagram 13-14.)
- **Train back sets and side sets to the right side attacker.** The setter is positioned in the pass target and moves to receive a toss from you. The setter back sets on balls along the net (0–2 feet) and side sets on balls farther off the net (3–15 feet). You alternate tosses close and off the net. The setter accumulates points on good technical execution and accuracy. (Refer to Diagram 13-14.)
- **Train back sets and side sets to the right side and front sets to the left.** The setter moves to receive tosses from you 0–15 feet off the net. You call out the command to set forward or back just prior to setter contact. Emphasis is on squaring the shoulders to the zone 4 target, each time ready to set in any direction. The setter accumulates points on good technical execution and accuracy. (See Diagram 13-15.)

> **KEYS:** Provide the setter with sufficient in-system (good passes) and out-of-system (average to poor passes) tosses/passes according to the percentage of times that they occur in the game. Out-of system passes are very common at most levels.

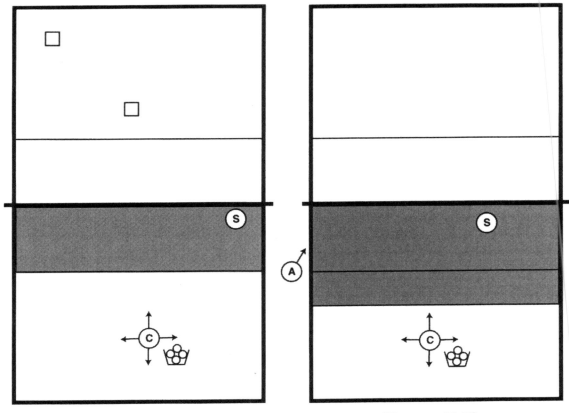

Diagram 13-12.   **Diagram 13-13.**

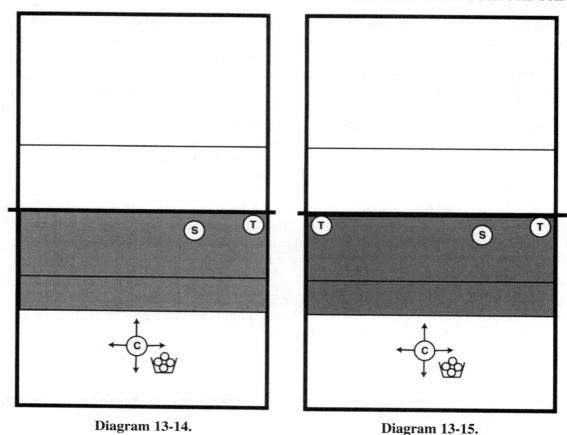

Diagram 13-14.   **Diagram 13-15.**

Provide the setter with tosses that simulate high and low passes and passes tight to the net and off the net in and outside the target area.

Provide the setter with tosses initiated from various positions on the court as they might occur in the game.

Setter Responses to Visual Cues from Coach Toss/Hit from Zone 4.   You are positioned in zone 4. Setters set 10–15 balls and switch out or rest before returning to the drill. Emphasis is on training setters to see more than the ball.

Repeat the drill with emphasis on the following training goals.

- **Train the setter to respond verbally to your visual cues.** You toss the ball to the setter in a variety of locations and immediately place your hand near your chest in an open or closed position. The setter evaluates the toss, takes his or her eyes off the ball to read your hand signal, and responds to it by calling out "open or closed" accordingly before setting the ball back to you in zone 4. (See Diagram 13-16.)
- **Train the setter to respond to the coach's visual cues with proper set execution.** You toss the ball to the setter 0–10 feet off the net and immediately place your hand near your chest in an open or closed position. The setter evaluates the toss, takes his or her eyes off the ball to read the signal, and responds by setting forward (fist) or back (open hand). (Refer to Diagram 13-16.)

- **Train the setter to respond verbally to visual cues on the opponent's side.** You toss the ball to the setter and the setter evaluates it before taking a quick look to the opponent's side to read the hand signal given by the middle blocker (open or closed fist held near chest). The setter calls out the appropriate signal and sets back to you. (See Diagram 13-17.)
- **Train the setter to respond to the opponent's signal with proper set execution.** You toss the ball to the setter and the setter evaluates it before taking a quick look to the opponent's side to read the signal given by the middle blocker (index finger pointing to the right or left sidelines). The setter responds by setting the ball forward or back in the direction of the signal. (See Diagram 13-18.)
- **Train the setter in an overload situation to dig, read cues, and set.** You hit the ball to the setter who is playing defense in zone 1 or 2. Immediately after the dig, toss another ball for the set. Emphasis is on playing defense first before releasing to set. Prior to the set, the setter looks for the cues from you or the blocker and responds to them as in each of the above drills. (See Diagram 13-19.)

First- and Second-Tempo Sets with Coach Same-Side Toss

- **Train first-tempo sets to a stationary attack target.** You toss to the setter who sets a first-tempo set to a teammate who is standing on an elevated platform with arms extended. Setters have an opportunity to set to a stationary target and see clearly where the ball must be directed for a successful contact. You move the setter within the target area for in-system passes. Emphasis is on setting the ball with the hands high and a quick release. (See Diagram 13-20.)

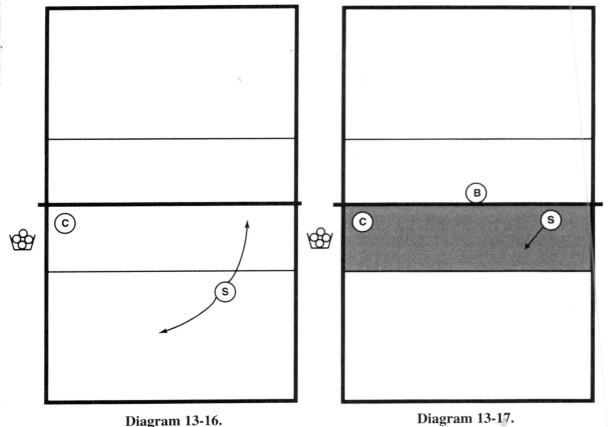

Diagram 13-16.   **Diagram 13-17.**

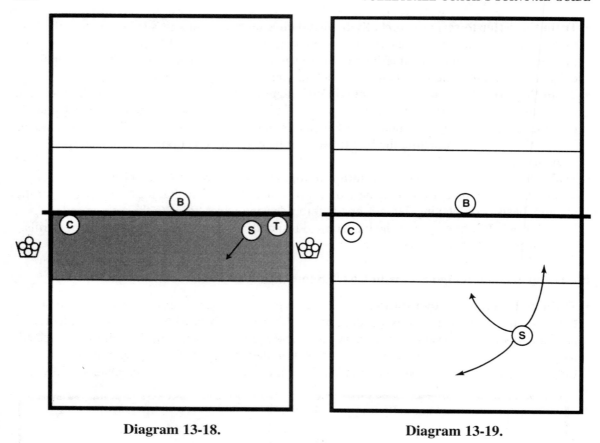

Diagram 13-18.   **Diagram 13-19.**

KEY: Emphasis is on training the setter to jump set.

- **Train first-tempo sets to a "live" attacker.** You toss to the setter who sets a "live" attacker. Vary the origination of the toss and its location within the target area for in-system passes. First, the setter sets single set options, that is, attackers hit only 1's, only back 1's, only 3's, or slides. Emphasis is on the setter "seeing and hearing" the quick hitter and establishing good timing and set accuracy. After successful execution, quick hitters vary their calls with emphasis being placed on the setter responding to multiple audible calls. (See Diagram 13-21.)
- **Train first-tempo "1" set vs. a middle blocker.** A blocker is added to the above drill. You toss to the setter who sets a first-tempo "1" to the attacker. Emphasis is on the setter seeing the opponent's middle blocker's position in his or her peripheral vision and setting out of the range. If the middle blocker commits to blocking the angle (the attacker's right shoulder), the setter sets beyond the middle blocker to the attacker's left shoulder, forcing the cutback. If the middle blocker commits to the cutback, the setter sets straight up to the attacker's right shoulder to force an angle hit.

    The setter/attacker team accumulates points with successful plays. It needs five kills before the middle blocker stuffs one ball.

    Train all first-tempo set options versus a single block.
- **Train second-tempo play sets.** You toss to the setter who sets only the second-tempo attacker. The first-tempo attacker approaches for a "1" followed by the second-tempo play set attacker who hits a "2." Emphasis is on establishing second-tempo set heights, timing, and positioning between the two attackers. Train all desired play combinations. (See Diagram 13-22.)

- **Train first- and second-set play combinations.** You toss to the setter who sets either the first- or second-tempo attacker. Emphasis is on proper set heights, timing, and positioning between the setter and attackers. If the first-tempo attacker is not set, the second-tempo attacker should be jumping up as the quick hitter is landing. (Refer to Diagram 13-22.)
- **Train first- and second-play combinations versus a middle blocker.** You toss the ball to the setter who sets the first- or second-tempo attacker. Emphasis is on setting the correct attacker based on the actions of the middle blocker. If the middle blocker jumps with the quick hitter, the setter sets the second-tempo hitter. If the middle blocker remains on the ground, the setter sets the first-tempo hitter. The setter accumulates points based on appropriate responses. (See Diagram 13-23.)
- **Train the setter to respond to the middle blocker's cues to set outside or quick.** The setter models the block in zone 2, lands, and looks for your toss. The setter sets based on the cues received from the middle blocker's movement. The setter sets the zone 4 attacker if the middle blocker jumps with the first-tempo set. The setter sets the quick hitter if the middle blocker remains on the ground or releases early. The setter accumulates points for appropriate responses. (See Diagram 13-24.)
- **Setter–middle blocker challenge.** The setter models the block in zone 2, lands, and looks for your toss. The set is directed outside if the middle blocker jumps to block the quick attack. The set goes to the quick hitter if the middle blocker remains on the ground.

    Points are awarded based on correct responses. A point is awarded to the setter if the blocker is faked. A point is awarded to the middle blocker if the middle blocker correctly

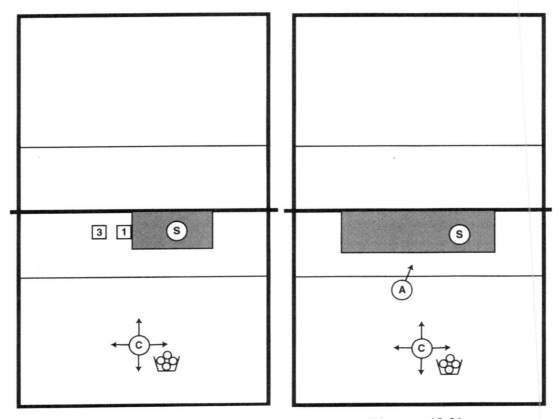

Diagram 13-20.   **Diagram 13-21.**

reads the setter. The first to reach 5 points wins. The game is over if the middle blocker stuffs the ball. (Refer to Diagram 13-24.)

The Setter Off "Live" Passes.   Include the components of the above drills with sets off free ball passes, off serve receive, off digs, and in live game situations as quickly as possible.

- **Train sets off free ball passes.** The coach/player tosses the ball from the opposite side of the net to a receiver for a free ball pass. (See Diagram 13-25.)
- **Train sets off controlled digs.** The coach/player hits from a box on the opposite side of the net to a receiver. (See Diagram 13-26.)
- **Train sets off serve receive.** The coach/player serves to receivers. The setter accumulates points for sets to a specific target. Emphasis is on the setter reading the receiver's body position and platform for clues of the pass direction. Train in specific reception formations and rotations in small groups or with the entire team. (See Diagram 13-27.)
- **Train sets off "live" digs (setter exchange).** Setters and/or secondary setters (zone 2 players) are positioned for defense in zones 1 and 2. You are positioned on the same side of the net in zone 4 and attack the ball to one of the receivers; one digs and the other sets the ball back to you. After the set, players "change" positions front to back or "stay" as indicated by their court position. After the set, both players hustle back to their base defensive positions. Emphasis is

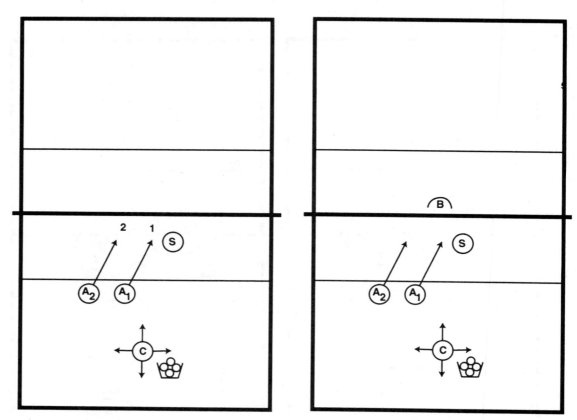

Diagram 13-22.   Diagram 13-23.

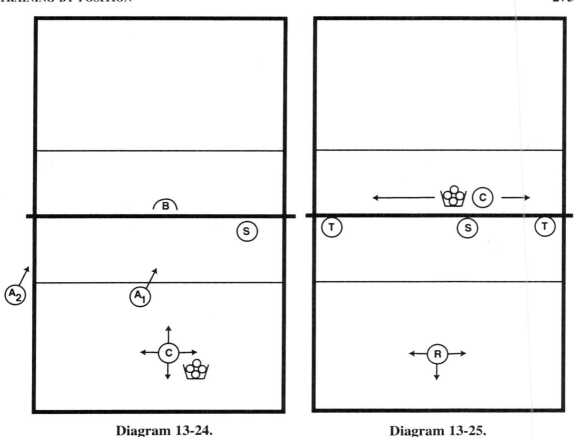

Diagram 13-24.   **Diagram 13-25.**

on good communication between the setters, calling out "I set" and "stay or switch" to communicate where they are returning to play defense. Setters accumulate points for proper execution and accuracy. (See Diagram 13-28.)

Repeat the drill with you on an elevated platform in zone 2 on the opposite side of the net and add a left side and/or middle attacker. (See Diagram 13-29.)

- **Offense–defense challenge.** One, two, or three attackers plus a setter challenge the full defense. The ball is initiated by you from the same side as the offense or over the net as a free ball. The offense must score two consecutive little points to earn one big one. The offense needs six big points to win. The defense receives a point each time it returns the ball to the offense side and two points when it successfully attacks the ball. The defense needs 15 points to win. The losing side sprints. (See Diagram 13-30.)

  KEYS: There are numerous point variations to determine the winner, but both sides must have an equal opportunity to win to make it fun and challenging for both the offense and the defense.

  Train the setter to be responsible for leading the offense through accurate and smart setting. The setter can give a tactical advantage to the attacker by calling the right plays and setting the correct person. It takes time and experience to learn how to make good tactical choices.

- **Train team side-out work in specific rotations.** The second team serves to the first team and the entire game is played out in one rotation. Starting scores vary depending on the strength or weakness of the rotation and how much time is desired training it. Handicap the starting team

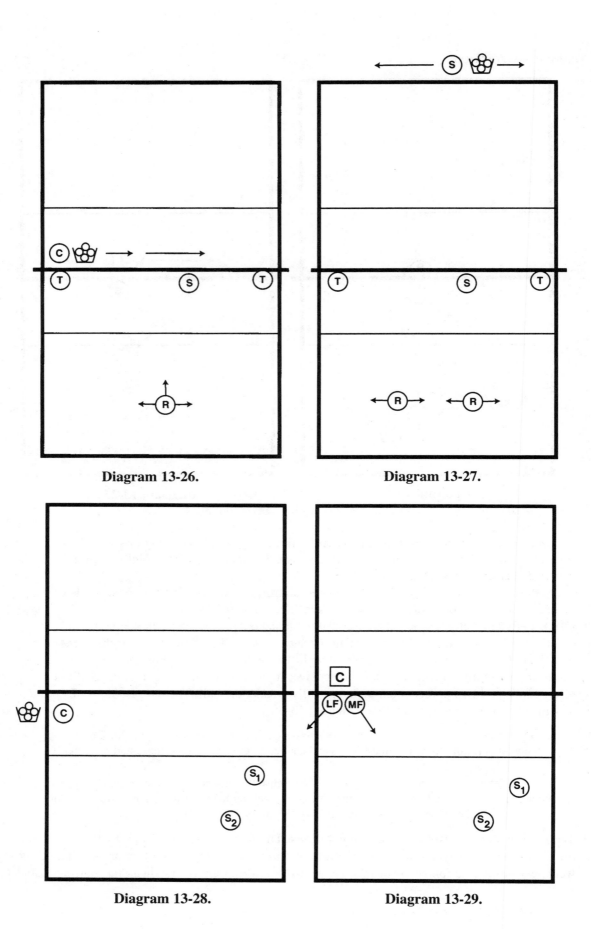

Diagram 13-26.

Diagram 13-27.

Diagram 13-28.

Diagram 13-29.

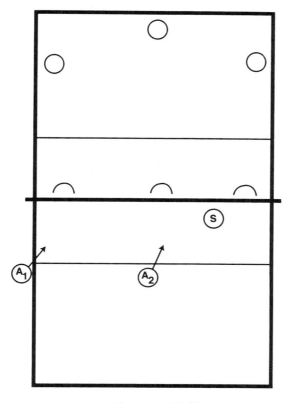

Diagram 13-30.

to make it challenging for both sides. A starting point is 6–10 in favor of the second team. The losing side sprints and the game begins again in another rotation. The setter is given the freedom to change the reception formations, and the setter and/or attackers call the plays.

KEYS: Train setters to problem-solve within the drill. Give them ideas and options but let them experiment their way to success.

Always use antennae and have them placed in the correct positions. Antennae are a guide for set placement.

Stress quickness of the setter to the target area in free ball and serve receive situations. The setter should arrive early to present a visual and verbal target for the passer.

Stress the use of the "hand" set on low or distant balls, rather than setting the ball with the forearm pass. Allow setters to mishandle balls in practice in order to train them to extend their range of legal "hand" sets in the game.

Stress ballhandling skills for setters. Setters must set many balls to develop good control. The more opportunity setters have touching the ball, the better.

In addition to the drills mentioned above, setters can train alone utilizing self-sets. *For example:*

- Self-set within a limited space to see how many sets can be done consecutively.
- Alternate self-sets with forearm sets in a limited space.

- Alternate self-sets with other tasks, such as: self-set, drop to a kneeling position, get up, self-set, drop to a sitting position, get up, self-set, lie on back, get up, self-set. See how many sets can be done consecutively without dropping the ball.
- Select various spots on a wall and set consistently to these spots.

Communication Training Keys

- Train communication in every drill.
- Train setters to be responsible to set every second ball unless a teammate calls "mine" and is clearly in better position to set.
- Train setters that they must never assume or never ask another player to set the ball.
- Train setters to communicate vocally, with body language, and by their body position that they intend to set the ball.
- Train setters after they dig the first ball to call out the name of the intended secondary setter, such as, "Janet, set."
- Train setters to call out the name of the intended attacker when the ball is set between two players, such as, "Margie, hit it."
- Train setters to be communicative with teammates and coaches, working together to execute the tactical aspects of the offense.
- Train setters to communicate with attackers before, during, and after each play.
- Train setters to request feedback from attackers to determine which sets they feel are most effective for them.
- Train setters to call "tight," "low," "inside," or "off" on sets to help the attacker more quickly evaluate the set and their options.
- Train setters the importance of "reading" attacker attitudes, encouraging and instilling confidence in them.
- Train setters to apologize for inaccurate sets and assume some of the responsibility for attacker errors.
- Train setters to "over talk" in stressful situations to instill confidence in the team and keep the team's thoughts directed on execution.

Setter Leadership Training Keys

- Train setters to lead the team offensively and emotionally under good and difficult situations.
- Give deserving setters the responsibility of being court captain.
- Emphasize the importance of having a positive outlook, thinking clearly, and maintaining composure.
- Stress setters in drills by overloading them technically, tactically, physically, and emotionally. Stretch their limits so they will be able to function in pressure situations in the game.
- Train setters to deal with attacker breakdowns and poor passing. Help them with solutions and options so their play is not affected negatively.

Tactical Setter Training Keys

- Train setters through drills, game tapes, and discussions to lead the offense. Emphasize the importance of problem-solving and decision-making.

- Train setters to make good tactical selections by understanding the strengths and weaknesses of each option, and in what situations each option is most applicable.
- Train setters to make set selections based on the opponent's defensive strengths and weaknesses.
- Train setters to make set selections based on their team's strengths and weaknesses in general and specifically in the current situation.
- Train setters to make set selections based on attackers' performance and attitude in the current situation.
- Train setters to make set selections based on the position of the pass.
- Train setters to be responsible for all set selections.
- Test setters in scrimmages and drills by stopping the action, after both good and poor choice selections, to question why a particular set was made. Require them to defend their selection.
- Train setters to analyze the game by asking "what if" questions about situations that could occur in the game and how they would handle them.
- Train setters to make good choices by recalling a series of sets. Question the setter periodically in practice, "What were your last five sets? Who attacked the ball and what was their success ratio?"
- Train setters to record in their head's mini-computer how points are won and lost and to use the information to determine future strategy.
- Train setters to know to whom they are delivering the ball. Who has received the most sets and how effective were they? What is the ratio of quick to outside sets? Question setters in practice and aid them in the game with statistics.
- Train setters in traditional side-out scoring to distinguish between side-out and point-making situations. Train them to take more risks when there is not a possibility of losing a point.
- Include setters in the development of the game plans prior to the match.
- In time-outs and between games during the match, share important statistical information and observations with setters. Discuss any adjustments that should be made.
- Evaluate after the match the setter's performance technically and tactically. Include personal observations, statistics, and the game tape.

TRAINING THE OUTSIDE ATTACKER
(Zones 2 and 4)

Attributes of a Successful Outside Attacker

See Chapter 5.

KEY: Stress aggressive, explosive approaches every time.

Outside Attacker Skills

Right Side Attacker (Zone 2)

- Attack second- and third-tempo sets from zone 2. (Train right-handers to keep the ball over their right shoulder so they initially face their range point and have the ability to attack the line or angle with power.)
- Attack the second-tempo right side cross (X) in zone 3.
- Attack first- and second-tempo back slides for right-handers and the front slides for left-handers.
- Attack from the back row.
- Set when the primary setter digs the first ball.
- Block the opponent's power attacker.

Left Side Attacker (Zone 4)

- Attack third-tempo high sets of good and poor quality in zone 4 as well as from the back row.
- Attack second-tempo shoot sets in zone 4 and second-tempo play combinations in zone 3.
- Block right side play combinations.

Movement Training

Model Approach Patterns.   Model the three- and/or four-step approach patterns from the standard tag-up points in zones 2, 3, and 4 to their corresponding attack zones at the net. These patterns allow attackers to most easily face their range point. After successful approach patterns have been established, train outside-in, inside-out and/or straight-in pattern variations. (Refer to Diagram 5-2.)

Attack Options

- **Train to attack with a variety of options.** The setter receives in-system tosses (passes within the target area) from you and sets attackers in zones 2, 3, 4, and/or back row. (See Diagram 13-31.)

MAXIM: Poor technique limits the players' present and future successes.

Attackers accumulate points for proper technical execution of the tip, power, and off-speed attack. They receive additional points for disguising the option until the last moment by making the same approach and arm swing each time. Feedback is based on technique rather than the result of the hit; *for example:* high contact, contact in front of the body, and proper follow-through. Repeat with out-of-system tosses (outside the target area) from you and set attackers in zones 2, 4, and/or back row. The setter begins in the target area. The attacker evaluates the set and calls for the desired option. (See Diagram 13-32.)

> ***MAXIM:*** *Only players with great height and jumping ability have the luxury of being successful by attacking hard in one direction only.*

KEY: The majority of sets off poor passes (behind the 10-foot line) should be directed to the on-side attacker. An attacker is considered on-side when the ball is contacted before it crosses the body and, thus, is an easier angle to adjust to and hit with power and placement on out-of-system passes. The on-side attacker is a right-handed left side or middle attacker and a left-handed right side attacker.

- **Train Attack Off Sets from Zone 6.** You toss or bounce the ball to a player in zone 6 who sets to the zone 4 attacker. Vary the tosses, making them easy as well as difficult for the setter to reach. The attacker focuses on making good attack choices depending on the quality of the set, that is, going hard after the "kill" on a good set or keeping difficult sets in play. (See Diagram 13-33.)

- **Train attack vs. the block.** Repeat the drills, adding a double block and one or two defensive players. Two attackers and the setter compete against the defense. Attackers work to gain +7 kills, that is, add one point for a kill and subtract one point for an error. The score remains neutral on balls kept in play by the defense or for a successful recovery of a blocked ball by the offense. If the attackers go into the negative, the game is over and the defense wins. (See Diagram 13-34.)

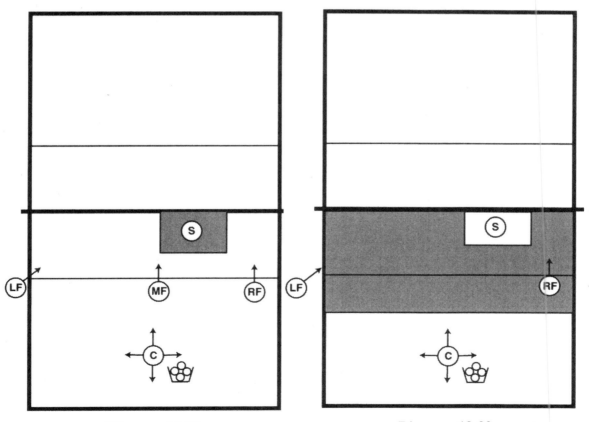

Diagram 13-31   **Diagram 13-32.**

- **Train to Attack Overset.** The coach/teammate tosses the ball from the opposite side of the net for the attacker to hit or redirect with a sweeping block motion. (See Diagram 13-35.)

Attack Placements

- **Train placement.** Repeat the above drills training a variety of placements from each option and each zone. Attackers accumulate points on proper technical execution and placements. Use cones, towels, or chairs for targets.

  KEY: Always stress placement of the attack, especially in drill situations where attackers are not hitting against a block. Use targets.

The Counterattack

  KEY: Avoid spending a great deal of training the attack using hitting lines. It is most advantageous to train the attack in a game-like situation where movement is made from different court positions transitioning to the attack.

Counterattack from a Free Ball Pass. The coach/player tosses the ball over the net and the attacker passes the ball to the setter and transitions for the attack. Repeat from various positions on the court and transition to various attack zones along the net. (See Diagram 13-36.)

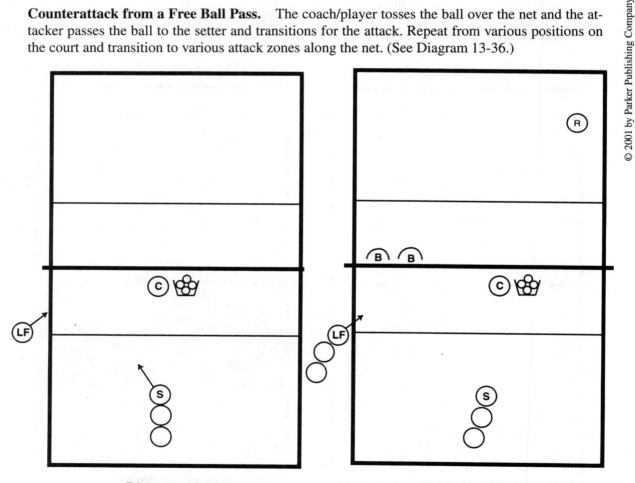

Diagram 13-33   **Diagram 13-34.**

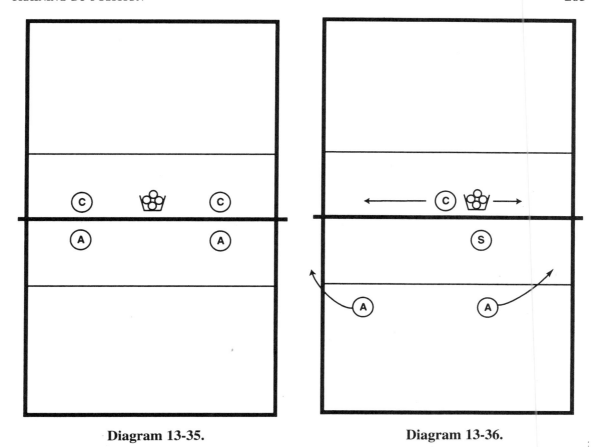

Diagram 13-35.   Diagram 13-36.

Counterattack from Serve Receive

- **Receiving from right and left back.** The coach/player serves short or deep to a receiver in the left back position. The receiver passes the ball to the setter, tags up, and transitions for the attack in zone 3 or 4. After a specific number of successful attacks, the receiver passes from the right back position and attacks in zone 2 or 3. (See Diagram 13-37.)

  Emphasis is on the attacker focusing on passing first, tagging up for the approach, calling the desired set, and attacking the ball.

  KEY: Use targets for attack placements or blockers and defenders.

- **Receiving from middle back.** The coach/player serves to a receiver in the middle back position. The receiver passes the serve and has the option of hitting in zone 2, 3, or 4. After the attacker successfully hits the desired target a specific number of times, add three blockers in standard base positions and emphasize that the attacker moves toward the weakest blocker. Blockers vary their positions to force the attacker to look at the defense. (See Diagram 13-38.)

- **Receiving in 3's and attacking against a full defense.** The serving team of six serves to the receiving team, which consists of three receivers and a setter. The receiving side passes, sets, and attacks. Left back and right back are designated as front row attackers and after each attack, the hitter switches to receive in the middle back position. (See Diagram 13-39.)

  The rally begins again with the serve. The drill is completed when 30 balls have been successfully served. Statistics are taken on the quality of the pass and the effectiveness of the attack. The defensive side transitions to the attack and the play ends.

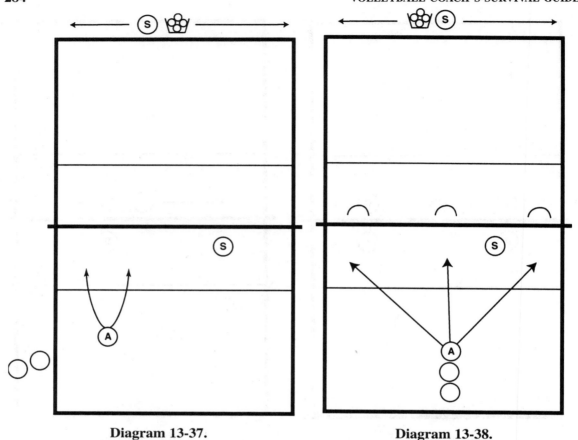

Diagram 13-37.   **Diagram 13-38.**

Variation: The designated attacker receives in the middle back position, and has the freedom to attack anywhere along the net. After each attack attempt, the hitter switches to the right or left back position and a new passer/attacker moves into the middle. (See Diagram 13-40.)

> **KEY:** Train attackers to differentiate between sets that are good percentage options to "kill" and those that are best to keep in play. The attacker must "go for it" when the percentages are good because the rally will end after both sides have had an opportunity to play the ball only one time.

Counterattack from the Dig

- **Attacker's challenge.** Two attackers compete against a double block and one or two defenders. You initiate the ball with an attack from the floor or over the net from an elevated platform. Attackers alternate receiving the ball and transitioning to the attack.

  The game ends when one attacker gains +5 points or the defense forces both attackers into a negative score. Attackers earn points on successful hits (only one tip or off-speed shot is allowed). Each error reduces by one any successful attacks. An attacker loses and is eliminated if his or her score goes into the negative. The single attacker continues until one side wins. The defense wins if both attackers go into the negative. (See Diagram 13-41.)
- **6's challenge with coach on elevated platform.** Two teams compete. The defensive team has six players, while the offensive team consists of six players plus you on an elevated platform.

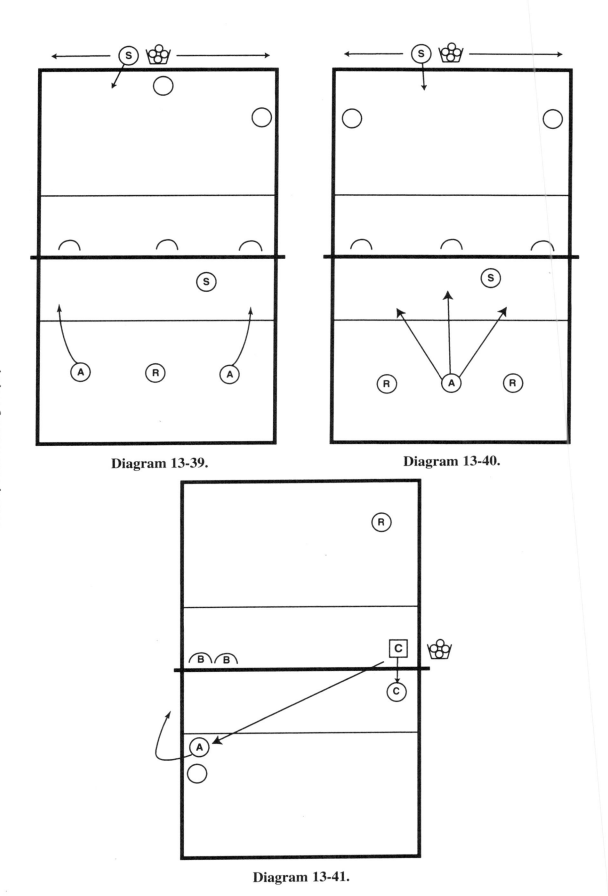

Diagram 13-39.

Diagram 13-40.

Diagram 13-41.

You initiate the ball in zone 2, 3, or 4, or the ball is tossed to the offensive team to be attacked in standard fashion. On your side, the attack options are limited to the zones not occupied by the box. The first team to 15, rally score wins. At 8 points, each team has the option to switch its front row players to back row positions, especially if the middle blockers need a rest. (See Diagram 13-42.)

• **3's cross-court attacker challenge.** Three players on a side form a team that consists of an attacker, setter–blocker, and a digger. The ball is initiated from a coach/player on the sidelines and alternately tossed to each team. The ball must be attacked in the cross-court half of the court and all options are permissible, that is, tip, roll shot, and power. Points are scored on successful attacks rather than on opponent errors. Players rotate on their side of the net when their attacker has scored three kills. The first team to rotate back to its start positions wins. (See Diagram 13-43.)

Counterattack from the Block.   Two players are positioned opposite one another and model the block. As the blocker/attacker lands, you toss the ball to the setter. The attacker transitions off the net, tags up for the approach, and calls for the desired set. Players switch positions after three attacks or one successful stuff block. (See Diagram 13-44.)

Repeat the drill blocking in various zones along the net appropriate to the team's defensive tactics and each player's role.

© 2001 by Parker Publishing Company

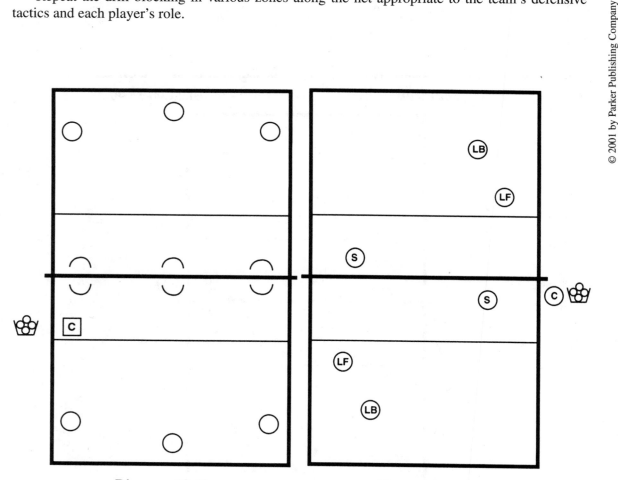

Diagram 13-42.   **Diagram 13-43.**

Visual Training

To See the Block.   The majority of attack drills should be performed with blockers. All of the above drills should be repeated adding a single, double, or triple block. Train attackers to see the block and openings or seams between the block.

- **Attackers hit line or angle around the block.** Blockers are first positioned only to block the line, then only to block angle, and finally to block line or angle at random. Attackers hit around the block to the defensive player. Repeat from zones 2 and 4. (See Diagram 13-45.)
- **Attackers hit the open spot.** Three blockers are bunched together to block a single attacker. The blocker in the middle position signals (by touch) to the outside blockers to jump or not to jump prior to each attack. One blocker remains on the ground to create an opening for the attacker. The attacker looks for "daylight" and attacks through the open spot. Repeat in zones 2, 3, and 4. (See Diagram 13-46.)
- **Attackers hit the hole or seam of the block.** Three blockers are in wide base block positions. You toss to the setter who works to deceive the direction of the set to create a hole between the middle and outside blockers. The attacker sees and attacks the hole or seam. (See Diagram 13-47.)
- **Attackers hit over the smallest or weakest blocker.** Two or three blockers of unequal height are positioned next to one another to block. Blockers switch positions just prior to the set and the attacker hits over the smallest blocker. Repeat in zones 2, 3, and 4. (See Diagram 13-48.)

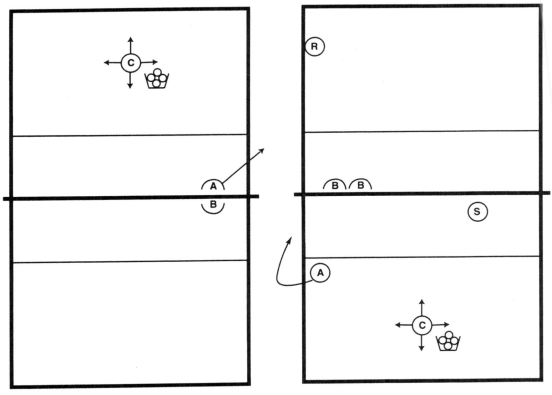

Diagram 13-44.   **Diagram 13-45.**

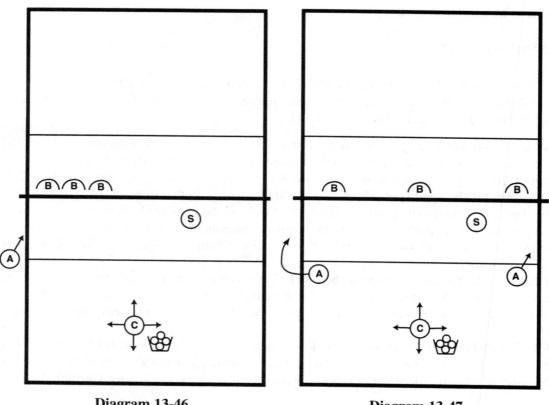

Diagram 13-46.   **Diagram 13-47.**

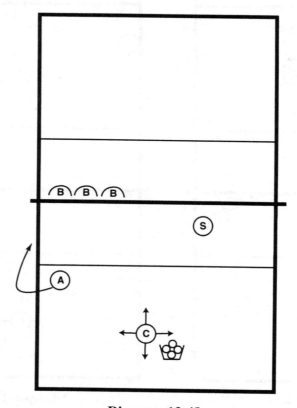

Diagram 13-48.

- **Attackers make the best tactical set selection according to block start positions.** Blockers vary their initial base position, such as, wide to the antennae or pinched inside. (See Chapter 9.) The zone 2, 3, or 4 attacker calls the set that makes the blockers move from their original positions. *For example:* The outside blockers are positioned wide, and the zone 2 attacker calls a second-tempo cross to the middle of the court. (See Diagram 13-49.)

To Hit Off the Block.   Train attackers against blockers on an elevated platform. This allows tight sets without the fear of injury that could occur if the attacker goes under the net. Blockers can use boxing sparring gloves or garden gloves to protect their fingers. Repeat drills with "live" blockers jumping from standard positions.

- **Attackers hit or tip horizontally off the block.** One tall blocker stands on an elevated platform near the sideline. You toss or a setter sets the ball tight to the net and near the sideline. Attackers hit or tip off the block. Attackers accumulate points for successful "kills" off the block. (See Diagram 13-50.)
- **Attackers hit vertically off the block.** Two tall blockers stand on an elevated platform opposite the attacker. You toss or a setter sets the ball a few feet off the net and the attacker hits high and flat off the top of the block. Attackers accumulate points for successful "kills" off the top of the block. Repeat from zones 2 and 4. (See Diagram 13-51.)
- **Attackers hit vertically or horizontally off the block.** Two tall blockers are positioned opposite the attacker on an elevated platform. You toss or the setter sets randomly tight to the net

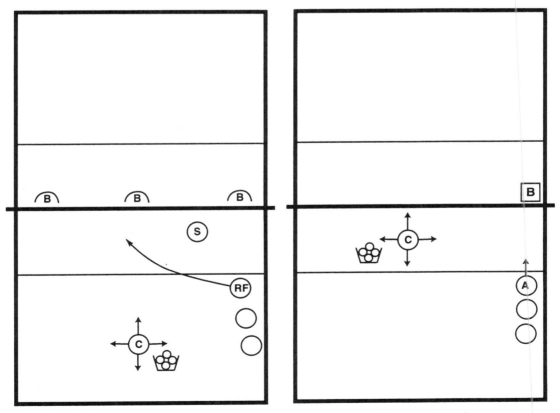

Diagram 13-49.   Diagram 13-50

and the sideline or one to two feet off the net. Attackers hit off the block vertically or horizontally according to the set. Attackers accumulate points for successful "kills" off the block. Repeat from zones 2 and 4. (See Diagram 13-52.)

To See Back Row Defenders.   Train attackers to look at the opponent's initial defensive positions prior to the set. Advanced hitters can make another quick eye check just after the set is made.

- **Attackers hit away from defense.** You toss to the setter who sets the attacker. The middle back rotates to the corner or remains middle back during the set. The attacker hits to the spot left vacant by the receiver, that is, deep line or middle. Repeat from zones 2 and 4. (See Diagram 13-53.)
- **Attackers hit or tip.** The left back receiver starts deep on the line and remains back for a line attack or moves up during the set for the tip. The attacker hits deep if the receiver moves up. The attacker tips if the defender remains deep. Repeat from zone 4. (See Diagram 13-54.)

Attack Against a Full Defense

Gladiators.   Two attackers and a setter (gladiators) compete against a team of six. You initiate the play with a free ball toss to the gladiators' side. They pass the ball to the setter and attack anywhere along the net. The rally continues until the ball is down. Rally score to 15. If the gladiators

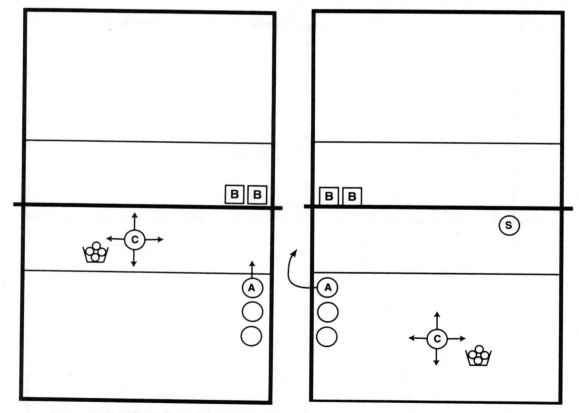

Diagram 13-51.   **Diagram 13-52.**

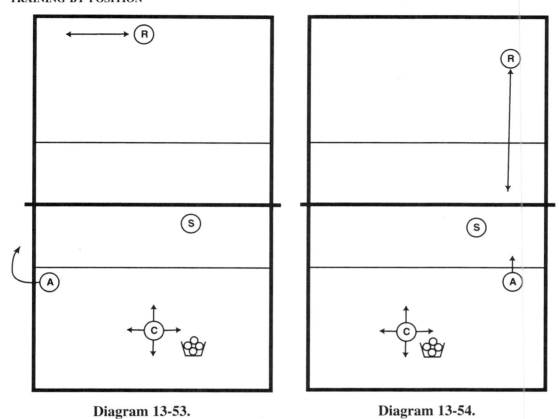

Diagram 13-53.   **Diagram 13-54.**

win the first contest, a second contest begins with the gladiators receiving serve instead of a free ball. (See Diagram 13-55.)

5's Left Side Attacker Challenge.   Form teams of five on each side. The coach/player alternates initiating the ball with a toss or serve to each side. The only players who are allowed to score points are the left side (zone 4) attackers, and they score only with kills. No points are scored on errors. If a player other than the left side attacker scores, that team wins the right to receive the next ball, but no point is scored. The first attacker to score 4 points wins. Only a single block is permitted. Repeat with the right side attackers. (See Diagram 13-56.)

5's Left vs. Right Side Attacker Challenge.   Form teams of five on each side. The coach/player alternates initiating the ball with a toss or serve to each side. The only players who are allowed to score points are the right side (zone 2) and left side (zone 4) attackers, and they can only score off kills and stuff blocks. The first attacker to score 4 points wins. Attackers switch their position from right side to left side or vice versa when one attacker reaches 2 points. (See Diagram 13-57.)

6's Challenges.   Form two teams of six. Points are scored on the attack and/or the block of the designated "go-to person," that is, left vs. left, right vs. right, and right vs. left as in the 5's challenges. Blockers release to the side of the point-scoring attackers. Double and triple blocks are

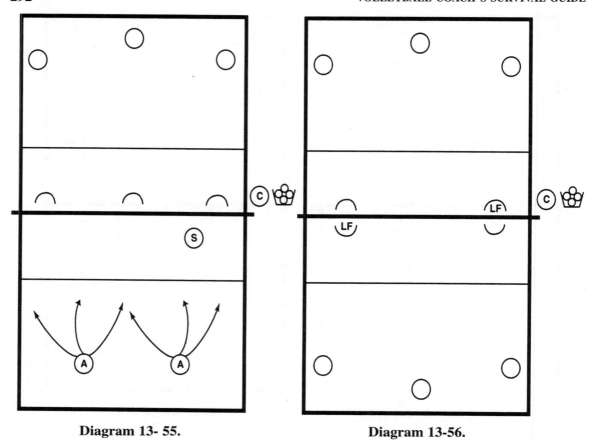

Diagram 13- 55.   **Diagram 13-56.**

encouraged. The coach/player alternates initiating a free ball to each side. The first attacker to reach 5 points wins for his or her team. (See Diagram 13-58.)

Second Contact Set and Attack for Zone 2

The right side (zone 2) player has set responsibilities when the primary setter receives the first ball. The following are minimum requirements for the position. See Chapter 3 for more training options.

Transition to Set from the Block.   The zone 2 player models the block and turns to find the ball tossed by you. The set is directed to the middle or left front targets or "live" attackers. The coach/player tosses the ball as the blocker is landing. The ball is initiated from right back, simulating a dug ball by the setter in the right back position. Setters accumulate points for proper set execution and placements. (See Diagram 13-59.)

Transition to Set from a Dig.   You hit from an elevated platform in zone 4 to the primary setter playing defense in zone 1. The zone 2 player jumps with your hit, comes out of the block looking for the ball, and sets a second- or third-tempo set to the middle or left side target and/or attacker. Setters accumulate points on accurate sets. (See Diagram 13-60.)

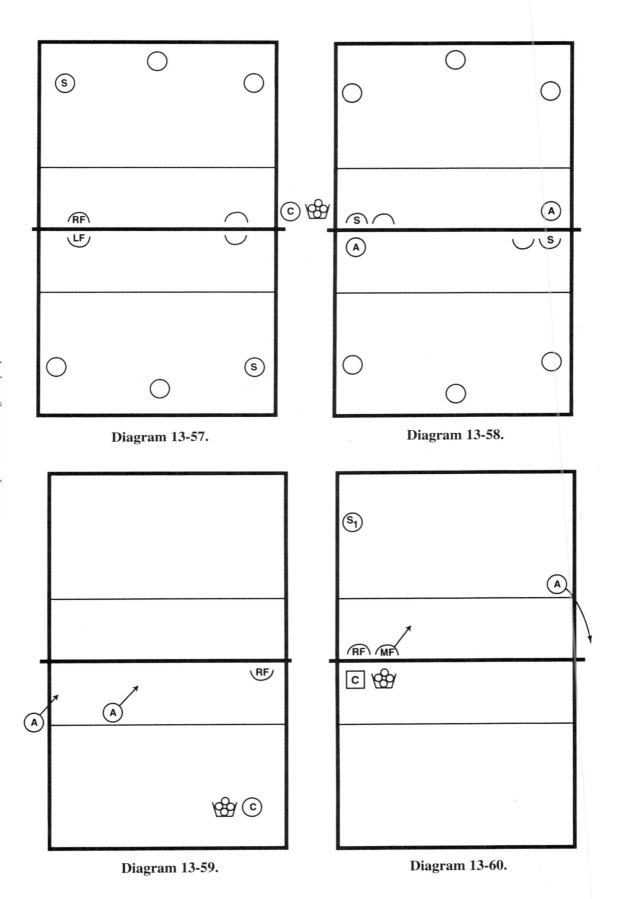

Diagram 13-57.

Diagram 13-58.

Diagram 13-59.

Diagram 13-60.

Transition to Second Contact Attack.   The zone 2 player models the block, lands, receives a tossed ball from you, jumps, and attacks the ball with the right or left hand to the targets. Setters accumulate points for proper attack execution and placements. (See Diagram 13-61.)

Transition to Set or Attack.   The zone 2 player models the block, lands, and receives a tossed ball from you. Just prior to setter contact, you call out to jump set to the zone 4 target or attack the ball to a specific target. Setters accumulate points on successful execution and deception. (Refer to Diagram 13-61.)

TRAINING THE MIDDLE BLOCKER
(Zone 3)

Attributes of a Successful Middle Blocker

Also see Chapter 7.

Height.   Height has its advantages for the middle blocker. Taller blockers cover a bigger area at the net. They require less time to jump to block first-tempo sets, and less time to recover from misreads blocking quick sets to move to the outside attacker.

Quickness and Agility.   The best middle blockers are not always the tallest; rather, they are quick and agile. They are able to control their body on the ground and in the air in transition blocking and attacking. They are quick enough to arrive on time to block high and quick sets and to recover to transition to attack.

Intensity and Aggressiveness.   Successful middle blockers pursue attackers with the attitude that every ball is blockable. They are intense and determined to get to every ball.

Tactical "Smarts."   Successful middle blockers are aware of the opponent's offensive system. They predict setter selections and know setter and attacker strengths and tendencies. They are constantly evaluating attackers' positioning and movements for cues to help establish proper block position.

Good Peripheral Vision.   The best middle blockers have good wide and narrow focus. They see first-, second-, and third-tempo attackers coming into and/or leaving their zone.

Good Communication.   Middle blockers are the captains of the front row defense and must communicate blocking switches and responsibilities. This communication begins prior to the play and continues throughout the rally.

Conditioning.   Successful middle blockers are in great shape physically to block and attack with maximum effort throughout the match.

> **KEY:** It is ideal to have middle blockers who are equally strong blocking and attacking, but this is not always possible. It is your role to determine which of these skills is more important to winning at your level and base the selection of the middle blocker on these merits.

Middle Blocker Skills

Block first-, second-, and third-tempo sets in all zones.

Drills

Drills are performed generally with three to four middle blockers.

Training the Block Without the Ball

Train block mechanics and footwork patterns without the ball. Blockers accumulate points on successful technical execution.

Model Blocks in Zone 3.   Middle blockers start in a ready position in zone 3 and model the block for first-tempo sets. Emphasis is on high posture, high hands, and very little bend prior to take-off. Repeat the drill, modeling the block using the technique for second- and third-tempo sets. Emphasis is on a half-squat bend just prior to the block for a maximum jump. Repeat adding quick sidesteps to the right and left prior to each block to simulate positional adjustment steps. (See Diagram 13-62.)

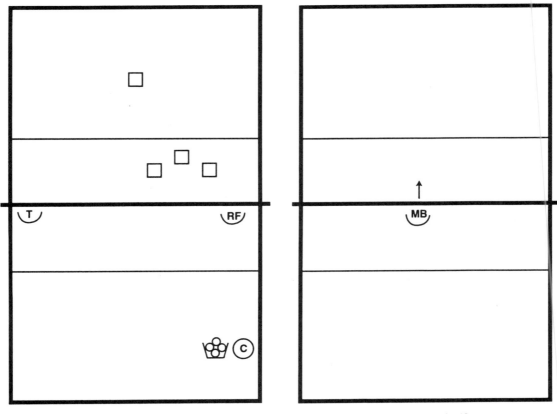

Diagram 13-61.   Diagram 13-62.

Model Blocks in Zones 2 and 4.   Middle blockers start in a ready position in zone 3 and move to block in zone 2. Blockers shuffle back to the middle and move to block in zone 4. Return to the middle each time. Repeat the blocks, moving to the outside position with the three-step crossover.

> **KEY:** Use tape marks near the sidelines to indicate take-off points for middle blockers to insure that they cover the desired distance necessary to present a solid block with the outside blocker. (See Diagram 13-63.)

Variations.   Middle blockers must always make the attempt to block. Misreads happen, but blockers must never "give up"; rather, they readjust and aggressively pursue the ball. If late, blockers use a one-hand block technique to reach the ball. Blockers accumulate points on proper technical execution.

Repeat the above drills with emphasis on the following technical training goals:

- **Train to block with each hand independently.** Middle blockers move to the outside to model the block. Emphasis is on reaching with the outside hand to cover the seam or the inside hand to cover the cross-court ball. Blockers can reach farther with one hand than both and still penetrate the net. This technique is frequently utilized on late blocks, sharply angled hits, and blocking quick sets in the middle.
- **Train for first-tempo set misreads.** Middle blockers misread the first-tempo set, jump to block it, land on one foot (the opposite foot of the intended direction of movement), and push off to quickly move to the right or left sideline to model the block in zone 2 or 4.
- **Train for second- and third-tempo set misreads.** Middle blockers misread the direction of the outside set and take a step in the wrong direction, then push off to change directions and model the block in zone 2 or 4.
- **Train middle blocker quickness.**
  1. **Middle blockers mirror challenge.** One middle blocker is designated as the leader and blocks anywhere along the net. The other middle blocker, the chaser, follows and blocks in a mirror image. Repeat the drill, reversing roles. Emphasis is on quick foot speed into the block position and quickness off the ground into a block position in the air.
  2. **Middle blocker–setter challenge.** The setter is positioned in the team's pass target area. (See Chapter 9.) The middle blocker is in a ready position on the opposite side of the net in zone 3. Targets are positioned in zones 2 and 4. You toss the ball to the setter, who sets front, back, or middle as deceptively as possible. The middle blocker reads the setter's body position and release and moves to block in the appropriate area. After the block, the blocker returns to the initial base position and targets return the ball to you. (See Diagram 13-64.)

Blockers must complete ten consecutive blocks without misreading the setter to complete the drill. If the middle blocker is "faked" and does not make a move to block, the score returns to zero. Emphasis is on reading and pursuing the ball every time.

Block with the Ball

You are on an elevated platform two to three feet off the net hitting into the block. The middle blocker can perform these drills alone or with a corresponding outside blocker. Emphasis is on block mechanics and footwork to the ball. Blockers accumulate points on proper technical execution.

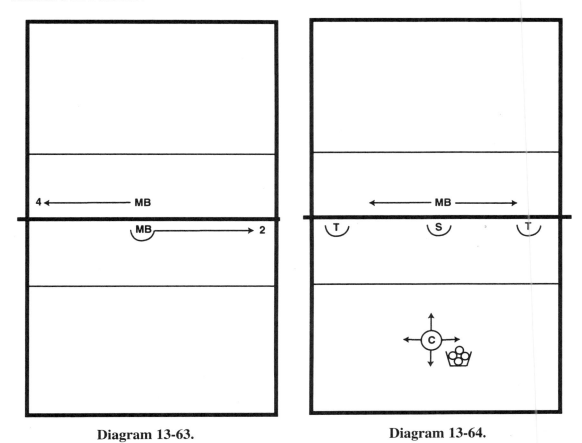

Diagram 13-63.   Diagram 13-64.

Movement to the Outside Block Position.   Middle blockers begin in zone 3 and move with their preferred footwork (shuffle or crossover) to block your attack in zone 4. Repeat in zone 2. (See Diagram 13-65.)

Repeat the drill with the following training goals.

- **Misreads of quick sets.** Middle blockers misread the quick attack and block in zone 3. They realize their mistake, land on one foot, and push off to move to block the outside attack in zone 2 or 4.
- **Misreads of the direction of outside sets.** Middle blockers misread the direction of the outside set and take a first step in the opposite direction of the attack. They realize their mistake, immediately turn, and push off to move to block on the opposite side.
- **Blocking with one hand independently.** Middle blockers begin in zone 3 and move to block your attack in zone 2. You turn your body to indicate the direction the ball will be hit and the blocker responds by using the closer hand to block the ball. Repeat the drill with you positioned in zone 4. (Refer to Diagram 13-65.)

Follow the Ball Attacked Around or Off the Block.   Middle blockers jump to block and immediately come out of the block looking for a ball tossed by the coach/player simulating a back row dig. The blocker digs or attacks the ball accordingly. (See Diagram 13-66.)

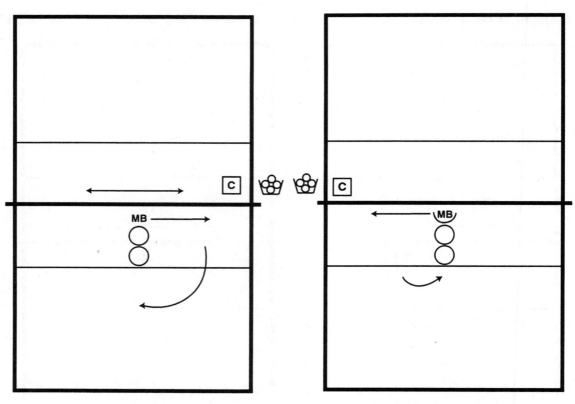

Diagram 13-65A.   **Diagram 13-65B.**

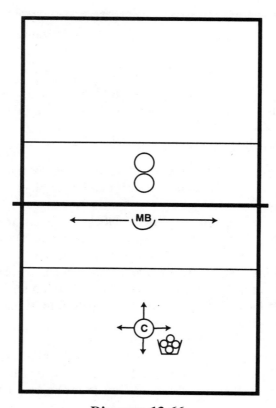

Diagram 13-66.

Block Against Attack Line(s).   Emphasis is on repetitions of block footwork and mechanics and reading the attacker cues that help establish proper block position.

- **Train blocker focus on the cues rather than the ball.** The setter sets to attackers in zone 2 or 4 at random. Middle blockers move to block but *do not jump*. Blockers call out the type and direction of attack prior to hitter contact, that is, line, angle, or tip. Emphasis is on reading the setter and attacker cues, quick movement to the outside, and establishing a block position that takes away the attacker's angle of approach or tendency. (See Diagram 13-67.)

    KEY: Emphasis is on quick movements to the block take-off position. There is time to make more adjustments if the middle blocker arrives early.

- **Train blocker response to a single option.** Middle blockers are positioned middle front to block the zone 3 attacker only. Emphasis is on good positioning based on the attacker's angle of approach or tendency. Repeat the drill, moving to block only the zone 2 attacker and then only the attacker in zone 4. (See Diagram 13-68.)
- **Train blocker response to two options.** Middle blockers are positioned in zone 3 and alternately release to block the attack in zones 2 and 4, 3 and 2, and then 3 and 4. Repeat the drill with the setter directing the ball at random to two of the above options. (See Diagram 13-69.)
- **Train blocker response to three options.** Middle blockers defend attacks set at random to zones 2, 3, or 4. Attack options include three front row attackers, two attackers, and a front row setter and/or back row attackers. (See Diagram 13-70.)

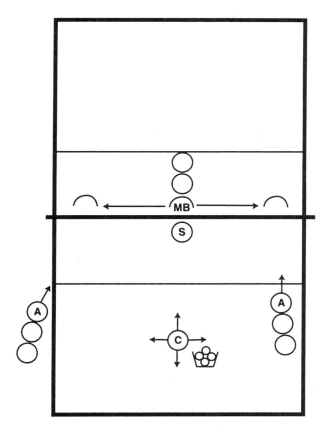

Diagram 13-67.

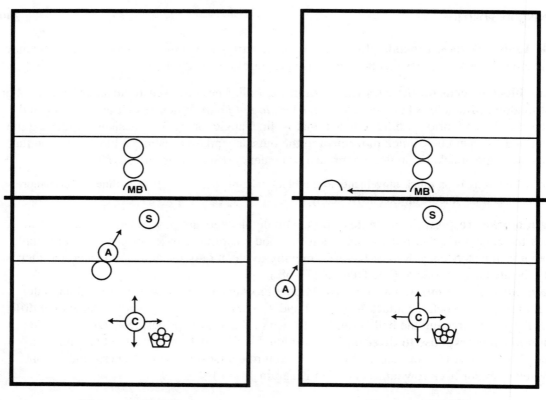

Diagram 13-68A.   **Diagram 13-68B.**

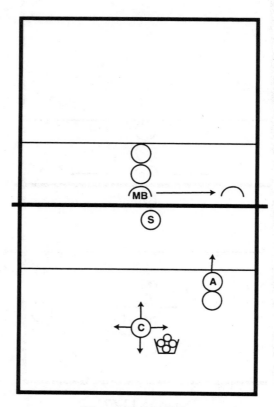

Diagram 13-68C.

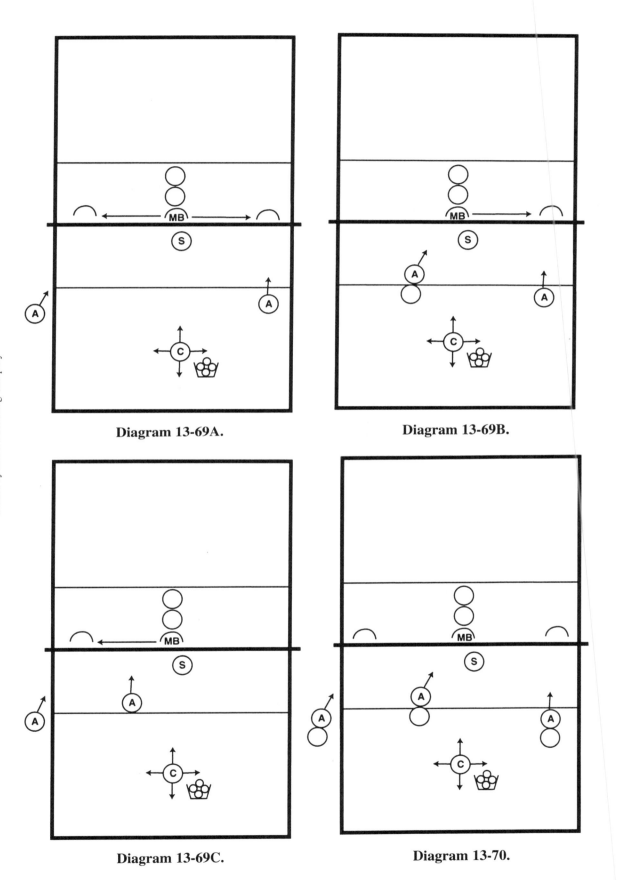

Diagram 13-69A.

Diagram 13-69B.

Diagram 13-69C.

Diagram 13-70.

KEY: As the options increase, so does the response time of the blocker. Good reading ability, efficient lateral movement along the net, and quickness off the ground aid the middle blocker in reaching the attack position on time.

Middle Attacker Skills

• Train middle blockers to attack first-, second-, and third-tempo sets in zones 2, 3, and 4. Do not limit their options.
• Train middle blockers to attack with a variety of shots, such as, power, tip, and off-speed.
• Train middle blockers to attack with a variety of placements, such as, the deep and sharp angles, the cutback, the tip directly over or to the sides of the block, and the deep corners.
• Train middle blockers to hit or redirect overpasses with a sweeping block motion and slight wrist movement.

First-Tempo Attack on In-System Passes

Mechanics and Placements.   You toss to the setter who sets for the first-tempo attack. Emphasis is on proper tag-up start positions, footwork patterns, approach routes, and attack mechanics. Repeat the drill with all first-tempo attack options. Attackers accumulate points on proper technical execution and placement. (See Diagram 13-71.)

For more information, see Chapter 3 for first- and second-tempo sets; training the outside attacker for attack options and placements; Chapter 5 for slide and quick attacker mechanics checklists; and Chapter 9 for set options and combinations.

KEY: Emphasize tagging up to the same spot every time in transition and making a strong approach. Avoid revealing the option by the tag-up position.

Repeat the drill as necessary with emphasis on the following areas.

• **First-tempo set timing.** Train middle attackers to arrive to the attack position in the air at the proper time. You toss balls to the setter at different heights, trajectories, and locations within the target area for in-system passes, and the attacker approaches and jumps. The setter catches the ball and the other middles call out "late," "early," or "perfect" to indicate the timing of the quick attacker. Middles accumulate points by properly adjusting the timing of their approach and take-off. Middles approach three times in succession, returning each time to the tag-up position.
• **Proper take-off positions.** Train middle attackers to evaluate the position of the pass and the setter in order to select an appropriate option, approach route, and take-off point. You toss balls to a variety of locations and vary the origination point of the tosses. Middles accumulate points on proper take-off positions.

KEYS: Train attackers to open up to the setter.

Train attackers to keep the ball, the setter, and the net in view at all times.

Train attackers to give the setter room to set the ball.

Train attackers to take off far enough off the net to allow the setter room to deliver a set off the net and out of the hands of the blocker.

Tape a line one to two feet off and parallel to the net. Train the attacker to jump on or behind the tape.

- **Judgment of in-and-out-of-system passes.** Train middle attackers to distinguish between in- and out-of-system passes. You toss balls inside or outside the taped target area that indicates in-system passes. Middles run first-tempo plays whenever possible. Emphasis is on learning to judge the pass, knowing when the first-tempo set is possible, and when another option must be called. Middles accumulate points for consecutive correct judgments.
- **First-tempo attack on passes along the net.** You toss a series of balls at different locations along the net within the target area to the setter. The first few tosses are to the right. With each subsequent toss, the passes move farther along the net toward the left. Train attackers to evaluate the pass in order to select an appropriate option, approach route, and take-off point. Repeat the drill with the tosses along the net at random. Attackers accumulate points on proper selection of options, good execution, and placements. (See Diagram 13-72.)
- **First-tempo attack on passes various depths off the net.** You toss a series of balls to the setter, varying the depth of the pass from the net but within the target area. The first few tosses are tight to the net. Each subsequent pass moves the ball farther off the net. Train attackers to call the best option in each situation. Attackers accumulate points on proper selection of options, good execution, and placements. Repeat the drill with the tosses at random distances. (See Diagram 13-73.)

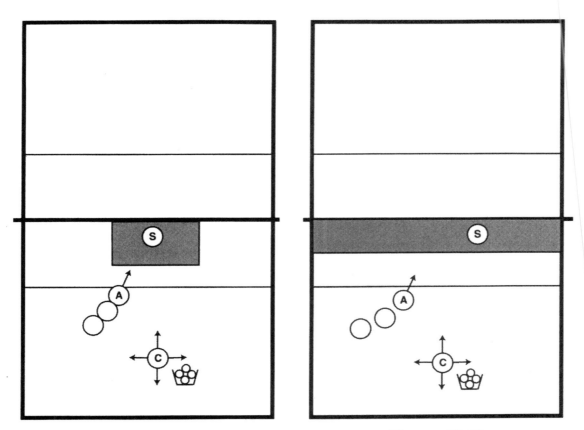

Diagram 13-71.   **Diagram 13-72.**

© 2001 by Parker Publishing Company

KEY: Train attackers on tight passes to jump with the setter, ready to attack as the setter contacts the ball. Emphasis is also on the attacker staying off the net, allowing the setter to redirect the ball off the net and out of the blocker's range.

- **First-tempo attack on random in-system tosses at different heights, locations, and depths.** You toss balls at random to the setter. Emphasis is on middle attackers making an audible call for the set when the ball is at the midpoint between the passer and the setter and establishing a good take-off position. Attackers accumulate points on proper selection of options, good execution, and placements. (See Diagram 13-74.)

KEY: Vary the origination of the toss in all drills.

Attack Options on Out-of-System Passes

The play has been called for a first-tempo set, but the pass does not allow the option. It is an out-of-system pass. You toss balls at random to simulate this situation, which requires middle attackers to call second- or third-tempo set options. Emphasis is on middle attackers establishing an attack position or knowing when the attack is not possible and releasing to cover another attacker. Middles accumulate points for proper judgments, good execution, and placements. (Refer to Diagram 13-74.)

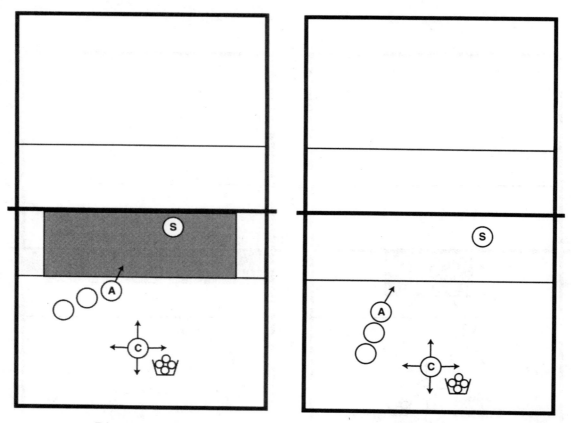

Diagram 13-73   Diagram 13-74.

Attack on the Overpass

The coach/player tosses the ball from the opposite side of the net to simulate an overpass. The blocker gathers and jumps to hit or redirect the ball with both hands in a sweeping block motion with a slight wrist movement to direct ball down. (Refer to Diagram 13-35.)

Options for Common Attack Problems

Correct Arm-Swing Mechanics

- **Attack with a badminton shuttlecock.** Middle attackers approach the net holding the shuttlecock in their hitting hand, jump, and throw it over the net toward the angle or cutback target.

    Shuttlecocks are an effective method for training a quick, compact arm-and-wrist motion for middle hitters because they are small and light. The size and weight of the shuttlecock makes it easy to hold in one hand, and its lightness forces a powerful and quick arm-and-wrist action for the shuttlecock to go down properly.
- **Attack from an elevated platform.** The middle attacker stands on an elevated platform with a basket of balls close by. The attacker self tosses the ball and hits it over the net toward the angle or cutback target. Emphasis is on a quick and compact arm swing and snap initiated from the elbow and wrist. Repeat the drill, adding a setter. You toss the ball to the setter, who sets the stationary middle attacker.

Transition to First-Tempo Attack

From the Block

- **Train footwork to first-tempo attack without the ball.** Middle blockers are positioned in zone 3 and move to model the block in zone 2 or 4, tag up to the approach base position (a taped X on the floor), approach, and model the attack. Attackers call for a specific set as they begin the approach. Attackers accumulate points with proper block and approach footwork. (See Diagram 13-75.)
- **Off coach toss.** Middle blockers alternate modeling the block in zones 2 and 4. You toss the ball to the setter as the blocker is landing. The blocker finds the ball, and the setter, allows the setter to get to the ball, and transitions off the net. The blocker calls for the desired set and approaches for the attack. Attackers accumulate points with good execution. (Refer to Diagram 13-75.)

    KEY: Vary the timing, height, and location of the toss. Some passes allow middle blockers adequate time to transition off the net, tag up, and take a full three-step approach. Others force attackers to shorten their approach to two steps, or turn and jump with almost no approach. Train the attacker to be available every time the setter has the ball.

- **Off free ball pass.** Middle blockers move to block in zone 2 or 4. You toss a "free ball" to the receiver and the blocker transitions off the net, calls for the set, and approaches for the attack. Emphasis is on the attacker calling the play vocally, attacking from various locations along the net and to different targets on the court. (See Diagram 13-76.)
- **Off a down ball.** Middle blockers move to block in zone 2 or 4. You hit a down ball to a receiver. Just prior to contact, the blocker calls "no block" and transitions off the net for the attack. (Refer to Diagram 13-76.)

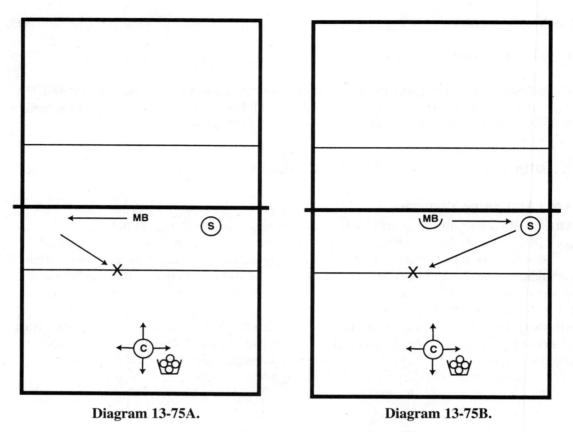

Diagram 13-75A.   **Diagram 13-75B.**

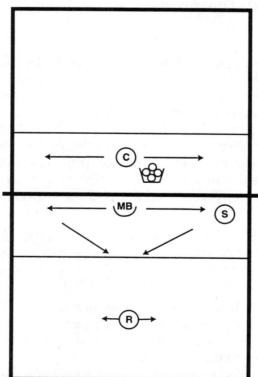

Diagram 13-76.

- **Off a controlled dig.** You are positioned at the right or left corner of the net assuming the position of an outside blocker. The middle blocker is positioned in zone 3. You slap the ball and the middle blocker moves to block the ball on the side nearest you. You hit the ball to a receiver for a controlled dig. The middle attacker transitions off the net to the tag-up position, the setter releases to set, and the middle attacker approaches for the attack. (See Diagram 13-77.)
- **Off a "live" dig.** You stand on an elevated platform and hit the ball to a receiver. Middle blockers move from zone 3 to block the attack. They transition off net and approach for the attack if the ball passes them. Middle attackers judge the pass to determine if a first-tempo attack is possible. If not, they call for a higher set or cover another attacker. Repeat with you hitting from zones 2, 3, and 4. (See Diagram 13-78.)

From Serve Receive.   The ball is initiated with the serve to one or more receivers. The middle attacker and setter vary their initial start positions in accordance to the team's reception formations. Emphasis is on the middle attacker evaluating the pass, finding the setter, and establishing the proper approach route and take-off point. Emphasis is on using different attack options. (See Diagram 13-79.)

First-Tempo Attack Against the Block

Train the first-tempo attack against a single, double, and triple block as soon as possible. All the above drills should be repeated adding a block.

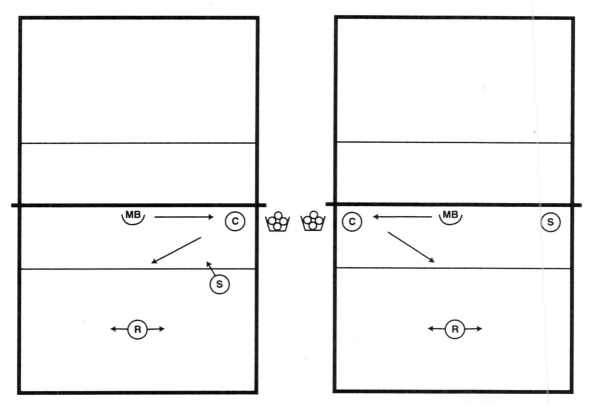

Diagram 13-77A.   **Diagram 13-77B.**

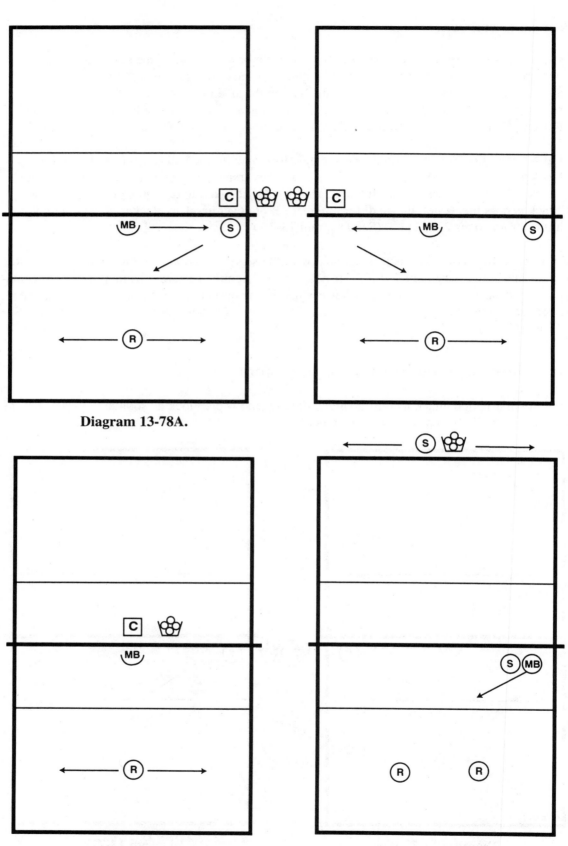

Diagram 13-78A.

Diagram 13-78C.

Diagram 13-79.

Attack Against a Single Block

- **Train to see and hit the opposite direction of the blocker movement.** You toss the ball to the setter. The middle blocker takes a step toward the right or left sideline just prior to the set. The middle attacker hits in the opposite direction of the blocker's movement. (See Diagram 13-80.)
- **Train to see the block and call a play moving away from the block.** You toss the ball to the setter who sets the middle attacker. The attacker alternates hitting locations; *for example:* alternating hitting a "1 and A," "1 and 3," or "1 and slide." Emphasis is on initiating the approach from the same tag-up position each time, but varying the position of the attack along the net, forcing the middle blocker to move from their original position. (See Diagram 13-81.)

Attack Against a Double Block.   Set up specific game situations where middle attackers face a double or triple block. Emphasis is on:

- utilizing a variety of options and placements
- setting the ball off the net to give the attacker room to hit around or off the block
- going to seams in the block and making the middle and outside blockers move
  (See Diagram 13-82.)

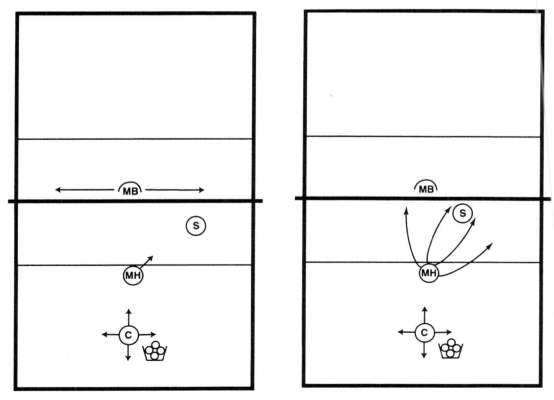

Diagram 13-80.   **Diagram 13-81.**

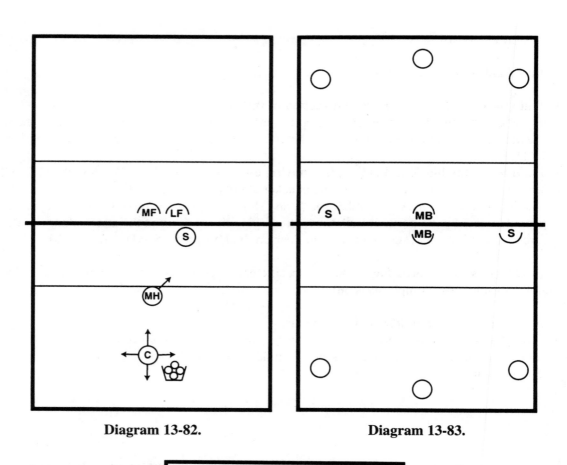

Diagram 13-82.

Diagram 13-83.

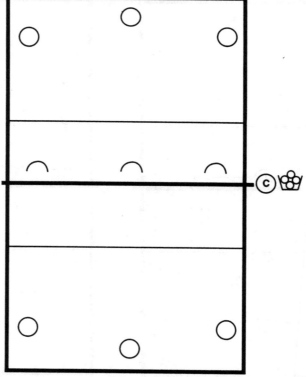

Diagram 13-84.

First-Tempo Attack in Live Situations

Give middle attackers many opportunities to have real-game practice situations through modified games and scrimmages.

- **5-on-5 middle attacker challenge.** Two teams of five each compete. The setter is positioned in zone 2 and the middle attacker is in zone 3. There are three back row defenders. The first team to reach 5 points wins, rally score. You initiate a free ball at the beginning of each rally, alternating sides each time. Points are scored only by the middle attackers and only on successful attacks or stuff blocks. No points are awarded on player errors. If another attacker wins the point, that side is awarded the next ball but not a point. (See Diagram 13-83.)

    KEYS: It is important for middle attackers to be in air when the setter has the ball, especially when the pass is tight.

    It is important that the middle attacker be creative in using attack options to create holes and seams in the block.

- **6-on-6 middle attacker challenge.** Two teams are positioned as in a regulation game. The first team to reach 20 points wins, rally score. You initiate a free ball at the beginning of each rally, alternating sides each time. Three points are scored when the middle attacker kills a first-tempo set. All other attackers score 1 point for a kill. No points are awarded on player errors. Emphasis is on overloading the middle attacker with a double or triple block. (See Diagram 13-84.)
- **Setter exchanges with a middle attacker.** See "training the setter" earlier in this chapter.

CHAPTER 14

THE INTANGIBLES

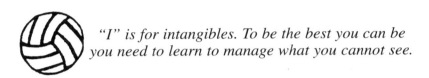 *"I" is for intangibles. To be the best you can be you need to learn to manage what you cannot see.*

The mind is the key to improving performance, as well as its biggest obstacle. Mental thoughts can be friends or enemies. They can act as motivators or create self-doubts that impede an athlete's progress. Only when players fully utilize their mental skills will they be able to consistently achieve their best performance levels.

> **MAXIM:** *Ninety percent of sports is mental. The other half is in your head.* Yogi Berra

THE ERROR PROBLEM

Making mistakes is a natural part of the learning process; it takes time and experience to develop fundamental technical and tactical skills. Thus, it is understandable when errors are made in the early stages of players' development, but players at every level are going to make some mistakes. If they worry too much about committing them, they will not take sufficient risks to play their best and continue to advance. Therefore, critical to players' success is not the elimination of errors but the reduction of their overall number.

Along with eliminating unnecessary errors is learning to manage those that have been made. It is often athletes' reaction to errors—rather than the errors themselves—that is the greatest hindrance to performance. Successful athletes learn to master the many forms of failure and frustration in a positive way.

In *Extraordinary Tennis for the Ordinary Player,* Simon Ramo, Ph.D. (Crown Publishers, Inc., New York, 1970) uses the term "botch" to indicate an unnecessary error. It is defined as the type of error that cannot be blamed on a teammate or the opponent, rather an act that one does entirely on his or her own. It is something unnecessary that results not from one's inability to play in the physical sense, but by not using his or her head. In addition to the botch is the S.O.B., the "son of a botch." This second-generation botch unfortunately is the consequence of an earlier botch. Most players focus their attention on the son-of-a-botch and fail to realize that the botch is really the culprit.

Errors are not created equal and athletes must learn to distinguish between "acceptable and avoidable" ones. Errors happen but botches and sons of botches can be avoided through better use of the "thinking department." Players can greatly facilitate the reduction of errors through appropriate responses in the categories of personal, teammate, thought, tactical, and match decisions described here.

Personal Decisions

Personal-decision errors are big enemies of successful players and teams. They are to blame for as many losses as faulty techniques or tactics. The problem is that players often do not recognize them as errors, nor do they understand the depth of their consequences. If left unchecked, personal decision errors are responsible for many subsequent errors.

See Beyond the Moment.   Although athletes know what is right, they often make the decision not to do it. They are distracted by the immediate pleasure of the moment. Help athletes make future-looking decisions by pointing out the consequences of their actions. Show how the first poor decision or error is the cause of more serious consequences that negatively affect their performance and future goals. Help them reassess their personal priorities with regards to keeping an eye to the future. These errors are avoidable for those athletes who have the desire.

Budget Time Properly.   An athlete cannot attend practice because of the necessity to write a paper or study for an exam. Not only is the athlete affected, but teammates as well because the player is not available to participate in team drills.

Eat Properly and Get Sufficient Sleep.   An athlete lacks energy and gets sick more frequently because of poor nutrition and sleep habits. This player is not so effective in practice or the classroom and has a higher absenteeism rate. A player is tired during the match and does not perform up to standard. The athlete, as well as teammates, suffers the consequences.

Learn the Fundamentals.   Players must pay their dues in time and effort to learn to do the fundamentals correctly. Good technique insures consistency of performance and the reduction of errors. It takes lots of repetitions to develop good technical skills. There are no short cuts. Tactics are not a consideration without the basics.

Do Weights and Conditioning.   Some athletes decide not to work out because they "just don't feel like it." This attitude becomes the norm and makes it easier and easier not to do it. This attitude begins to affect how teammates feel about working out because then they feel "if she doesn't have to do it, then why do I?" Athletes cannot be their best if they are not physically in top form.

MAXIM: You can't get much done by starting tomorrow.

Discipline Yourself to Focus.   Errors dealing with mental lapses are completely unnecessary. Players are responsible for what they are doing, and this starts with good focus and good movement. They must always know what is being said and done. Players who are lazy or inattentive must not be allowed to remain in the game or in practice.

Don't Be Lazy in Practice. A player has a careless practice attitude that causes the loss of that day's practice. Going through the motions does not help the athlete improve or even maintain current levels. It would have been just as effective not to practice at all.

Stay Alert. Players cannot apply game or drill instructions because they did not hear them. Players cannot make a good play on a ball that is "playable" within the realm of their abilities because the ball suddenly appears and they are not prepared to react to it properly.

Keep Your Feet Awake. Players are unable to make a good play on the ball because their feet fell asleep, that is, they are standing still while the ball is in play. They must be in a continual "active" ready position and be ready with both the eyes and the feet. They cannot assume or hope that the ball is going to someone else.

Make No Excuses. It is easy to make excuses for poor play or losses; *for example:* "I was sick . . . the car ride was so long . . . it was hot in the gym . . . everyone was playing poorly . . . the sets were bad . . . no one was talking." Excuses, however, are only ineffective ways of not accepting responsibility for failure. Athletes who continue to blame others for their mistakes never get any better.

Say It, and Do It. It is really easy to talk about the things necessary to be good, but it is quite a different matter to actually do them. Talking the talk, but not walking the walk, gets the athlete nowhere. If an effort is not made to make a change, there is a good chance that the change will not be made. It is hard to give it your all when you are not feeling well. It is difficult to always meet the commitment of weights or extra conditioning. It is harder and more tiring to approach and swing hard every time, to be low on defense and go for every ball, but players who want to be the best find a way to do them.

MAXIM: Talk is cheap because supply exceeds demand.

Teammate Decisions

Dcision errors dealing with teammates are also big enemies to successful teams. They also go unrecognized as errors but often are equally harmful as poor personal decisions.

Be Considerate to Teammates. It is easy in a moment of thoughtlessness to alienate a teammate by responding in a cold manner or not responding at all when being with other friends is seemingly more important. It is easy not to respond to a teammate's request for help because it is not convenient at the time, but there is no justification for it. The teammate is then offended and there is no valid excuse that can be given for an apology. Encourage players to be kind to one another.

Do Not Gossip. It is wrong to gossip about teammates even if what is said is true. Embarrassing, criticizing, or joking about teammates behind their backs might seem insignificant at the moment, but it damages relationships. Encourage athletes not to participate in gossip, rumor spreading, or reputation bashing. Encourage them to apologize immediately if they have offended someone.

No Negative Talk or Finger Pointing. There is no room for the negative on or off the court. It can be the downfall of the team. It is easy to criticize or put the blame somewhere else but it does not do anything to change the situation; rather, it worsens it. Encourage players to accept responsibility for searching for solutions instead of being negative.

Be There for Teammates. Athletes must know that their teammates can rely on them. Athletes must support and help each other when they are down or frustrated. They must keep an eye out for each other, lend an ear, encourage teammates when they are discouraged, and congratulate them when they are successful.

Make Teammates Feel Liked and Included. Everyone wants to be accepted and fit in. All teammates must be included in conversations and functions. Teammates at group gatherings should sit with those who they are standing closest to rather than forming cliques and "rejecting" certain teammates. Players must remember the lessons of the golden rule. If you want to be treated with courtesy, kindness, and respect, then it is very important to be conscious of your behavior toward others.

Forgive and Forget. Team members may unknowingly hurt another's feelings even under the best of circumstances. Athletes must overlook some "relationship mistakes" and give teammates the benefit of the doubt in "gray areas." Teammates must not let these mistakes and/or small differences of opinions affect positive relationships.

> **MAXIM:** *No matter how far you have gone on a wrong road, turn back.* Turkish proverb

Thought Decisions

Athletes' thoughts have the power to make or break them. Help athletes improve their mental approach to the game by first making them aware of potential problem areas, and then training them to develop effective coping strategies. They can learn to use their minds to work for them rather than against them by directing and redirecting their concentration to the positive and to the controllable.

A major inhibitor of performance is fear of mistakes. Do not let players magnify or give too much importance to them; it is unproductive. Help players conquer their fear of making mistakes by allowing them to make errors rather than trying to avoid them. Encourage players to learn from mistakes and avoid making similar ones. Players perform not only in accordance with their ability or reality, but also in accordance with their perception of reality. Convince them that they can be successful and their chances have increased greatly. The following are examples of thought options for players.

> **MAXIM:** *If you constantly direct your attention to all the negatives, you cannot possibly see the positives.*

Think Constructively. Minimize the influence of errors by *dealing* with them, rather than dwelling on them. You cannot change something that has already happened and you cannot afford to let it ruin your concentration or future play. Getting too caught up in previous errors affects the things you normally would be capable of doing. Leave the error behind and narrow your concentration to the task at hand. Focus on what you want to do instead of dwelling on the past.

> *MAXIM: Success comes in cans, not in cannots.* Unknown coach

See Errors as Mini-Lessons.   Think of mistakes in terms of mini-lessons, and as opportunities to improve and grow. There is a lesson to be learned from each error. Failure should be used only as a guide to signal in which direction to go. What you learn from errors determines whether or not you will attain success in the future.

> *MAXIM: Focus on the ball, not the scoreboard.*

Be Nonjudgmental.   Learn to recognize mistakes without judging, criticizing, or blaming yourself for the action. Analyze what happened and how to make the proper adjustments to avoid similar errors in the future. Strive for perfection, but at the same time, understand that no one can play the perfect game. Everyone makes mistakes, but champions learn from them and move on.

Avoid Self Put-Downs.   Do not turn against yourself with self-imposed limitations; *for example:* "I always screw up . . . That was sure a stupid shot . . . We'll never win if I keep playing like this . . . I'll never be able to do it . . . I'm just not that good an athlete . . ." Do not sabotage yourself. Redirect your focus to correct execution and effort. Avoid taking a single negative event or a few consecutive errors and seeing it as a pattern of defeat. A bad warm-up does not have to indicate a bad game. A few mistakes do not mean you are playing terribly or that you will not get better.

> *MAXIM: Athletes, who anticipate failure, are never surprised.*

Choose Positive Internal Dialogues.   When the mind speaks to the body, it listens, and it greatly affects performance. Tune into your thoughts and identify positive and negative messages. The quality and content of your inner speech is within your control. Reinforce what you want to happen by programming yourself to substitute positive words, statements, and thoughts for unproductive or detrimental ones. Facilitate success through positive talk or exaggerate the problem by excessively dwelling on it. Replace self-doubts with positive, constructive conversation (self-talk); *for example:* "I am an effective attacker . . . I make good tactical choices . . . I am aggressive . . . I become more confident in my passing everyday . . . I know that I can make the difference . . . I enjoy playing against tough competition."

> *MAXIM: Think positive; it doesn't cost any more.*

Be Supportive.   Avoid attacking or criticizing yourself for your mistakes. Eliminate negatives. You cannot concentrate on your job once you let yourself become involved in "negs." No matter how tough things get, stay positive in body language and self-talk.

When too many errors threaten to overcome you, turn your focus to teammates and how you can be helpful and supportive of them. If you go down mentally, make the fall alone.

MAXIM: *Focus on the rose rather than the thorn.*

Maintain a Simple Focus of Attention.   Maintain a single-minded focus. Identify the most essential elements of each technique or tactic and specify these in the form of personal "performance cues." Repeat these "cues" through self-talk to help focus on the essentials without distraction; *for example:* "Stay low . . . high contact . . . wrists locked . . ."

Focus on Controllable Factors.   Have a positive and a winning attitude no matter what the situation is. Know you cannot always control the decisions made by coaches, officials, or teammates. You cannot always control whether you will play or not or whether you will win or lose. The most effective tactic is to be positive rather than negative and work to control those things within your reach, such as, technique, thoughts, feelings, actions, and energy levels. Focus on what you want and how you are going to accomplish it. Focus on better shot selection and placement for the next attack, rather than on the previous attack error. Focus on effort, rather than on results. Sustaining focus is a constant effort. It is normal for the mind to wander, but as soon as you are aware of the distraction, bring your mind back to the immediate task and refocus as often as necessary.

Identify Stress Triggers.   Be aware of specific situations that create physical or emotional tension and learn coping strategies to deal with these "stresses." Rehearse mentally the "new" responses so when these situations arise in practice or the game, you are prepared to deal with them more effectively.

MAXIM: *Whether you think you can, or you can't, you are usually right.* Henry Ford
---

Tactical Decisions

Help athletes reduce the number of tactical errors through carefully thought-out practices that set up tactical situations in drills and modified scrimmages. Through repetition, athletes improve their ability to judge situations and make good decisions. They learn to "see, evaluate, and respond" correctly to the game in front of them. The following are examples of tactical options for players.

Play the Percentages.   Read each circumstance and consider which responses offer the highest percentage of success. It is a good choice to go for the "kill" when the situation has a high success ratio according to your abilities. Know when to gamble and when it is better to play it safe.

Avoid Overplaying.   There is at least one appropriate tactic for every contact. Consider the best options according to the situation and your abilities. Resist the desire to attempt shots in the game that you have not mastered or placements that are too difficult according to your position on the court or the position of the ball. Resist the temptation to go for the winner in a difficult situation. While it may lead to an occasional spectacular shot, the smarter option is to keep the ball in play and give the opponent the opportunity to make some errors.

When the team is behind and the opponent appears to be much better physically, it is permissible to take a few more chances, but avoid going for low-percentage, one-in-a-million plays. Play smart and go aggressively after the point with plays that have been effective in other situations.

Serve Within Your Ability. Many service errors are caused by the misconception that "tough" is related to speed and the harder and faster the serve, the better. Unfortunately, gravity cannot keep some of these balls in the court. A tough serve is a ball with a low trajectory and good placement. Serve within your strengths and limitations. Aiming directly for the lines and just over the top of the net is dangerous. Allow a safe margin for error by serving higher above the net and farther away from the lines according to your ability.

Resist Overplaying the "Juicy Ones." Concentrate on making good tactical choices in "easy" situations. Errors under these circumstances are psychologically deflating to the team and give the opponent a "boost." *For example,* take care in playing an overpass that is tight to the net. The prospect of getting a "kill" is so exciting that it is easy to overhit it and commit a net error on the follow-through. Control the shot with a compact swing or a redirect.

MAXIM: Serve errors do not give the opponent an opportunity to show their weaknesses.

Avoid Underplaying. Some tactical choices are not recognized as errors, but it is precisely that action that created the problem; *for example:* sending the ball to the opponent's side with a free ball when it should have been attacked. The free ball did not appear to be an error, but it ultimately caused the loss of a point because the opponents had an easy opportunity to run the offense and score. Serving too easy is another example. Although it does not appear that the server has made an error, it gives a good opponent an easy opportunity to secure the side-out and/or point.

Take Calculated Risks. Underplaying is just as bad as overplaying. The key is knowing when it is appropriate to go aggressively after the ball and take some risks, and when it is more appropriate to be more cautious and play it safe. Do not sit back and wait for opponents to miss; rather, take some risks and go after the win. Keeping the ball in play against an opponent of equal caliber only delays the agony of defeat. Give opponents enough easy balls and eventually they will come back at you with "kills."

Make an Adjustment. Make an adjustment if something is not working. Hit the line if they are digging you at the angle. Tip to the middle of the court if they dig you on the line. Place it to another target if they pick up the tip in the middle of the court. Change your study habits if you got a "C" on your midterm.

Don't Change a Winning Game. Continue to aggressively go after the win when ahead. Avoid the tendency to get conservative and hope that the opponent will make errors. Stick with the game plan and continue to do those things that got the team in this position. Have confidence that you can continue to play at this level.

Don't Succumb to Pressure Dynamics.   The farther the team is behind, the less pressure you feel and the better you begin to play. The closer the team is to achieving an important goal, the more pressure you feel and the harder it is to keep control mentally. The tendency is to be more conservative, trying not to lose rather than to win. Focus on the moment and on the effort, rather than on the scoreboard.

Simplify Difficult Plays.   Avoid pinpointing passes on hard-driven spikes or difficult serves. In these situations, it is best to pass the ball high and toward the center of the court, giving the setter an opportunity to reach it. Setters, as well, must avoid pinpointing sets on difficult passes. It is more important to give the attacker a high hitable set off the net than risk a more difficult set with a poor percentage for success.

Stay in the Point as Long as Possible.   Even in the most hopeless and futile situations, do everything possible to get one more ball over the net. Every time the ball gets to the opponent's side, it translates into another opportunity for them to make an error and lose the point. Stay in the point long enough to give opponents an opportunity to beat themselves.

> *MAXIM: The difference between the impossible and the possible lies in one's determination.*

Match Decisions

Never Underestimate the Ability of Opponents.   Respect all opponents and never assume they will be easy to beat. Know that either team has the opportunity to win and there are always obstacles to overcome.

Act Like a Winner.   Present a powerful image. Exude confidence, fight, and determination. Fake it if you do not feel it. Show opponents that you have no fear of their game or ability. Never show opponents that you are tired, frustrated, or lack confidence. Believe you can win. Develop an attitude that the opponent is always beatable despite the score or the odds. Challenge yourself to find a way to win. Believe that you can overcome the obstacles.

Better the Situation.   Look to yourself first to remedy difficult situations. If teammates are playing poorly, step up your own game to compensate. If someone is not getting the job done, play harder to inspire by your example. If you are not being successful in one area of the game, work hard in order to contribute more in another.

Focus on Execution.   Focus on what needs to happen technically and tactically to win and less on winning. Focus on what you want to achieve, rather than what you want to avoid. Focus on performance, rather than the outcome; strengths, rather than weaknesses.

Learn as the Match Progresses.   Every match has a different life. Always be learning and adjusting to the opponent's tendencies offensively and defensively. Identify what is working and not working for you and for the opponent. Consider, after each point, how to play the next one. Know which attacks scored for you individually and why others did not. Ask yourself, "Who is blocking and digging me?" Look, find, and focus on the opponent's weaknesses.

Do Not Overreact.   Control your emotional reactions. Anger feeds on itself and magnifies the problem. Let anger go and deal with frustration in a positive way. "Cool down" by counting to ten, but do it quickly and get back into the drill or game.

Do Not Groan on Bad Calls.   Do not acknowledge your frustrations visually or verbally. This can be a signal for the official to make a call; a teammate, an excuse for his or her poor performance; or opponents, a psychological "boost." Getting upset does nothing to make the situation better. In fact, it generally makes it worse because you cannot concentrate and, at times, the official seeing this reaction is upset as well. Officials' calls are out of your control. It is best to ignore them and concentrate on playing.

Don't Try to Prove Anything.   Do not try to prove something to yourself, your coach, parents, friends, or the opponent, which just puts you under an emotional strain. Concern yourself with being your best for your own satisfaction and do not worry about anything else.

Communicate with Teammates.   Focus on good communication with teammates, especially in losing situations. This is where teams often break down and become silent. Pump up teammates with high fives and verbal support. What specifically is said is less important than being positive.

Maintain a Game Focus.   Confide your thoughts to the world inside the boundaries of the court. This is where your efforts are needed.

Focus on the task—not the crowd, the score, internal doubts, bad calls, or previous errors. Resist the temptation to give in to frustration, anxiety, or negative thoughts. Celebrate the good things and learn from the others. Focus on intensity and effort, point after point. Place all efforts and energy toward competing well.

> MAXIM: *The height of your accomplishments will equal the depth of your convictions.*
> William F. Scolavino

TRAINING THROUGH VISUALIZATION

Although a great deal of time is spent training players for the physical aspects of the game, their minds need to be trained along with their bodies. Research indicates that learning can be accelerated when mental practice is combined with physical practice.

One effective tool for mental training is visualization. At some fundamental level, visualizing an action and performing it appear to be almost the same because the mind cannot completely distinguish between actual experiences and ones that are vividly imagined. Imagery is not only visual, it also involves the whole body. Even though there are no outward movements in imagery, there are eye and muscle movement, body temperature changes, and changes in the heartbeat. The body perceives the imagined task almost as if it were the actual physical performance.

Repeated visualizations of performing technical and tactical skills correctly builds visual and motor pathways in the brain. Over time, the information is absorbed and imprinted in athletes' minds, helping them to give the correct response quickly and easily in "live" game situations.

Studies have shown that those things we visualize begin to happen with increasing frequency. Athletes learn to comprehend and evaluate the game in front of them by reviewing options mentally and making good choices in visualization sessions. These practices help the athlete perform with greater ease, confidence, and poise.

Performance inconsistencies are often a result of psychological factors as much as physical ones. Visualization not only gives athletes the opportunity to work on the technical and tactical aspects of the game, but the emotional ones as well. Athletes can learn to control negative thought patterns, enhance their ability to maintain their concentration, and build confidence and overall good mental habits.

Visualization, like other skills, must be practiced to become an effective learning tool. Train players to vividly imagine skills and tactics by analyzing films, videos, slides, photographs, or live performances of top athletes. Guide them to analyze movements and tactics by pointing out relevant cues. Ask the athletes to "put themselves into the body of the viewed athlete" and imagine themselves performing in the video. Immediately following the video, have them close their eyes and imagine themselves repeating the same performance.

Research indicates that replays of the athletes' own successful performances can greatly improve their play. Make highlight tapes of the players' successful performances for them to view and study.

Visualization can be utilized in a variety of other ways, too. It can be integrated into the practice, for example, as part of the cool-down. Review the most important aspects of practice, while players visualize proper execution and correct their previous errors so the body experiences the correct response. Visualization can either be guided or athletes can be given the freedom to select their own scenarios. Visualization work can also be given as homework.

Athlete Visualization Work-Out

The athlete performs the work-out as part of the training session or as homework. It can be included in the cool-down as a natural way to close out the practice. Divide the work-out into two parts: the relaxation phase and the imagery phase. This session can be performed in 10–15 minutes.

"Chill-Out" Relaxation Phase.   Visualization is most effective in a relaxed state when the mind is most favorable to accepting positive suggestions. Studies show that it is difficult for the body to experience anxiety when muscle tension is reduced. Have athletes follow these steps:

"You," in this scenario, is the athlete.

- Find a quiet spot with as few distractions as possible to sit or lie down.
- Close your eyes and begin to breathe deeply and rhythmically. Control your breathing by counting from one to four as you inhale and again when you exhale. Take long, deep, and even breaths.
- When your breathing is relaxed and easy, begin to focus on systematically relaxing the muscles in each part of your body. Start with your toes and work your way up through your legs, back, chest, shoulders, arms, and face, tensing each muscle, holding it, and then releasing it in its relaxed state.
- Take as much time as necessary to calm the body and the mind.

Imagery Phase.   See yourself on the court looking, acting, thinking, and feeling exactly as you want to in these various scenarios. Choose from one or more of the training areas—technical, tactical, or emotional—and visualize yourself being successful in each scenario.

Technical (mechanical) work. Picture and feel yourself executing correctly and successfully the fundamentals of the game, such as, the movements of the attack, block, pass, set, serve, and dig. Visualize yourself in flawless slow-motion and game-speed sequences, and performing the skills under favorable and difficult circumstances. Overlearn them to the point that you will do them automatically, in relaxed as well as stressful game situations. Focus on correcting any errors you have previously made in recent practice or game situations.

Tactical work. Picture and feel yourself executing tactical game options. Set up game situations and see yourself recognizing them rapidly and choosing the appropriate tactical option. Strengthen your ability to make good choices in game situations by reviewing all "what if" situations offensively and defensively and playing out all possibilities. Visualize seeing the cues and simultaneously responding confidently with the correct tactical choice. See yourself "seeing" what is necessary to do before it needs to happen.

Emotional work. Prepare for and deal with the emotional aspects of the game by recalling past game and practice situations that elicit disruptive emotions. Recognize the warning signals and create a "solution bank" to help cope with these problems in the future. Accept that you will have these thoughts and feelings and visualize how you want to react. Recreate stressful and anxious moments and see yourself working them out in a positive way. Rehearse your new actions over and over in your mind until you feel comfortable and confident coping with them. Visualize your ideal performance state and your ideal performance. Practice being the perfect you.

Coach-Guided Visualization Work-Out

Guide your players through the visualizations while they are in a comfortable and quiet location in the gym or a classroom. Speak softly, slowly, and calmly in a comforting, soothing, and steady manner. Leave spaces of time after each suggested image.

"You," in this scenario is the athlete.

Guided Visualization Work-Out

- Close your eyes and relax.
- Imagine yourself sitting in a soft and comfortable chair in a big room with a movie screen. You slide down into your chair to watch the movie. The movie starts and *you* are the show.
- You see yourself putting on your uniform and shoes and getting ready for the game.
- You enter the gym and place your personal items on the team bench.
- You then place all your distracting thoughts, worries, and problems on the "volleyball problem tree" behind the bench. Your mind is immediately clear and focused on playing good volleyball.
- You feel poised, confident, and ready.
- You see your opponents, but you have no fear of them.
- You warm up with complete concentration and enthusiasm, preparing physically and mentally to play the match.
- The whistle blows and the match begins. You feel completely prepared and ready for the challenge. You are excited to test your skills in this volleyball battle. You feel "good vibes" from the other gladiators on your team.
- You react quickly and with confidence controlling the ball on your side of the court. You see yourself working hard on every play, playing poised and making smart tactical decisions.
- You keep the opponents guessing on defense by utilizing different attack options and placements.

- You frustrate them with your "scrappy" defense. You relentlessly pursue every ball. You move quickly to your base positions after each play and begin thinking about the next play.
- You see by your positive attitude that you are in control of what is happening in the match.
- You recognize winning opportunities, set them up, and capitalize on them.
- You totally support yourself and teammates when difficult situations occur.
- You see yourself bounce back from disappointing situations.
- You remain confident, determined, and in control. You feel yourself become stronger mentally and physically as the match progresses.
- Visualize yourself doing each skill—serve, pass, set, dig, attack, and block—correctly.
- Create a situation where you successfully exhibit mental toughness.
- Create a situation where you are ahead and spin a successful ending.
- Create a situation where you are behind and spin successful endings.
- Create a situation where you are hot and experiencing great success.
- Visualize yourself making the big play.
- Visualize yourself as the player you want to be—playing your best in an optimal performance state, with your competitive juices flowing.
- When you are ready, take a few deep breaths and begin to bring yourself back to the present.

> **MAXIM:** *Visualize enough and it will become the present.*

More Visualization Work-Outs.   The following visualizations can be guided by the coach or utilized individually by the athletes.

Success Images

- Visualize yourself in uniform, walking into the gym looking poised and confident. You feel excited and ready for the challenge. You are nervous, but confident, because you have practiced hard and are prepared for battle. Picture the court and see yourself on it. See yourself performing each skill correctly and successfully; serving tough; spiking for the kill; making the perfect pass, set, dig, block, and cover. You feel in control of your game. You know you can do anything you set your mind to.
- Visualize your ideal volleyball self. See yourself with the skills, attitudes, and characteristics you want. Create your perfect "self" and "team" player. Create your perfect "feeling" and "anxiety" level. Visualize yourself in perfect harmony with yourself and teammates. Visualize yourself in complete control of your game technically, tactically, and emotionally.
- Imagine yourself going to the line to serve. The score is close. A tough serve will help the team win and an error will give the opponent an opportunity to get back in the game. Look to the bench for the coach's signal to see which zone you are going to serve. Eyeball the target, look at the ball, take a deep breath, and serve tough. Move quickly into your defensive position.
- See yourself ready to pass the serve. You want the ball to come in your direction because you feel confident. You move quickly to get behind the ball and angle your arms to the target. You are balanced and relaxed and see the ball go perfectly to the setter in the target area. You immediately prepare to attack or cover for a teammate.
- See yourself preparing for the attack. You make a good strong approach, analyze the position of the set and block, and select the best attack option. Visualize yourself attacking with a vari-

ety of shots according to the situation. You smile because your opponents are confused and frustrated trying to guess what you will do next.

- Picture yourself experiencing great success. Your "competitive juices" are stirred up positively and you are at your optimal performance level. You are playing with great self-confidence. You are making "big" plays at critical moments in the match. See yourself sneaking your hand under the ball just before it touches the ground to make the great save. See yourself attacking the ball off the block and blocking the opponent's best attacker. See yourself playing "hot."

- Visualize yourself competing against opponents. They are playing extremely well. They are hot. You are nervous but confident that you can compete with them. See and feel yourself enjoying the challenge of playing against a tough team. See yourself giving 100 percent mentally and physically and feeling good about your attitude and effort. Imagine the opponents serving, with you making a good pass. They hit hard, tip, hit off the block, and you dig it. You hit and tip for kills and block for points. Imagine yourself performing the skills correctly and making good tactical choices. See yourself utilizing all game plan information. Go through all situations you might face in the game and spin successful endings.

- Review the last match you played. Playback all the positives and turn the negatives into successful endings.

- Visualize a situation where you or a teammate exhibited mental toughness. Recall situations where you needed to exhibit toughness, but did not. Spin a successful ending.

- Visualize one extremely long point where everything possible, both positive and negative, happens. See yourself work through difficult tactical and emotional situations. Repeat the point from every position that you play on the court.

- Think of a time you played extremely well against a tough opponent. Think of how you felt and picture how you played. Remember how you responded to difficult situations and continued playing well.

- See yourself playing relaxed, poised, and with enthusiasm. Visualize yourself doing those things that you must do to play well against a current opponent. See yourself making the big play, the exceptional dig, the pressure pass, and the smart hit. Visualize yourself with perfect focus. Your attention is only on the ball and the "cues" that tell you what to do. You play point by point, working your way through the match. You become stronger mentally and physically as the match progresses.

Failure-to-Success Images
- Visualize situations where you have been or might become angry, frustrated, "rattled," "up tight," or stressed. See yourself work out positive solutions to each difficult situation that you encounter. Visualize yourself choosing positive ways to change what is not working, rather than surrounding yourself with negative thoughts. See yourself learning from each difficult situation and then aggressively going after the next ball with confidence.

- Create situations that are tough physically and mentally for you in practice and the game. See yourself doing those things that give you the opportunity to come out on top. See yourself in a series of ups and downs emotionally, but where you continue to play your best to overcome each obstacle as it crosses your path.

- Create a situation where you are experiencing failure. See yourself struggling and frustrated with yourself and/or teammates. See yourself channel your energy to find positive solutions and making the adjustments for a successful ending.

- Visualize a situation where you are losing badly. The court is very quiet and it seems that no one has any confidence. See yourself pulling out of your "bag of tricks" tremendous enthusiasm and spirit. See yourself inspiring the team by your example. See yourself totally supporting the team. See yourself going all out, giving 100-percent effort mentally and physically, playing every point as if it is the most important one of the match. Imagine that as you gain more confidence in yourself, so do your teammates. Your enthusiasm and team spirit become contagious.

- Visualize yourself tolerating mistakes (yours and teammates). See yourself accepting them as part of the process, not a deterrent to success. See yourself using mistakes as information and an opportunity to learn, then make your adjustments.
- Picture yourself playing points you are afraid of. See yourself gathering all your strength emotionally to push forward to play your best. Visualize yourself being mentally tough and dealing with each situation. Visualize yourself replacing fear with fight. You feel an inner calm and strength at the same time. See yourself helping yourself and teammates find a way to win.

COMMUNICATION AIDS

Provide athletes with many opportunities and methods of communicating their thoughts. Each player communicates in a different way. Verbal communication is easy for some; for others, it is more effective to write it down. The more you know and understand your athletes, the more effectively you can work with them.

Team Communication Announcement

It is every team member's responsibility to **DIG** in and accept the responsibility for good communication. Neither the coach nor a teammate should **PASS** up an opportunity to compliment a member of the team on his or her efforts or accomplishments. Nobody should **BLOCK** the team's progress with negative talk. Do yourself a **SERVICE** and **RECEIVE** communication with a receptive mind. Everyone should **ATTACK** conflicts in a positive way, talking of solutions. Each team member must **SET** a good example and **APPROACH** teammates and coaches to work out problems.

"From Me to You," and "From You to Me" Messages

- It would be more comfortable and beneficial to me if you would . . .
- Please do the following things more or better . . .
- Please do the following things less, or stop doing them . . .
- Continue doing the following things . . .
- Start doing these additional things . . .

Response Questions

Personal

- What is it like to be you?
- What is the most important comment you can make about yourself?
- What would you like teammates to know about you?

- List three things you value most in life.
- Describe your ideal day.
- Things I like about myself . . .
- Things I like/dislike about school . . .
- Things I like best/least about myself in practice . . .
- Things I like best/least about myself in the game . . .
- List five adjectives to describe yourself.
- What do you like most (what are you proudest) about your culture?
- What stereotypes do you dislike?
- How are you alike and how are you different from others?
- What is an interesting fact teammates don't know about you?
- How is your personality reflected on the court? In what ways does it help you? What ways does it hurt you?
- Who do you most respect and why?
- List attributes and characteristics of people you respect.
- What do you perceive as your role on the team?
- How can you contribute to the total team success?
- List five "rights" to be included on the "Athlete's Bill of Rights."
- List five "responsibilities" you have as a team member.
- What is the best part of your game (technical, tactical, emotional)? How do you want to change the other parts?
- What builds your confidence? What can you do? What can teammates do? What can the coach do?
- Name those teammates in whom you have the greatest amount of confidence.
- One thing I like about the team is . . .
- I wish the coach would . . .
- What are the obstacles you must overcome to reach your potential? How will you do it?

Successful

- In what areas of your life have you been successful? How did you do it and what impression has it left on you?
- A big success I experienced in athletics . . .
- A big success I experienced outside of athletics . . .
- List in order of their importance things you deliberately did to accomplish your successes.

Unsuccessful

- Recall an unsuccessful situation in which you were involved. As you look back, were you prepared or could you have been ready to make the outcome more to your liking?
- Describe a situation when a negative game expectation came true.
- Describe an occasion when you blamed someone else for your errors in practice or the game.

Problems/Solution Bank

- List problems that have occurred in the past and might occur again in practice or the game. What was your self-talk? How will you cope with these problems the next time?
- What do you personally feel when you start to get "uptight" in a match? How do you want to cope with this?

- What is your worst volleyball fear? Why do you think you feel this way? How do you want to cope with it? How do you want to remedy it?
- What single thing impedes your success the most? What is your plan to remedy this?
- List your positive and negative technical, tactical, and emotional sports-related tendencies or patterns. Be specific. How do you want to deal with the negative tendencies?
- What rattles you most in a match? How can you regain your composure?
- Explain a negative emotion you have had in practice and/or the game and tell how you are going to eliminate it.
- How do you react when in trouble or behind in a game? How do you want to react?
- You begin to make some errors (serve, receive, attack). What is your plan to pull out of it and play well?
- In what (practice and/or game) situations do you lose control or confidence in yourself or the team? How can you deal with this better?
- What is your plan to change things around when you are not performing well in practice or a game?
- Have you ever determined the outcome of the match before it is over? Why? In what ways can you avoid doing it in the future?
- How do you prepare yourself mentally for a match?
- What do you think about during the pregame warm-up?
- Describe your match self-talk.
- What things do you think about on the court during the match?
- In a close match, does your mind drift to similar matches that you have lost?
- What is mental toughness? Describe a situation in which you or a teammate exhibited this quality.
- How do you deal with skill errors, both yours and teammates? Is your tolerance level different? Would you like to handle the situation differently? Do you ever blame others for your errors?
- Describe one new, positive habit you will develop that will help you play better in the match.

Teammates

- What can a teammate or the coach do for you when you get down in practice and/or a game?
- What affects you most positively and negatively on the court that teammates do?
- What affects you most positively and negatively that the coach does?
- List teammates who always give 110 percent at practice. Are you one of them?
- How can you make a teammate feel valuable?
- What can you do to help a teammate play his or her best?
- In what ways can you get teammates "up" when the team begins to play poorly or lose confidence?

Practice

- What can you do each practice to get you off to a good start?
- What must you do to have your most productive practice? How do you achieve this?
- In practice, it really irritates me when. . . . How do you want to cope with it?
- Do you practice with the same intensity you play the game? Explain.
- Are you as hard on yourself in practice as the game? Explain.

Game

- I play best when . . .
- After a loss I feel . . .
- List five starters you would like to see on the court with you.
- What is your most productive game attitude? How do you achieve it?
- What must you do to have your best performance in the game?
- I feel pressure in the game when. . . . How do you deal with it? How would you like to deal with it?
- At what level of activation do you perform the best?
- If winning is based on you, what do you need to do?
- If you could have done one thing better in the match, what would it have been? Explain.
- What do you like/dislike to see and hear from the bench?
- List "igniter words" (uppers) that help you in the game.
- List "killer words" (downers) that hurt you in the game.
- You have five seconds before you serve. How do you want to direct your thoughts?

Scale Questions 1–10 (10 Being Highest)

- What is your level of desire to play volleyball?
- What is your intensity level in practice?
- What is your intensity level in the game?
- What is your level of confidence?
- What was your effort level in practice today?
- How receptive were you to corrections?
- How hard are you working in practice mentally and physically to reach your goals?

ATHLETE GOAL-SETTING

Goal-setting is the first step in helping athletes focus on what is necessary for success and how to attain it. The athlete's concentration must be directed and redirected toward these objectives, whether they are volleyball, academics, or other endeavors. Help athletes make their goals specific, realistic, and measurable. Suggest that they post their goals in their school locker and at home. The chances of them realizing their goals greatly increases when goals are put into written form and seen on a daily basis.

MAXIM: Limited expectations yield limited results.

The following five worksheets will help your athletes set goals for themselves and evaluate their feelings about competition. They also are a valuable tool to help you better understand each individual player as well as the group dynamics that contribute to the success of the team.

Player Worksheet:
INDIVIDUAL GOALS

Who are you now and who do you aspire to be? Success or failure is a decision you make. The commitment comes from you. Completing this worksheet is the first step in your journey along the road to athletic, career, and personal success. You have the choice to become the person you want to be. The coaching staff has high expectations for each of you. Past tradition sets lofty goals for future teams to reach. Begin today to become your best.

> *Maxim: It is not only what you say, it is what you do!*

Rank each category 1–10 (10 being the highest) in order of importance in your life: volleyball, school, family, and social activities.

RANK	CATEGORY

List three of your strengths that will assist you in volleyball.

-
-
-

List two of your weaknesses and indicate which of the following you want to do: change, improve, or eliminate.

-

-

List two academic goals.

-
-

List two career goals.

-
-

List three technical volleyball goals (dealing with a skill).

- **First goal:**
- **Action plan:**

- **Second goal:**
- **Action plan:**

- **Third goal:**
- **Action plan:**

List three tactical volleyball goals.

- **First goal:**
- **Action plan:**

- **Second goal:**
- **Action plan:**

- **Third goal:**
- **Action plan:**

List three emotional volleyball goals.

- **First goal:**
- **Action plan:**

- **Second goal:**
- **Action plan:**

- **Third goal:**
- **Action plan:**

List three obstacles you might encounter in striving to reach your goals.

-
-
-

List one method to successfully deal with each obstacle.

-
-
-

List three goals you have for the team.

-
-
-

List three practice goals you have for yourself.

-
-
-

List three weight-training or conditioning goals for yourself.

-
-
-

List two things that must happen for the season to be a success.

-
-

List three ways you can contribute to the total team effort other than playing in the games.

-
-
-

I truly desire these goals and believe they are possible for me to attain. I fully commit myself to achieving these goals.

Sign and date:

Player Worksheet:
MONTHLY GOAL EVALUATION

List goals you have reached.

-
-
-
-

List problems you have encountered and how you have dealt with them.

-

-

-

List the changes to your current goals or new goals.

New goal:

Action plan:

New goal:

Action plan:

New goal:

Action plan:

New goal:

Action plan:

Player Worksheet:
SEASON-ENDING GOAL EVALUATION

List five goals you have accomplished this season.

-
-
-
-
-

Who on the team did you most respect?

-

Explain.

-

List two things you would have done differently.

-

Explain.

-

Explain.

List three things that have made this season successful for you.

-
-
-

List three goals you want to make for next season.

-
-
-

List three things you want the coach to continue to do next season.

-
-
-

Player Worksheet:
TEAM EVALUATION

The coach will insert the names of your teammates and you check the name(s) to whom the statement applies, excluding yourself. Through your honest participation, the coach can identify individual and group feelings that can be potentially helpful or harmful to the team.

TEAM EVALUATION															
Favorite pepper partner															
Players I respect															
Gives 100% in practice															
Talks behind others' backs															
Feels above being subbed															
Always cheers from the bench															
Blames others for her/his errors															
Has a tendency to sulk on the bench															
Practices harder than most															
Is sometimes dishonest															
I want these 5 players on court with me															
Is always competitive															
Talks negatively about teammates															
Refuses to give up when the team is behind															
Tends to make errors when the pressure is on															
Doesn't contribute to positive team chemistry															
Blames hitting errors on poor sets															
Is reliable to win pressure points															
Is someone I would confide in															
Is popular with everyone															
Does not abide by team rules consistently															
Is dedicated															
Exhibits team leadership qualities															
Accepts blame for own errors															
Is truthful															
Is a favorite player for group drills															
Is a negative influence															
Is supportive of teammates															
Is a good teammate															
Brings out the best in others															
Enjoys the challenge of a close match															
Respects authority and coach's judgment															
Sacrifices personal desires for the team															
Pulls out a little extra in tough situations															
Loses confidence when the team is behind															
Poised and confident in critical times															
Leads by example															
Is easy to play with															
Has fighting spirit															

Player Worksheet:
ATHLETE SELF-EVALUATION

The more you and your coach know about how you feel about competing, the better opportunities you have to achieve success. Analyze your feelings through this worksheet.

5 = Almost always, 4 = Sometimes, 3 = Seldom, 2 = Almost never, 1 = Never

_____ I am confident in my abilities.

_____ I am intimidated by better players.

_____ I dwell on my errors.

_____ I work out on my own to improve.

_____ I am eager to share with extra responsibilities.

_____ I worry about what others think of my performance.

_____ It's hard to recover if I play poorly at the start of the game.

_____ I get distracted easily in games.

_____ I give 100% in every practice.

_____ I demonstrate good sportsmanship in games.

_____ I am a coachable player.

_____ I don't let mistakes discourage me.

_____ Small problems affect my game.

_____ I want to play the ball in critical game situations.

_____ Losing makes me feel bad for days.

_____ Teammates' negative comments affect my game.

_____ I like the challenge of playing good competition.

_____ My nervousness can ruin my game.

_____ I enjoy the pressure of important games.

_____ I enjoy practices and training.

_____ I encourage teammates often.

_____ I am confident that I will succeed.

_____ I am a very aggressive player.

_____ A personal pregame ritual helps me play better.

_____ I am committed to the program goals.

_____ I enjoy being a part of the team.

_____ My teammates make me feel worthwhile.

_____ I enjoy the friendships I have developed on the team.

_____ My teammates value my contributions to the team.

_____ I value my membership on the team.

_____ I support and respect my teammates.

_____ I am proud to be a member of the team.

_____ I feel prepared mentally and physically to compete.

_____ I feel accepted as a member of the team.

_____ I am often not satisfied with my performance.

_____ I choke when I put pressure on myself to win.

_____ I get overly nervous before I compete.

_____ Repetitive corrections destroy my confidence.

_____ I don't believe it is true when the coach praises me.

_____ I play best at home games.

_____ If we lose, but I perform well, I feel good.

_____ I prefer playing away games.

_____ I play best when my friends come to see me.

_____ I have excuses ready when I play poorly.

_____ I lose confidence when I compete against tough opponents.

_____ I often decide the outcome of the match before it begins.

_____ I am not satisfied with less than my best effort.

_____ I am concerned more with effort than winning.

PLAYERS' COMMANDMENTS
FOR DEALING WITH CONFLICT

Most of these are appropriate for the coach, too!

- *You shall* understand that disagreement is okay. It is an expression of a genuine difference of opinion.
- *You shall* acknowledge that everyone has a right to his or her opinion, although you don't have to agree with it.
- *You shall* respect another's perspective, even while emphasizing your own.
- *You shall* remember that it is the responsibility of all team members—players and coaches—to learn to confront situations head on.
- *You shall* deal directly with the person(s) with whom you have the problem.
- *You shall* deal with differences immediately, before the situation is allowed to become more serious.
- *You shall* keep confrontations private.
- *You shall* talk to the captain or coach when no acceptable solution can be met privately.
- *You shall* avoid team meetings on serious issues that do not involve the entire team.
- *You shall* identify the problem and the options, and choose a route to a solution.
- *You shall* be a good listener.
- *You shall* listen with an open mind.
- *You shall* be open to new ideas. Every opinion is worthy of discussion.
- *You shall* strive to hear and understand the feelings and needs of others.
- *You shall* perceive the conflict from the other side.
- *You shall* listen with the ears, eyes, and heart.
- *You shall* listen without passing judgment.
- *You shall* respect the views of those who may not share your opinion.
- *You shall* be honest but tactful.
- *You shall* state your opinion in a way that does not offend or insult.
- *You shall* avoid putting anyone on the defensive. *You shall* attack the problem, not the person.
- *You shall* tailor communication in such a manner so as not to offend teammates or evoke negative connotations.
- *You shall* avoid put-downs. No one needs them!
- *You shall* be specific, objective, and nonaccusatory.
- *You shall* speak for thyself, not for anyone else.
- *You shall* remember that the only feelings you know are your own; therefore, affirm only what "I" think or feel.
- *You shall* keep control of your emotions.
- *You shall* be aware of your body language.
- *You shall* not gossip.
- *You shall* not hold grudges.
- *You shall* forgive.
- *You shall* respect agreed-upon decisions.
- *You shall* strive to make your point in a concise manner.

THE "IDEAL PLAYER" CHECKLIST

> *MAXIM: You get better or worse, there's no standing still.*

Strives for Perfection

✓ Continually seeks ways to improve performance.
✓ Strives for the highest degree of excellence.
✓ Makes the extra effort to do things the right way.
✓ Does not waste time or opportunities.
✓ Is not satisfied with less than his or her best.
✓ Always strives for a higher level.
✓ Dares to risk.
✓ Dares to step out of his or her comfort zone.
✓ Dares to try new things.

Is Mature and Responsible

✓ Is a responsible student–athlete.
✓ Shares responsibility for team management.
✓ Accepts responsibility for own success both on and off the court.
✓ Demonstrates consistent behavior on and off the court.
✓ Never places blame on others if things do not turn out in his or her favor.
✓ Takes the initiative to do what needs to be done without always being asked.
✓ Has the courage and determination to strive for his or her goals.
✓ Organizes and prioritizes time, school, work, practice, and social life to avoid conflicts.
✓ Is concerned with proper diet, nutrition, and rest.
✓ Sees both his or her own strengths and weaknesses.
✓ Thinks about own weaknesses constructively, exposes them, and strives to overcome them.
✓ Handles criticism and praise equally.
✓ Keeps personal disagreements away from the court.
✓ Is a leader of self and teammates.
✓ Leads and inspires by example.
✓ Honestly believes that the coaches are doing what is best for them individually and for the team.

Is a Good Sport

✓ Celebrates with the team after a good play, rather than "razzing" the opponents.
✓ Wins and loses with class. Never takes away from another team's win.
✓ Gives the winning team credit, rather than giving excuses.
✓ Does not moan or complain about official's calls, bad breaks, and self or teammates' errors.
✓ Has pride in the team and respect toward opponents and officials.

✓ Never gives up or makes excuses.

✓ Accepts responsibility for losses and works to improve his or her performance.

Has a Strong Work Ethic

✓ Has the attitude that no one will work harder than him or her.

✓ Has a willingness to challenge obstacles that stand in the way of reaching his or her goals.

✓ Pushes and motivates self to do the job.

✓ Practices hard every day with the same intensity.

✓ Practices beyond the point of what he or she thinks is good.

✓ Knows it takes constant effort to get results.

✓ Is willing to do the drudgery work as well as the "fun" activities.

✓ Has an intense desire to work on the things he or she cannot do as much as those he or she can.

✓ Is willing to put in the time and effort year round: in the weight room, on the track, in scheduled practices, and on his or her own.

✓ Works hard in drills and shags hard when not in the drill.

✓ Gives 100 percent, 100 percent of the time in practice and the game.

✓ Pays the price in time, energy, and effort to reach his or her goals.

✓ Practices hard when the coach is not watching.

Is Mentally Tough

✓ Is poised and calm in stressful situations.

✓ Never allows the frustration of errors to dampen his or her belief in self.

✓ Never gives up or turns against self.

✓ Has a strong belief in his or her ability.

> **MAXIM:** *It's hard to win if you've already decided that you are going to lose.*

✓ Focuses on effort and execution regardless of the distractions.

✓ Refocuses immediately when his or her attention "strays."

✓ Does not worry excessively about mistakes.

✓ Deals with errors and failure by regrouping and bouncing back.

✓ Knows that he or she can overcome any obstacle that gets in the way of his or her success.

✓ Projects a powerful image of success, determination, and fight.

✓ Knows that negative attitudes inhibit performance.

✓ Challenges self to deal with stress, frustration, and fatigue in a positive way.

✓ Works around obstacles and through tough times.

✓ Will not give up if he or she doesn't succeed right away.

✓ Plays with poise, class, confidence, and determination.

✓ Immerses self totally in the competitive battle.

✓ Enjoys the competitive battle.

Is Positive

✓ Is an optimist. Expects good things to happen.
✓ Never doubts his or her ability to succeed.
✓ "I can't" or "I'll try" is not in his or her vocabulary. It is, "I can," and "I will."
✓ Maintains a positive attitude through thick and thin.
✓ Acts like a winner or fakes it until he or she becomes one.
✓ Believes in self and teammates.
✓ Replaces "negs" with positive talk.
✓ Focuses on goals, not hardships.
✓ Inspires others with effort, enthusiasm, and determination.
✓ Stays positive in the game no matter how he or she feels or what the score is.
✓ Gives positive, supportive reinforcement to teammates.

Is Patient and Persistent

✓ Knows that it takes time to learn and that improvement is not a continuous upward path.
✓ Knows that one needs time to mentally absorb information as well as physically learn the skills.
✓ Does not get discouraged just because improvement doesn't come quickly.
✓ Knows that mistakes are a part of the learning process.
✓ Accepts that no one tries to makes mistakes, but knows that everyone does.
✓ Sees things through, no matter how long it takes.

Is Communicative

✓ Uses all game communications in practice.
✓ Supports and encourages teammates vocally.
✓ Voices his or her opinion in an intelligent and thoughtful way.

Confronts Problems

✓ Does not "bad mouth" or gossip about other players or coaches.
✓ Knows that negative talk destroys moral and team unity.
✓ Confronts individuals directly to talk of solutions.
✓ Works to resolve conflicts in a positive manner.
✓ Keeps team problems within the team.

Is Committed to the Program

✓ Follows all training rules.
✓ Makes a strong and continuous commitment to give his or her all to achieve the team's goals.
✓ Gives full commitment to improving his or her game.

✓ Knows that the commitment doesn't start and end with the scheduled season.

✓ Knows that what he or she does in the off-season determines what he or she will do during the regular season.

✓ Is willing to practice on own to improve his or her skills.

✓ Is willing to get up early if that is the only time to do conditioning.

✓ Is willing to work out year round, rather than only for two weeks before the season begins.

✓ Is willing to give up a little of his or her social life to practice and study, if necessary.

✓ Knows that if you are not getting better, you are getting worse.

✓ Knows that everyday you are not making progress, someone else will be moving ahead of you.

Is a Team Player

✓ Accepts his or her individual role within the concept of the team.

✓ Pledges support of teammates on and off the court.

✓ Always looks for ideas that will improve the well being of the team.

✓ Is willing to make sacrifices for the team.

✓ Does not put self higher than a teammate.

✓ Is as enthusiastic about the success of others as he or she is about his or her own.

✓ Is not threatened—but rather challenged—by teammates who play better than him or her.

✓ Strives to be his or her best while helping teammates to do the same.

✓ Concentrates on his or her improvement so much that he or she has no time to criticize others.

✓ Always thinks of "giving" before "getting."

✓ Recognizes and values contributions of each team member.

✓ Accepts all team assignments positively.

✓ Helps set up nets without waiting for an invitation.

✓ Looks for ways to help out. Asks the question, "Is there anything I can do to help?"

Is Passionate

✓ Loves the game, the training, and the competition.

✓ Has an intense desire to win and to be the best.

✓ Is driven mentally, physically, and emotionally.

✓ Receives satisfaction just from participating. The whole experience is fun.

Is Energetic and Enthusiastic

✓ Plays with joy, enthusiasm, and relentless energy.

✓ Has self-generated energy.

✓ Works with the same enthusiasm for the things he or she enjoys as those he or she does not.

✓ Plays and practices with the same high energy and determination during the highs, lows, and plateaus.

Is Competitive

✓ Loves to compete. Thrives on new and different challenges.
✓ Is ready for the best the opponents have to offer.
✓ Attempts to beat opponents as decisively as possible.
✓ Never gives up! Knows that it is not over until it is officially over.
✓ Strives to out-hustle and out-think opponents.
✓ Plays to win no matter what the score.

Is Disciplined

✓ Disciplines self so others won't have to.
✓ Plays within the team rules and follows team regulations.
✓ Is always punctual to team practices and events.
✓ Gives 100 percent concentration and effort.
✓ Has "will" power and "won't" power. Knows what is important to do and does it! Knows what is necessary to forego.
✓ Has stick-to-itiveness and does what is necessary to get the job done.
✓ Is disciplined to put tape, ice bags, and towels in their proper places.
✓ Is attentive in timeouts; listens and applies all game instructions.

Is Honest

✓ Admits mistakes.
✓ Gives credit where credit is due.
✓ Tells the truth even when it is very difficult.
✓ Acts, listens, and responds with sincerity.
✓ Maintains confidentiality.
✓ Does not participate in spreading rumors.

ATTITUDE PROFILE

Profile of a good attitude

Self-confident
Positive
Enthusiastic, cheerful, fun
Follow rules because it is
    important to the team
Confronts teammates and coaches
    with suggestions for problems
Is committed to team
Is coachable
Does not gossip
Supports teammates on and off the court
Is helpful and caring
Confident in self, team,
    and coaches
Pushes hard to improve
Trains to work hard on own
Self-disciplined
Gives 100% in practice
Leads by example
Is honest and reliable
Is appreciative
Has pride in team
Respects teammates
Respects coaches
Respects officials
Is cooperative
Has self-control
Is sensitive
Does not dwell on mistakes

Profile of a bad attitude

God's gift to volleyball
Finds fault with everything
Is gloomy and unhappy
Follows rules only if
    they have to
Complains but does not do anything
    to work out problems
Is loyal to self
Always has an excuse
Talks behind other's back
Is concerned more for own success
Cares mainly about self
Confident in self but does not
    believe in others
Poor practice habits
Trains only in practice
Undisciplined
Lazy practice attitude
Poor example
Dishonest and unreliable
Unappreciative
No pride in team
Does not respect teammates
Does not respect coach
Does not respect officials
Disagrees with everything
Loss of control emotionally
Overly sensitive
Dwells on errors